INSIDE OUR SCHOOLS

INSIDE OUR SCHOOLS

TEACHERS ON THE FAILURE AND FUTURE OF EDUCATION REFORM

Edited by

BRETT GARDINER MURPHY

HARVARD EDUCATION PRESS

Cambridge, Massachusetts

Paperback ISBN 978-1-68253-042-9
Library Edition ISBN 978-1-68253-043-6

Library of Congress Cataloging-in-Publication Data
Names: Murphy, Brett, editor.
Title: Inside our schools : teachers on the failure and future of education
    reform / edited by Brett Gardiner Murphy.
Description: Cambridge, Massachusetts : Harvard Education Press, [2017] |
    Includes bibliographical references and index.
Identifiers: LCCN 2016054434| ISBN 9781682530429 (pbk.) | ISBN
    9781682530436 (library edition)
Subjects: LCSH: Educational accountability—United States—Case studies. |
    School improvement programs—United States—Case studies. | Education
    and state—United States—Case studies. | Educational change—United
    States—Case studies. | Education—United States—Evaluation. | Academic
    achievement—United States—Evaluation.
Classification: LCC LB2806.22 .I56 2017 | DDC 379.1/580973—dc23
    LC record available at https://lccn.loc.gov/2016054434

Published by Harvard Education Press,
an imprint of the Harvard Education Publishing Group

Harvard Education Press
8 Story Street
Cambridge, MA 02138

Cover Design: Wilcox Design
Cover Photo: iStock/© monkeybusinessphotos
The typefaces used in this book are Sabon for text and Myriad Pro for display.

Contents

Introduction

I started teaching in New York City in 2006, four years into the implementation of No Child Left Behind and three years into Michael Bloomberg's mayoral control of the city's schools. The first school that I taught at was a test-prep machine, where music and dance classes were transformed into workbook-heavy sessions of literacy and math, and where students told me whether they were a "1, 2, 3, or 4"—their score on the previous year's exam—on the first day of school. The schools where I taught in the years after experienced budget cuts, annual threats of teacher layoffs, a charter school co-location, extensive teacher turnover, and an obsession with data and test scores that permeated each school's culture. The middle school where my students once held debates, role-playings, and simulations, read primary texts, and wrote analytical and personal essays has since been closed, the space transferred over to one of the many charter school chains that are now inescapable in Harlem. My experience is not unique among teachers in this era of accountability. Ask most teachers about what education reform has meant for their school and they'll have a list of examples just as long.

Since 2001, education reform has been largely defined by the sweeping federal laws under Presidents George W. Bush and Barack Obama that embraced an accountability agenda. The first was the No Child Left Behind Act in 2001 (NCLB), followed by Race to the Top (RTTT) in 2009 and the No Child Left Behind waivers in 2011. But education reform in this period has also been defined by a slew of other characters and groups who have honed a particular message about what's best for American public schools and the students they serve. They include a number of education nonprofit organizations like the Education Trust and alternative certification programs like Teach for America. High-profile state and local leaders like John White of Louisiana, Joel Klein in New York, and Michelle Rhee in Washington, DC, count themselves as education reformers. Major think tanks, including the Thomas B. Fordham Foundation, have contributed research and media content. And a number of very wealthy foundations, including the Bill & Melinda Gates Foundation, the Walton Family Foundation, and the Broad Foundation, have donated millions of dollars to the cause. Combined, they constitute what is now known as the education reform movement, and their collective goals have been defined by an aggressive push to measure and track student progress, hold educators and schools accountable for student learning, and expand school choice. They abhor the status quo and favor bold initiatives that can rattle a system that they see as impervious to change, arguing that education is the civil rights cause of our generation.

In many ways, this movement has succeeded in creating striking changes in public education over the past sixteen years. Consider the following: states are now mandated by the federal government to administer high-stakes tests in seven out of thirteen grades of school every year, almost triple the number required before NCLB.[1] The United States is the closest we've ever been to having a set of national standards, with forty-two states currently implementing the Common Core State Standards.[2] Teacher tenure laws, once seen as a hallmark of the profession, have been changed in at least eighteen states, repealed in four states, and are under court review in at least three more.[3] Teacher evaluation systems, most of which were previously based in principal observations, were tied to student test scores in forty-five states by 2015.[4] Large high schools that once defined urban school systems have been broken up in the nation's biggest cities, creating hundreds of small schools in their place.[5] School boards that used to dominate local decision making around education have been removed from power in many districts in favor of mayoral control, state takeovers, or management organizations overseeing portfolios of schools.[6]

In 2001 there were fewer than two thousand charter schools. In 2015 there were almost seven thousand, and the numbers continue to climb.[7] The first all-charter school district in the country was established in New Orleans in 2014.[8] Meanwhile, tens of thousands of schools have been shut down. In the year before NCLB, 1,193 schools were closed. Three years later, 2,168 schools were closed in that year alone. Zero-tolerance discipline policies, first introduced in the 1990s, reached their peak in the 2000s, with out-of-school suspension rates rising disproportionately for nonwhite students.[9] Major school desegregation policies were overturned, repealed, or neglected during this period, resulting in the highest levels of racial and economic school segregation the United States has seen in four decades.[10] The fact that so much of this appears to be part of the normal landscape of education now speaks to how much things have actually changed.

What has all of this meant for public education in the United States? What should happen now that the latest version of federal education law, the Every Student Succeeds Act (ESSA), has turned so much of the power of education back to the states? Before jumping headfirst into the next wave of change, we need to take stock of what just happened. And to get the full picture, we need to hear from some people who have been unwisely ignored when it comes to education reform and policy: teachers.

Inside Our Schools goes beyond the headlines, speeches, public relations campaigns, and glossy magazine covers to tell a different story of education reform since 2001, combining research with the voices of teachers from around the country who have experienced these reforms firsthand. The book is organized around five recurring buzzwords that the mainstream education reform movement has used to define their policies: accountability, quality, choice, failure, and equity. Chapter introductions give an overview of education policy and research in each of these areas, but the testimony of teachers makes up the bulk of the book by design. For all the time that we've spent talking *about* teachers, *Inside Our Schools* offers a much needed platform for their stories and experiences to be included in the conversation.

In creating the "primers" for each section, I've tried to squeeze fifteen-plus years of policy, rhetoric, media coverage, and research into about ten pages per theme. I've also attempted to show multiple perspectives on different issues and have sought to bring some nuance to how these conversations have played out on the national stage. Clearly, this is a fool's errand. There will be aspects of each topic that are no doubt missing. And, as a former history teacher, I found it painful to not reach further back in time to make broader connections between the trajectory of education reform and the much longer roots of educational inequity. Despite the omissions that page limits require, my hope is that these essays give readers enough of a picture about what has happened under NCLB and where education reform has landed that they can form their own opinions about what should happen next.

That being said, as a group of public school educators, we have a clear point to make about public education policy. Top-down education reform as it has existed since NCLB—often punitive, distrustful of those who do the actual work in education, and divorced from the realities of schools—has failed. We believe that local, state, and federal policy should empower educators and communities to create a more equitable education for all students. This is a vision that believes in the holistic development of all students in ways that honor and support their strengths, needs, opinions, communities, and cultures. It relies on capacity building, not threats, and views teachers, not policy makers, as the experts on student learning.

This point of view will come across through the introductions, but it will come alive in the stories from teachers. In my last year of teaching, I began to work on this book specifically to highlight their perspective. It felt like my experience with accountability-based reforms in my classroom was so different from what was being portrayed in the media and in politics; even my closest friends were confused about what was changing in education. I thought that if only people knew what was really happening, they would have a lot more to say. In 2013, I began outreach to every teacher organization, union, college and university education department, education writer and commentator, parent association, and community group I could find across the country to ask for other teachers who wanted to share their stories.

After four years and over a thousand e-mails, I ended up with the twenty-five contributors to this collection. As you'll see, they are an incredible group, full of writers, scholars, union leaders, parents, and activists. They include veteran teachers, award-winning teachers, and people brand-new to the profession. Collectively, they move the conversation about improving education from rhetorical abstractions to the real world, one that is populated with real kids who thrive and struggle in real classrooms every day. These teachers bring readers directly inside their schools, providing an honest look at what it takes to do the work of helping kids become their best possible selves. In the process, they provide a referendum on reform, calling out many of the policies that have made the day-to-day work of teaching students harder, more frustrating, and less just.

Anyone who has been a teacher knows that it's very hard to sit back and watch something go wrong in your classroom. Driven by a commitment to their students, many teachers have fought against the policies that they have found so harmful. Sometimes this shows up in the form of teacher activism, which has grown tremendously during this time period. But most of the time, teachers' responses to the failure of policy don't make the headlines. They occur in the myriad ways that teachers create and implement practices in their classrooms and schools that run counter to mainstream thinking about education. Each section of the book has stories of these alternatives too. This is not a "how-to" book, so there are not step-by-step instructions for how these practices could be implemented on a wide scale. They are included to spark a more imaginative conversation about what is possible for states, who now have more control to shape their own educational agendas under ESSA. While the stories themselves are based on real experiences, in almost every case, the names have been changed. A few times though, the author was so proud of the work that their school, students, or colleagues did, they asked us to keep the real names, with everyone in the story's full permission. In those cases, we've noted that in the text.

In the course of reading about the reality of how these policies have impacted schools across the country, and the care, passion, and intelligence with which many teachers work to provide a high-quality, equitable education in the face of obstacles, I hope that it becomes clear that educators must be collaborators in the next stage of education policy reforms. And if you are connected to a school yourself, I hope that you'll want to add your voice to the discussion, too. As a start, you can visit us at www.insideour-schools.com, share your experience, and watch, listen and read others' stories too.

I left teaching after six years because I was frustrated, and because, selfishly, it was hard to watch a never-ending stream of bad policy rain down on my students. It felt wrong to be a part of something that I felt morally opposed to. I quit teaching because the reforms enacted in this time period stand in stark opposition to what I believe schools can and should be for students, their families, and their communities. After working on this book, I think I made the wrong decision. The teachers in this collection call on me—and, I hope, on everyone reading their stories—to not accept and give up in the face of these challenges, but to work to make them better. In the process, their stories create the imperative for a new kind of change in education. As Dr. Andre M. Perry has said, "We need less 'reform' and more social justice."[11] In whatever role you play—as an educator, voter, student, parent, community member, politician, journalist, or activist—I hope this book leaves you feeling informed and inspired about what is possible inside our schools.

CHAPTER 1

ACCOUNTABILITY

High-Stakes Testing Takes Over

Sometimes education news can feel like it's on a continuous loop. Headlines about underfunded schools, teacher strikes, and contract negotiations alongside opinion articles about the crisis of public education and the need to prepare students for the next generation of jobs could appear in a number of different time periods in our country's history. And yet, in the past decade or so, there's been an entirely new kind of story about public schools: students and parents who are experiencing extreme levels of stress caused by standardized testing.

In Florida, a pediatrician reported new patients coming to her office every day during testing season from February to April with test-related anxiety. "Sometimes these kids get so worked up as early as third grade with having to pass the FCATs [Florida's state exam]," she said. She sees kids "that have such severe anxiety that we can't get them to school . . . Literally, they will not get out of the car."[1]

For a nine-year-old in New York, the month leading up to the state tests included rounds of timed practice exams that stressed her out so much that she stopped eating. Her parents took her to the hospital, where she was placed on Prozac to help calm her anxiety.[2] A mother of another third grader shared that after her son failed the state exam on his second try, he tried to hang himself.[3]

In a story out of San Francisco, a group of high school students with disabilities sued the state after they were on track to graduate high school but couldn't pass the California exit exam. They included a seventeen-year-old with cerebral palsy who dropped out of school before getting his diploma and another student who had previously earned As and Bs but gave up on his dreams of going to college. "I didn't feel like this before, but after the test, school feels worthless," he said. "I had my mind set to go to college and get a job. Then the exit exam popped up. I'm not capable of doing it. It makes me sad, because I'm pretty smart."[4]

These selected anecdotes are supported by research confirming that anxiety among students, including very young students, has gone up dramatically since the arrival of high-stakes testing.[5] Their stress is often linked to an inordinate amount of significance assigned to the exams and students' sense that their futures are dependent on the score they receive. When did performing well on a test become the purpose of education? How did it get to this point?

Tests have largely been introduced in federal policy as part of the periodic reauthorization of the 1965 Elementary and Secondary Education Act (ESEA), which established Title I federal assistance to schools that educate poor students. Much of our current accountability system comes from changes made to this law in the 1990s. During the administration of President Bill Clinton, grants were provided under a separate program called "Goals 2000" for states to develop and implement new standards and assessments. When the Elementary and Secondary Education Act was reauthorized in 1994, states receiving Title I funding were required to establish challenging standards in reading and math, test all students on these subjects at three grade levels, and report the results. For the first time, standards and assessments for all students were enshrined in federal education policy, making accountability the cornerstone of reform.[6]

In 1999, Congress asked the National Research Council to look at the use of high-stakes testing as it began to balloon across the country. Their report cautioned policy makers about tying tests to decisions about students' futures like graduation and promotion and argued that there was not enough information about the negative consequences of the tests vis-a-vis their supposed benefits. They advocated for the use of multiple measures of assessment that went beyond test scores, and they pushed for more support for teachers.[7]

Two years later, the No Child Left Behind Act of 2001 (NCLB) was passed as the next reauthorization of ESEA with bipartisan support and praise from across the political landscape. Instead of heeding the research on high-stakes testing, No Child Left Behind doubled down. States now had to administer annual tests in grades 3–8 in math and reading and were required to reach 100 percent proficiency by 2014. Progress was tracked using state-determined benchmarks known as Adequate Yearly Progress (AYP). Scores also had to be reported for subgroups of students, including English language learners, students with disabilities, students of color, and low-income students. Title I schools that did not meet AYP were subject to a series of escalating consequences that included withholding their Title I funds, replacing school staff, or shutting down the school entirely. In one stroke, the law almost tripled the number of federally required tests from six to seventeen and, in the process, set off an unprecedented obsession with standardized tests that would reshape teaching and learning in public schools across the country.[8]

TESTING UNDER NCLB

In the years that followed, a number of clear patterns emerged about how schools responded to test-based accountability. Curriculum was narrowed to focus on math and reading as schools either cut out or reduced time for classes like social studies, science, art, music, and physical education along with "free time" like lunch and recess.[9] Even within the math and reading classes, curriculum was further constrained to test-preparation activities and, sometimes, scripted lessons that covered discreet skills on the test. A meta-analysis done by Dr. Wayne Au reviewed forty-nine studies on the effects of high-stakes testing and found that content in classes was reduced to decontextualized "test-sized pieces." Au described how the tests changed the delivery of instruction as well. Teachers transitioned from using active, student-centered activities to lectures and more direct delivery of information.[10]

The influx of testing and the fear of potential consequences shaped educators' view of students. One way this became manifest was through what was known as "educational triage." Teachers and administrators would look at their data, find the students who were "on the bubble," or close enough to proficiency to have a chance of passing, and focus their efforts on them.[11] In more severe cases, educators tried to remove students who might drag down their numbers and cause the school to miss their AYP benchmark. Students were dissuaded from enrolling, suspended so they missed testing days, recategorized as being in a nontesting grade, counseled into GED programs, transferred to other settings, or otherwise pushed out.[12]

These kinds of damaging choices were particularly acute in urban areas and other places with high populations of students of color and low-income students.[13] In a panic to meet outsized expectations for large gains on test scores, and without the time and resources to address the underlying causes of differing achievement levels, district leaders capitulated to the belief that forcing students to learn the test was the only way to raise their scores.

Teachers in urban schools disproportionately narrowed their curriculum to teach to the test, but urban districts found new ways to ratchet up the pressure even more. They added their own local tests, so that, by high school, kids in urban schools were spending 266 percent more time on local testing than their suburban peers.[14] In addition to the high school exit exams imposed by many states, a group of cities added new grade-retention policies that prohibited students from moving to the next grade if they didn't pass the state exam. Many of these policies and practices destroyed students' lives, and the students that were hurt the most were often the ones who needed the most support.

Reformers often called test-based policies the "tough action" that was needed to produce results,[15] and some states and districts saw gains on their state exams in the wake of these changes. They used these numbers to make grandiose proclamations about the great strides in student learning that were happening because of accountability reforms, particularly for the most disadvantaged children. By 2004, success was already being declared. A statement released by the Department of Education that year proudly announced, "NCLB has already begun to make a difference . . . every state that has released results this year has reported progress in one or more areas." In New York City, Mayor Michael Bloomberg claimed that the achievement gap between white and Asian students and Black and Latinx students had been cut in half.[16]

Then the curtain fell. In the case of New York City, reanalysis by Dr. Aaron Pallas at Teachers College showed that the test scores Bloomberg lauded only closed the achievement gap by less than 1 percent, not 50 percent.[17] Amid accusations of test score inflation across the state and studies proving the tests were getting progressively easier each year, New York recalibrated scores in 2010 and almost all of the much-heralded gains disappeared.[18] Across the country, similar findings appeared. Because they were pushed to show all students were proficient, states had an incentive to lower their standards and make the tests easier to pass. When their students took other exams, like the National Assessment of Educational Progress, a low-stakes exam given to samples of students in all states each year, the results did not show the same improvement in learning.[19] On top of that, a number of cheating scandals erupted across the country, completely invalidating gains in test scores in cities like Atlanta[20] and calling them seriously into question in places like Washington, DC.[21] Smaller, less obvious examples of student and teacher cheating on the exams were discovered to be relatively common throughout the country.[22] In short, states' tests and standards had been seriously compromised as reflecting any real picture of student achievement.[23]

THE COMMON CORE AND OBAMA ACCOUNTABILITY

The Common Core State Standards (CCSS) were presented in 2009 as the answer to these problems. The standards were founded on the same principle stated in No Child Left Behind—that all students can learn if we just hold them up to high standards—but aimed to increase the rigor so that all students left high school with the "skills and knowledge necessary to succeed in college, career, and life, regardless of where they live." The intent was for the standards to be adopted nationally in order to remove much of the variation in independent state standards and tests. The standards were also supposed to emphasize "twenty-first-century skills" like critical thinking and higher-order skills—broken down in reading and math for each grade from kindergarten to twelfth grade—that would avoid "drill and kill" test prep.[24]

Then U.S. Secretary of Education Arne Duncan called the passing of CCSS a "quiet revolution" "driven by leaders in statehouses, state superintendents, local lawmakers, district leaders, union heads, school boards, parents, principals, and teachers."[25] Officially, the CCSS were developed by the National Governors Association and the Council of Chief State School Officers. They brought on Achieve, a nonprofit organization started by business leaders and governors, to write up the standards in less than a year's time. The Bill & Melissa Gates Foundation contributed significant funding to the process and, later, to the dissemination of the standards in schools around the country.[26] The design work was mostly completed by Achieve employees, people from college admissions testing companies, and staff from other education nonprofits, foundations, and think tanks. Review boards were largely composed of college professors. Despite Duncan's claims, the CCSS were definitely not written by teachers, only one of whom was included on the design and review teams, or principals, none of whom was brought into this process. The CCSS were not written by public school parents either, who, unless by chance affiliated with one of the well-connected groups listed above, were also absent.[27]

The standards quickly became news because of the Race to the Top fund, a $4 billion grant competition that was included as part of the stimulus package passed by Congress in the wake of the Great Recession. States were offered a chance to apply for a share of the funds by adopting a series of reforms outlined by the Department of Education. The first item on the list was the adoption of the CCSS or equivalent college and career ready standards. Race to the Top was announced at the end of July 2009. The first round of applications were due in November of that year, and new standards had to be in place by August 2010. In the limited time they had to pass new legislation and pull together their plans, states could scramble to create their own rigorous standards, a process that generally takes years, or go with the preapproved option, the Common Core State Standards. By 2012, as a result of Race to the Top and the administration's NCLB waiver process for continued access to Title I funds, forty-six states had signed on to the Common Core State Standards.[28]

Despite this problematic process, many educators were initially optimistic about the CCSS. They appeared to outline a more progressive approach to education, seemed to understand the importance of collaboration, questioning, and critical thinking, and they removed much of the emphasis on lower-level skills that had been the hallmark of NCLB accountability.[29] Unfortunately, the standards did not enter into the nation's schools alone. In addition to adopting standards, states had to develop assessments that aligned with these new standards, create new data systems that tracked test scores, reform their teacher evaluation systems to include test scores, and use test score data to identify and then intervene in struggling schools. This happened at the same time that states and districts slashed their education budgets and defunded major social services in the wake of the 2008 recession. The combination of these trends—higher demands, lower resources, and higher-stakes tests—doomed any potential the Common Core might have held.

TESTING 2.0

New tests were needed to match the new CCSS standards. Two consortia of multiple states were awarded $360 million in the form of a Race to the Top grant to pay for the development of the Partnership for Assessment of Readiness for College and Careers (PARCC) and the Smarter Balanced exams.[30] In a speech titled "Beyond the Bubble," Duncan explained how these new exams would revolutionize accountability and take us beyond the perils of NCLB:

I am convinced that this new generation of state assessments will be an absolute game-changer in public education. For the first time, millions of schoolchildren, parents, and teachers will know if students are on-track for colleges and careers . . .

For the first time, many teachers will have the state assessments they have longed for—tests of critical thinking skills and complex student learning that are not just fill-in-the-bubble tests of basic skills but support good teaching in the classroom . . .

For the first time, the new assessments will better measure the higher-order thinking skills so vital to success in the global economy of the 21st century and the future of American prosperity.[31]

The first rounds of tests quickly removed any shred of hope that educators had about the potential of the Common Core State Standards. The exams were often developmentally inappropriate, with material well above grade level and of excessive lengths that induced nervous breakdowns in kids as young as eight. As Elizabeth Phillips, a principal in Brooklyn, wrote in the *New York Times*, "It truly was shocking to look at the exams in third, fourth and fifth grade and to see that they were worse than ever. We felt as if we'd been had."[32] Carrol Burris, a former principal in Rockville Centre, New York, reported on a few examples of content from the new tests, including a reading passage for sixth graders that included words and phrases like "beaten curs," "absconders of justice," "surmise," "savve our cabin" and "let's maroon him," and an eighth-grade reading passage on playground safety that included "bowdlerized, habituation techniques, counterintuitive, orthodoxy, circuitous, risk averse culture and litigious."[33]

Major glitches, sometimes across entire states, botched testing days across the country, leading to suspended and canceled tests, score invalidation, and the loss of instructional time.[34] At the same time, states continued to report these scores in entirely independent and often arbitrary ways, meaning that a student who received the exact same score on the exact same test in two different states could be considered proficient in one state and not in another, just like the state tests under NCLB.[35]

On top of the many problems with the new Common Core exams, after fifteen years of accountability under NCLB and the expanded role of testing under the Obama-era reforms, students were taking an intense and growing number of tests. A study by the Council of Great City Schools found that, on average, students took 112 standardized tests between prekindergarten and twelfth grade, not including optional tests, tests to determine special education or English learner classification, or school- or teacher-designed tests. They also found that the hundred-plus tests given to students were being administered for twenty-three different purposes, including state and federal accountability, grade-to-grade promotions, English language proficiency, diagnostic information, end-of-year proficiency, program evaluation, and more, even though many of the tests were never designed for such use.[36]

The slew of tests and the push to make these tests digital have burst open a gigantic market for private companies to reap billions of dollars. The two consortia that were awarded federal money to develop the Common Core tests delivered over $300 million in contracts to companies like Pearson, CTB McGraw-Hill, and ETS to actually write the exams, and these companies received millions more in individual state contracts to administer the tests.[37] Sales in testing and assessment software and digital content in the 2012–2013 school year alone were almost $2.5 billion.[38] The education materials market as a whole was $11.8 billion in 2015, with a large share going toward Common Core–aligned materials.[39] Yet for all the money flying around in this world of accountability, these private companies often have none of it. A POLITICO investigation of Pearson, one of the largest testing companies in the world, found that states bought Pearson products in no-bid contracts without proof that they were effective, and that the company was not penalized when they failed to deliver products, meet deadlines, or implement testing programs without major problems.[40]

The letdown of new standards and new tests tied to new consequences, along with years of pent-up frustration over accountability policies, spurred a wave of antitesting resistance across the United States. Early examples of this activism were largely based in individual schools. In 2013, teachers at Seattle's Garfield High School voted to boycott the administration of a required reading and math test, and in New York City, nearly 100 percent of students at Castle Bridge Elementary refused to take tests that the city tried to impose on their grade K–2 students.[41] In the following three years, antitesting sentiment coalesced in what is now known as the "opt-out" movement. In 2015, 20 percent of New York State students opted out of the tests, with some districts within the state hitting nearly 70 percent.[42] A year later, opt-out movements were reported in Colorado, Illinois, New Jersey, New Mexico, Oregon, Pennsylvania, Florida, Maine, Indiana, Texas, and Washington.[43]

In response to the backlash over the amount of testing taking place in schools, state legislatures began to call for the rollback of the Common Core State Standards. Three states officially repealed the standards altogether, and they were brought under review in a number of others.[44] The Common Core tests faced a more thorough referendum. While initially forty-five states and the District of Columbia had agreed to use the two Department of Education–supported tests, in the 2015–2016 school year, just six states and the District of Columbia administered the PARCC exam, and fourteen used the Smarter Balanced test.[45] Since annual testing was still mandated, this set off yet another underfunded, rushed attempt by states to create new tests.

The Every Student Succeeds Act (ESSA), passed in December 2015, is the latest reauthorization of the Elementary and Secondary Education Act of 1965, nullifying the policies of NCLB. But the tests remain. Students continue to be tested—with an ever-increasing patchwork of state tests— once a year in reading and math in grades 3–8, three times for science and once in high school, exactly the same as it has been. Critics and protesters have not been completely unheeded, though. ESSA offers the opportunity for seven states to develop "innovative assessment" pilot programs for use in some school districts, though they still want those students to take standardized tests to compare the results and ensure the new assessments meet rigorous standards. And the law offers states the chance to include a school quality measure that goes beyond test scores.

NEXT-NEXT-GENERATION TESTS

Educators, reformers, and politicians have come to an agreement that the tests we have cannot fully measure everything that we want our schools to be able to do. Some states, like California, are trying to tackle this problem by developing assessments for socioemotional learning.[46] Dr. Angela Duckworth, best known for her studies of "grit," and Dr. David Scott Yaeger, who has researched successful psychological interventions in education, have explicitly argued against the measurement of noncognitive skills for accountability purposes.[47] The excitement over testing these kinds of traits highlights the continuing American obsession with accountability. We've learned that the tests are too narrow, but instead of deemphasizing them, we still just want to make the tests better, to get them right. In this case, instead of working with teachers to ensure that they access the research around socioemotional learning, equip them with tools and strategies to incorporate in their practice, and empower them to implement these in their classrooms, we skip to the end: how do we measure that they're doing this, with yet another untested test.

For their part, testing companies are also planning for the next-next generation of tests. Pearson put out a report in 2014 about the assessments they're working on, which they breathlessly explain "will create an explosion in data because they track learning and teaching at the individual student and lesson level every day." In their vision, testing is a daily event, with data tracked constantly through online systems that follow what students do in class.[48] This cutting-edge goal of testing essentially mimics what good teachers do: they take the information that students provide through their work and participation to plan and make adjustments for the whole class and for individual students in order to push everyone's learning to the next level.

We could use the money that's being poured into private companies to create new accountability systems to develop a world-renowned teaching force and well-funded schools, like many top-scoring countries do. Policy makers in the United States instead seem perpetually more interested in designing the measurement that shows the problem than in investing in solutions. We will never create equitable schools that serve all students well with this approach. A shift in the current understanding of accountability away from high-stakes standardized tests, no matter how new and improved they might be, is required. That includes pulling assessment information from multiple sources so that we can better capture the many skills that we want schools to help students develop and countering the pressure and inadequacies of standardized tests.[49] But, more importantly, it also means expanding who is held accountable for student learning. Dr. Linda Darling-Hammond talks about this as a system of shared accountability, where all levels of public education are expected to improve teaching and learning.

> States would be responsible for providing sufficient resources, for ensuring well-qualified personnel, and for adopting standards for student learning. School districts would be responsible for distributing school resources equitably, hiring and supporting well-qualified teachers and administrators (and removing those who are not competent) . . . [S]chools would be accountable for creating a productive environment for learning, assessing the effectiveness of their practices, and helping staff and parents communicate with and learn from one another. Teachers and staff would be accountable for identifying and meeting the needs of individual students as well as meeting professional standards of practice.[50]

In their book *Grading Education: Getting Accountability Right*, Dr. Richard Rothstein, Dr. Rebecca Jacobsen, and Dr. Tamara Wilder take this a step further, arguing for an accountability system that includes how public institutions help young people in their communities.[51] As of right now, accountability exists for those with the least amount of power in the system: students, parents, and teachers. If accountability is the idea that pushes us to a more equitable system, it's going to have to include a much broader group of people whose decisions shape opportunity and access for the nation's children.

TEACHERS' STORIES

In the first teacher story in this collection, Sarah Donovan takes readers through her work with one student across nearly a decade of reform efforts within their school, from NCLB testing to state mandates and finally to the Common Core, as they look for the space to create a meaningful and personal education. Graeham Dodd and Sean McAdam describe how standardized tests affected special education students and English language learners in their classrooms, creating unnecessary obstacles to real learning. Larissa Pahomov brings readers into her inquiry-based secondary school in Philadelphia, providing a model for how project-based learning can work as a form of assessment and what happens each year when everything pauses for the test. Finally, Kari Kokka details her teacher team's successful efforts to bring calculus to one of the New York State Consortium schools, where students are measured by Performance Based Assessment Tasks in place of standardized tests.

Snap If You Hear Me

Re-Forming an English Classroom

SARAH DONOVAN

"Colleen."[52]

Colleen stood up like a soldier. A quiet kid who was easily swayed off task by more extroverted students, Colleen loved to have side conversations with me about life. She was always curious about what we were learning and why.

"Okay, so this is a cento," explained Colleen. "I borrowed lines from other poems to make this one about how some pain can never be replaced or forgotten: This is a woman's confession:/She lived unknown, and few could/Know when/Pain froze you, for years—and fear—leaving scars . . ."

It was beautiful and haunting, and I could hear her trying out techniques like hyperbole. Pain cannot freeze you forever, but it sure seems like it at times. We had been reading about testimony and writing our own personal narratives, and while I know her cento was inspired by Wordsworth, in part, I couldn't help thinking about the pain I've heard in so much of my students' writing.

"Mrs. Donovan." It was my turn. Colleen gave me an apologetic look, being the one to call me out of my comfy and safe seat to share my own poem.

Every Friday our eighth-grade English class at Lincoln Junior High, a predominantly low-income, Latinx student community located just outside of Chicago, becomes Espresso Self Café. We hang up white "twinkle" lights, turn down the overhead lights, pass out cookies, and set out "the cup." I pull the first name from the cup, and a poet comes to the front of the room to speak his or her verse to the class. The poems tell stories or express an observation or experience. Some are poems we wrote in class to try out poetic techniques such as alliteration or allusion or to explore a theme such as fragile fortunes, truth and fiction, or dystopia. And some poems are inspired by heartbreak, death of a pet, friendship, or even surviving abuse. The audience of poets typically responds with a collective "aw," a giggle, or even a tear followed by snaps of appreciation for the art. The poet then draws the next name from the cup.

"Ah, you don't have to, Mrs. D.," said Jorge. "You've had a tough week. We don't expect you to have a poem ready."

"Oh, yes, we do. If we gotta do it, you gotta do it," said Dillon.

"Thank you, Jorge. And you're right, Dillon. It is only fair. I actually spoke a poem into my iPhone this morning. This just came to me, and I had to get it down."

"You mean you just came up with it?"

"Yes. I was reading this book, *The Things They Carried,* for the class I teach at UIC, and I was thinking about my dad. I was thinking about our parents and the 'things' they carry as human beings—like their history and the experiences that made them who they are before they had us. You remember how many kids are in my family right?"

"Ten," shouts Barbara. Barbara remembers all my stories.

"Yes, I have ten siblings. Thanks, Barbara. Imagine all those kids in one small house. Well, anyway, here it is. I'll just read the part about my dad, okay? The things they carried./Skippy carries a baseball glove waiting for his dad to come home./He carries his paintbrush and glue to make his model airplane/In his room./Alone./He carries the loneliness of being/ the only child/ . . ."

I finish the poem with tears in my eyes, and my students are sitting quietly. It is awkward, but they are supportive and snap for me. They hear me. They see me. And I see them.

"Barbara."

Barbara glances my way with her big brown, pleading eyes. I smile. And she slowly shifts in her seat, stalling as she opens her notebook before finally moseying to the front of the classroom. Leaning against the whiteboard, she begins to read slowly: "My stomach feels pain./The cabinets are empty./The children cry./They're hungry . . . Rain wets me./I'm freezing./I need a house to live./Will somebody help me?"

The room is silent, waiting for the next line.

* * * * *

I grew up in a middle-class family just outside Chicago, the ninth of eleven children. While I was in middle school, my father lost his job and never really worked again. While we continued to live in the same neighborhood, we were, in essence, living below the poverty line and surviving on donations from our Catholic church. Because of these early experiences, I considered myself somewhat well informed on social issues and even poverty. I studied social work in college and worked as a counselor for a number of years, where I had the privilege of listening to hundreds of life stories, virtually all of which included early school experiences. I later became a teacher, hoping to teach with and learn from the power of stories. Then I came to Lincoln.

What I found, at least on first impression, was that Lincoln Junior High was situated in a middle-class community much like where I grew up, but there was an underlying separation and racial mistrust that I did not remember experiencing in my own neighborhood. The elementary school taught the children from the neighborhood, who were mostly white, and the attached junior high taught those children *and* children from neighboring elementary schools who lived in rows of apartments just north of the school and who were mostly Latinx. The demographics changed so quickly in the early 2000s that the school purchased trailers for the expanded bilingual program for English language learners (ELLs).

I began teaching in the fall of 2004 at Lincoln Junior High. My first day there, I was assigned to a group of eighth graders who ranged from "gifted" to "newcomers." I had studied the school's demographics. I knew the school community, including many veteran Lincoln teachers, were unfamiliar with what it would mean to teach students from immigrant families, some still learning English and many from low-income families. It was, therefore, surprising that the two in-service days that preceded the first day of school were spent looking at data rather than talking about the social and economic needs of our changing school community.

In the first English department meeting of the school year, in room H103 two days before we met the students, each English teacher was handed student rosters with test scores from the previous school year. As I looked around the room of a dozen or so teachers furiously highlighting away, I quickly grabbed a highlighter, intent to look like I knew what I was doing, but indeed I had no idea. I was told to highlight the students who were "on the bubble." Noticing my confusion, the department head, Debbie, explained that a student "on the bubble" meant that the student did not "meet" the cut-off score on the Illinois Standard Achievement Test (ISAT) but was within a few points, so these students had the potential to actually pass this year. When I asked about all the other students who were below this range, she essentially said that they were too far behind in reading to bring up to grade level in one year. I went to work. When I asked what we were going to do with the highlighted pages, I was told that I needed to give extra attention to, or "target," those students on the bubble to raise their ISAT scores (administered in early March each year), and that the "district-approved" curriculum would help me. My department chair went on to explain what was at stake. In 2001 No Child Left Behind (NCLB) was signed into law, which meant that if our students' reading scores did not improve, we could be out of a job. This was my introductory lesson in data analysis and the institution of school.

Thinking about this now, I imagine Barbara walking out of her apartment with her backpack to get on a school bus for the first time. I can see her waiting at the bus stop along a busy street with cars zooming by while the local kindergartners walk to school with their parents. She would have been sitting in one of those trailers on her first day of kindergarten while others were in a classroom with windows. Was she finger painting, learning her numbers and letters, and loving story time, or was she subjected to some form of testing and goal setting? Barbara's parents are undocumented. They came to this suburb of Chicago for jobs and more affordable housing. Barbara represents all that was changing in this school, but the changes the school was experiencing did not tell Barbara's story. To tell Barbara's story, we would have had to listen to the stories of our students and their families, but instead we were listening to the data.

In a matter of hours, I received my next lesson on curriculum. I was presented a district-approved textbook written by Who Knows and published by Prentice Hall, a Pearson Education company. I was given the "bronze" level for my "regular" classes and the "gold" level for my "gifted" class. The school district paid Prentice Hall a lot of money for math, history, and literature textbooks that were "research based." For literature, we were presented CDs with recordings of every text, VHS tapes for "anticipatory activities," a database for test questions, three levels of consumables (i.e., workbooks), abbreviated versions of the literature for ELLs or struggling readers, and skills worksheets with every graphic organizer imaginable.

For a few years, the classrooms and hallways were covered with data and goals to raise reading and math scores. I had students charting their reading scores and setting improvement goals. I posted lists grouping students by skill deficits: word analysis, literary works, literary devices, and comprehension, among others. At one point in my first year, I even had visitors from other schools; they were mesmerized by my charts: weekly word analysis scores, comprehension competitions, and reading scores from quarter to quarter. I did not understand why teachers complained about being underappreciated. The district office was visiting classrooms and celebrating teachers for their efforts. It seemed like teachers were literally shining a light on the students who had been, or would be, "left behind" had we not looked at the data. It seemed like we were targeting their needs and filling them. There were, however, always students below the "bubble."

Year after year, Barbara and students like her who did not "meet standards" on the state test received more interventions. When goal setting did not work, Barbara was placed in a variety of specialized classes and tested more frequently than other students. The intervention classes were often expensive scripted programs devoid of teachers deciding what to teach, when to teach it, and how. Such curriculum has been coined "teacher-proof." After all, when a child is in a school for a number of years and does not pass the test, it must be the teacher's fault. By junior high, when Barbara still had not passed the state test, she had two math classes and three reading classes—there was no room in her schedule for music, art, a foreign language, or computer classes. So even though Barbara was no longer spending her days in the trailers outside the school, she was still segregated.

For me, when I wasn't looking at charts, I was fighting for survival. Of the six classes that came to me each day, none was easy. The diversity of students was overwhelming. Students' reading levels ranged from second grade to high school. Some students did homework; some did not. Some students wrote pages and pages, and others could barely put a sentence together. While over a third of my students were "Hispanic," I also had some students from Poland, Azerbaijan, India, and China along with the local white students. Lincoln, once a fairly homogenous, white, middle-class school, was now incredibly diverse, and I feared that we were not being responsive to students' lived lives. It seemed to me that the focus on testing and interventions failed to address the underlying social forces that brought us all together from 7:55 a.m. to 2:25 p.m. every day.

In 2011, our paths finally crossed. I met Barbara. In fact, I met Barbara in one of those reading intervention classes. In late summer, I was informed that my assignment for the coming fall, my eighth year at Lincoln, would be as a reading intervention teacher. The course was a new, highly prescriptive curriculum designed for "long-term" ELLs, English language learners who have attended U.S. schools for seven years or more. It was an expensive and intensive three-period reading program that came with a teacher's guide with explicit, integrated daily lessons to develop phonemic awareness, build vocabulary, and increase reading fluency. Insulted by this "teacher-proof" curriculum, I asked to meet with the school administrator.

"With all due respect," I said, "you are paying me a lot of money for my experience, judgment, and skills as a teacher. I have a master's degree and am halfway through a doctorate in English education. Please, let me do my job."

"Will all due respect," I was told, "we've been paying teachers to do their job for years, and still we have these students who cannot read and write on grade level. Follow the program."

I understood where they were coming from. There was a lot at stake, and after a long discussion, we agreed that there would be about twenty minutes a day when I could do my own curriculum. While I contemplated resigning, I knew how fortunate I was to have a job while so many were unemployed.

Barbara was a wonderful student of this curriculum. She filled in vocabulary blanks. She read the fluency passages with fluency. She matched sounds and letters quickly in the phonics section perfectly. And she followed the writing models well. In fact, all the students did well, and we finished the program in a few months, plenty of time for "my curriculum." They would write the stories of their lives and listen to countless other stories as we tried to make sense of our place in the world.

I had not anticipated the silence. When I gave them a journal for writing their own stories, it was as if the blank page was a ghost. They seemed afraid to mark it. At one point, Barbara said, "Just tell me what to write. I do good when the teacher just tells me." Instead, I told her one of my stories.

"When I was your age," I began, "I shared a bedroom with three of my sisters. We would roll up our blankets in the morning and store them in the closet, and at night we'd roll them out again to sleep. On some mornings before school, my mother would creep into our bedroom gently stepping between the bodies curled up on the floor looking for a few to take to work with her."

"Huh? You had to go to work before school?" one boy, Jorge, asked.

"It's not that strange. I help my dad at work all the time. Let her finish," Maria said.

"I was not a good sleeper," I continued, "so I was an easy target. We'd get dressed in the dark, pile into the car, and help her clean the bank at the local mall. I still remember the smell of the cigarette ashes as we dumped them into the garbage. Then we had to wipe out the remaining specks of ash. I can taste it in my mouth right now."

"So that's what you want to know," said Barbara.

"About your everyday life. Yes, I want to know the small stories that make up your life. Stories that only you can tell."

This was very different from the scripted lessons we had done earlier that year, where virtually everyone's essay about the Kush or Objects in Motion would be the same.

"I can do that."

And Barbara told me about how she makes coffee for herself in the morning, and how she feeds her brother breakfast. She included a poem about how her brother's laughter makes her happy, and she told me about a time her mother explained to her why she was different: a childhood accident that caused head trauma. Barbara told me that she has a hard time remembering what she learns.

When we began to read literature, I shared *Broken Memory,* a story about a Hutu child who survived the Tutsi-led genocide of Hutus in Rwanda. Barbara took copious notes. Even so, she seemed upset when the test did not have multiple-choice or fill-in-the blank options. Instead, I asked her to write about Emma, a Tutsi, who was saved by a Hutu woman. I wanted her to talk about the *gacaca* courts, and if she thought it was an example of democracy. I wanted to hear what she thought of America's response to the genocide. And she told me everything.

Still, we were segregated now. We spent three class periods together while the other students moved across classrooms with a variety of teachers and students. When Barbara and her classmates finished our three-period reading class, they went on to a double math class. I can say that the writing and reading we did that year helped Barbara's test scores, but she did not pass the state test. Our school became a "failing school." It was clear to everyone that NCLB indeed left some children behind.

The following August, I was moved to the very classroom where I learned to bubble, H103, and was informed that my assignment would be eighth-grade reading and writing. This school year, the Common Core State Standards were being implemented for the first time. I was happy to learn that the prescriptive curriculum was boxed up, but I was worried about Barbara and her classmates. I did not want her to spend her last year in our school district still segregated. I met with my building administrators and proposed that Barbara and her classmates be integrated for eighth-grade reading and writing. Coteaching with a bilingual teacher, we were careful to differentiate instruction to meet their needs. And I designed a curriculum *with* the students to really look at the social forces that shape our society, consider the sort of development we need to respond to our needs in a globalized world, and to uncover the darker side of modernity.

We took the global focus of the new standards seriously. And we began with an explicit agenda to understand globalization, to make a lot of time for students to lead discussions and generate their own writing topics, to use minimal worksheets or multiple-choice-style assessments, to grade using a portfolio and conference-based assessments, and to avoid, as much as possible, the phrase "you have to know this for the test." Because I had spent the previous three years in a doctoral program on English education teaching prospective teachers, I knew a lot about the Common Core State Standards, and I knew that it was a transition year. I wanted to see how we could use the new standards to *serve our* purposes rather than have them *be* the purpose.

In the months that followed, this eighth-grade English class studied the social, political, and economic causes and consequences of cultural intersections with dozens of first- and second-generation immigration stories and poetry; learned about testimony and bearing witness by writing personal narratives and listening to Loung Ung, a Cambodian-born American human rights activities and genocide survivor; considered consumerism and fragile fortunes with Steinbeck's *The Pearl* and Greenfield's documentary *The Queen of Versailles;* and explored the darker side of progress and climate change through contemporary young adult texts like *The Carbon Diaries, The Maze Runner, Divergent, Matched, Ship Breaker,* and *Among the Hidden.*

We read these texts with the same critical eye with which we began our year: with deliberate attention to the rhetorical and aesthetic nature of narrative and informational texts, and all with no test prep, textbooks, or purchased curriculum. We wrote about our lives, our ideas about the world, and the experiences that shape us. We learned the beauty and power of language with music and poetry. Student-led discussions captured nuances of ideas and showed how texts transact with experience. We all learned to listen to each other's stories and interpretations with sympathetic and critical ears, pushing interpretation and calling attention to how ideas are constructed for audience and purpose. And when we came together on Fridays to speak of our lives and our learning, what seemed most evident was that the poets were showing their unique contributions to the larger conversation about sharing this world, about being human, and about how language shapes our understanding. Don't we want to see and hear those unique contributions? Isn't that what living in the twenty-first century is all about?

In that year, I was able to take advantage of this transitional moment between the old and new policies to reimagine what an English classroom in the twenty-first century can do, to "pop the bubble." One student wrote: "This [year] helped and strengthened my thinking because now I look beyond and I think beyond. I wrote more and if I don't know what to write in my head I just let my pen think and write for me." I like the word "beyond," and think students were developing a way of writing and reading beyond what they had before. They began to believe that their voices matter, that what the world needs is their unique contribution, their story.

My school district is now fully invested in the Common Core State Standards (CCSS). I can see the same narrowing of curriculum as with NCLB, now under the guise of "college and career readiness." The accountability measures are still in place with new (and more) tests: the new PARCC test, which included a three-week interruption in instruction to test every student on math and reading; the Next Generation Science Standards (NGSS); and continued periodic progress-monitoring testing. As the Every Student Succeeds Act is implemented, as teachers use CCSS, and as PARCC data is analyzed in these next few years, my hope is that our nation will be free to return to conversations about education and how better to spend our time with the human beings with whom we are entrusted.

* * * * *

"Somebody, somewhere, somehow, some when, some time," Barbara concluded. There was a delay, but then came the snaps. She smiled at the sound of her peers snapping in appreciation of her verse, of her ideas, of her heart. Barbara was a somebody, the body we almost left behind with our targets and interventions. Her vision of the world survived, and I hope it will thrive through these next rounds of tests as she moves on to high school.

As the snaps subsided, she smiled and approached the cup. "Kevin."

"Purpose. A seven letter word./But what does it mean?/What is my purpose?" he began.

Sarah J. Donovan has been teaching junior high English language arts for twelve years and is an adjunct professor at DePaul University, Illinois, where she teaches graduate courses in adolescent development. She earned a PhD in English from the University of Illinois at Chicago, specializing in young adult genocide literature and English education. Three classroom projects she is developing with her seventh graders include a No-Grades Classroom, Bearing Witness: Documenting the Stories of Our Community, and the Inclusive Literature Workshop. She has a forthcoming book, Genocide Literature in Middle and Secondary Classrooms: Rhetoric, Witnessing, and Social Action in a Time of Standards and Accountability.

Nurturing Struggling Learners' Spirits in the School Testing Culture

GRAEHAM DODD

One sultry August afternoon while I was preparing for the coming school year, my classroom phone rang. The registrar asked if I could assess an incoming third grader to determine his current reading level. I did this sometimes when I was at school and a new student came in to enroll. It was part of my school's effort to start the school year off with as much knowledge of our students as possible. In Spanish, I explained the work that I would be doing with him to his mother, and when she smiled and nodded in agreement, Alvaro and I took the first step into our year together.

Alvaro told me that he and his mother had just moved to northern Virginia from California. When I asked him what prompted the move, he shrugged, not sure. "You don't know?" I asked. His face retained its original uncertainty. I asked him what he liked to do. He said he liked to play soccer. I sensed that he was nervous. He fidgeted, and his answers consisted of only a few words each. Still, he beamed brightly as often as he wrinkled his brow. Despite the way his eyes were fervently searching mine for something in them to trust, he seemed amiable and excited about his new school.

I began guiding the conversation toward the reading assessment I was about to give Alvaro. "Do you like to read?" I asked. He said yes and that he was really good at it. I asked him to name some of his favorite books. He grinned sheepishly and shrugged yet again. I asked him to name a book he had read recently. He squirmed in his seat and then said he hadn't been reading because of moving. I knew this was not a good sign, because a pattern had emerged in my then still-short career: students who cannot think of a single book they love or a reason to read are often struggling, inexperienced readers. I will never forget the way my first class, filled with fidgety second graders, gazed at me blankly in the early days of school as I enthusiastically read to them after lunch every day. After many afternoons of laboring through what should have been, from my perspective, among the most anticipated parts of each day, one of my students raised his hand. "I just . . . don't understand," he said, clearly trying to be as polite as he could. "Why are you reading to us?" And almost the whole class twisted in their chairs to look from him to me, laughing and murmuring all over the room about how they had been wondering the same thing, breathing out in relief because finally someone had asked so it could stop. I put the book back on the shelf, where it stayed. Reading aloud for the sheer joy of it in class has become taboo. And when I interview my students about their reading habits at the beginning of the year, most of them struggle to tell me what books they enjoy, and many don't understand the question about what book they last read with an adult.

I hoped that Alvaro's assessment of himself as a strong reader was accurate. I introduced the reading assessment—designed and provided by Teachers College at Columbia University—and we began. With reading assessments, if a student does not demonstrate proficiency on any given assessment, the teacher administers the one at the next step down. When a student is on level or close to it, the reading assessment can take approximately fifteen minutes. I spent nearly an hour with Alvaro, going backward until I was finally able to place him at the level of a midyear first grader. By the time we stopped working, he was fatigued and regarding me with obvious wariness. I could see that reading innumerable passages and picture books and answering so many questions after each one had baffled him. The truth was that he *did* read well. But he didn't understand what he read, and his voice was shapeless and emotionless as he raced from the top of each page to the bottom, indicating that he was not engaging with the stories. Probably no one had ever given him this kind of indication that he wasn't a "good" reader. In fact, Alvaro would go on to take a standardized reading test required by the state of Virginia two months later and score on a fifth-grade reading level. Perhaps this is why he had always been deemed a strong reader: he could ace reading tests that were graded primarily on the basis of a student's ability to recognize and decode words and recall bare-bones facts about the text. But when viewed holistically as a reader and pushed to deeply and critically comprehend high-quality literature, he faltered.

Alvaro had to have known that the texts I put before him were getting progressively easier. It is difficult to explain this to students and their parents alike, especially when they have come to believe that everything is all right, if not ideal, in the child's education. I returned Alvaro to his mother. The conversation about his reading level would come when school started. As they left, all I could think about was how could this have happened and what would it take to bring Alvaro up to a third-grade reading level, and quickly. I felt bewildered by the paradox of reading "achievement" in Alvaro's life: in a matter of one hour, I had identified him as a reader in need of aggressive remediation, after he had spent his learning career believing he was at the top of his game. In reality, he had been educated to "win" at tests.

Meanwhile, he needed English language support, and when school started, I would find that he needed considerable support in all of his other subjects as well. I wondered what his previous school had been up against. Alvaro was in my hands now, and there was so much to do that I spent a few days in despair. I've learned that every solution starts somewhere, so sometimes you just need to pick a spot and start chipping away. To begin with, Alvaro (and most of his classmates) required a bolstered vocabulary to assist with thinking and talking deeply about learning.

There's a riddle among educators that goes like this: from what country do the most English language learners (ELLs) originate in United States classrooms? The answer is the United States. Alvaro is one of them. A beginning English speaker, he was among the 50 percent of my class that spoke English as a second language. I have had classes with varying percentages of ELLs; in one, nearly all of my students spoke another language as their first. Teaching English learners, whether they were born here or lived part of their lives in another country where English is not the primary language, is a skill set that general educators need just as much as teachers who focus on teaching language. Ensuring the success of English learners in school is uncertain work. We are still figuring out the best pedagogy and learning to be culturally relevant for all students.

It can take years for students to become proficient with social vocabulary, and many more on top of those to become proficient with academic vocabulary. It has become the work of teachers to learn the theories of language acquisition and practice its implementation. It is one of the most critical and powerful equalizers in public education. It yields extraordinary results, including the blossoming of student language skills and confidence, but it is laborious and difficult. The scaffolding of vocabulary is what must be done in order to make reading (and all learning) accessible and enjoyable for students like my third graders. Furthermore, vocabulary instruction can be difficult for many parents to practice at home when the parents themselves are learning English, when parents must work more than one job or late hours in order to make ends meet, or when parents need a stronger understanding of the impact they can make on their children's learning. In my time working as a public school teacher, I have found myself wearing many hats: teaching children, teaching parents, advocating for children and their families, and trying to become a better teacher through a myriad of professional development. Teachers work tirelessly to identify and give students everything they need. Alvaro was no exception to this. He received intensive reading remediation, English support, and constant attention in all of his other subject areas.

Alvaro both blossomed and struggled. Three teachers came together to provide instruction and reading opportunities for an hour and a half each day to help him develop into a more inquisitive, careful reader. In this model, he rapidly made up lost ground and was legitimately on level by the middle of the school year. We celebrated this triumph and the quashing of the idea that reading is saying the words on a page out loud. Alvaro became a leader in his small guided-reading groups and seemed to gain confidence in himself as a learner. He reflected that he was able to comprehend what he was reading more meaningfully. He slowed down and seemed to enjoy what he read.

Yet Alvaro and other students still didn't really *want* to read. I try to foster in my students that feeling of urgency to connect to book characters and plots and themes that compels readers to read. Alvaro read in school, where books were selected for him and his reading was carefully guided so that he could learn to use an array of comprehension skills independently. But left to his own devices, he read one less-than-robust book over and over for the duration of the year, and with strict district reading guidelines to follow, I felt that I didn't have time to teach him how to make more meaningful book choices or to help him build the stamina he needed to sit and enjoy a book. I once taught a book to a remediation guided-reading group of rising third graders about Luis Soriano, a Colombian teacher who took it upon himself to provide access to a library to remote villages by way of traveling donkeys. After we read and discussed the book for two days, I asked my group why they thought Luis Soriano believed so strongly that all people should learn how to read. One of my students solemnly explained that the reason students are taught to read is so that they can pass standardized tests. The other students in the group did not counter this opinion.

As the year went on, the thinking was getting more difficult. The cultivation of independence was growing more constant. The lessons were not meant to be easy. They were meant to foster perseverance, problem-solving skills, and creativity in my students, along with a tolerance for devoting time to their efforts. Yet right around the time that my third graders began to handle more cognitively demanding and abstract tasks, I began to feel pressed to integrate testing techniques and practice into my teaching.

It is at this point that I began to lose credibility as Alvaro's teacher. I had coaxed my students to think deeply and critically, urged them to feel comfortable making mistakes and recognizing them as learning opportunities, and developed them into team players, but now I was telling them all to think in one specific way. After many months of insisting on excellence, I changed my tune. Simultaneously, I was stretched thin between trying to maintain a rigorous, exciting classroom environment and teaching directly to the four tests that my eight- and nine-year-olds would take over the course of six designated days. My own energy waned, and I felt torn between going to students like Alvaro who were struggling with the critical, open-ended assignments that I wanted him to think through and the data that shows he was still unable to correctly answer standardized questions similar to those he would encounter on the English Language Arts state tests. I couldn't stay torn for long, though, because I needed him to pass those tests. Good or bad, our names would be chained together on every score report.

By the end of the year, I'd lost the student who had come to me in need and had incited me to do everything in my power to provide him with an equal-opportunity education. The time I had had to teach him with every progressive, aggressive trick I had had eventually run out, not because the school year had ended, but because it was time to start testing. I thought I'd had him hooked on learning, but I hadn't had enough time to both bring him up to speed and help him realize a love for learning. As testing season began, Alvaro turned on me, focusing his attention on fitting in with some new friends. His effort and work completion waned.

Every year my colleagues and I exhaust our resources and test our own inner strength as we reach for the many students who come to us in need of remediation in both basic skills and elasticity of mind. At the still-young ages of eight and nine, I find that most third graders are at a place in their lives where they are developmentally ready to start seeing themselves as contributing members of their communities, and they believe that learning primes them for this. As their teacher, I strive to teach them to think critically and analytically, to strategize, and to problem solve. I do everything in my power to inspire love of learning in children. I also demonstrate my own determination that "the test" will not entirely consume the spring of every year.

Educators who push back on testing mentalities and all-consuming test preparations are fighting an unbelievably exhausting fight. They are working to counter the very beliefs that our now well-developed testing culture fosters: that standardized thinking is valuable, meaningful, and urgent. They are working for those moments when they hear a student say, "I think maybe I really love school." In many ways, my school and district have taken on this fight since the height of the testing craze when Alvaro was in my class. Educators at all levels in our district and across the country have begun the work of rethinking how to make education meaningful, personalized, and rigorous for our students. I am hopeful that it means Alvaro's experience is relegated to a particular time in our history—one where testing took over and left little room for students and teachers to fully develop—and that we can now focus on teaching and learning that inspires imagination and innovation in our students.

Graeham Dodd teaches at the elementary level in the Alexandria City Public Schools of Virginia, located just outside of Washington, DC. She is currently in her sixth year of teaching. Graeham also taught English at the elementary level as a Fulbright Fellow in Madrid, Spain. She earned both her bachelor's degree and her master of arts degree in teaching at Smith College and will complete her graduate degree in administration and supervision from the University of Virginia in 2017.

What Happens When Common Doesn't Address Everyone

SEAN MCADAM

I never intended to become a teacher, or even to work with children at all. I had just finished my master's degree in speech-language pathology and wanted to work in a hospital setting with adults. At that time, all hospital-based jobs were looking for candidates with a minimum of three years of experience, so I found myself walking into one of the consistently lowest performing schools in the state in one of the most violent neighborhoods in Boston with no idea about what to expect. It took a few months of doing all the wrong things to finally figure out what I should do. Once I did, my career took a turn I would never have expected.

I worked with a variety of students, some with physical disabilities like cerebral palsy, some with cognitive disabilities like Down syndrome, some with autism, and a significant percentage of students with learning disabilities. I loved working with all of my students, but quickly found that my true passion was working with students with learning disabilities.

I remember the first students that I ever felt like I had reached. Their names were Sid and Fernando, and they both struggled breaking down words when they were reading. I met with them outside of class for thirty minutes twice a week, going over the rules of phonics: a "apple" /a/ (representing the short vowel sound for a); e "egg" /e/. I was nervous about having to start here with them because they were in seventh grade, and it seemed almost insulting to be teaching them things that are taught in kindergarten. But this kind of teaching is what they needed, so I gave it a shot. By the end of the year, Sid had made about two grade levels of progress in his reading and had passed the seventh-grade English language arts state assessment for the first time ever. Fernando made improvements throughout the year, though not at the same levels. After I had worked with him for three years, he left for ninth grade, and I worried if there would be someone else following him carefully. Without that, I feared that he could easily slip through the cracks.

Working with these amazing young men, I realized that I needed to change what I did if I wanted to see the greatest positive change for the students I had in front of me. I signed up for a teacher licensure program to become a special education classroom teacher and began in the fall of 2010 at my new school. It was a middle school of 550–600 students in one of the smaller neighborhoods of Boston. Most of the students were bused in from other neighborhoods, mostly tougher parts of the city. They were considered low income, and a significant portion of them also had learning disabilities and intellectual impairments. Despite these variables, my school had made great gains over the previous four years and was the fastest-growing middle school in the city on state assessments.

That was the first year I ever really had to worry about the Massachusetts Comprehensive Assessment System (MCAS), our state achievement test that students took every year in grades 3–8 and again in grade 10. Passing these tests is a requirement for high school graduation. I had worked with students on their reading comprehension and phonics, and had even used a few MCAS materials in some of my work with students as a speech and language therapist, but this year the test dominated all of my thoughts and plans as a teacher. MCAS review days, MCAS practice tests, test-taking strategies, open responses: that is what many of my teaching days had become. I was the special educator for the sixth-grade team, and most of my students that year had failed the math MCAS consistently from third through fifth grade. Based on the No Child Left Behind Act of 2001, it was expected that all students were supposed to be proficient on state achievement tests by 2014. How do you go from failing to proficient in three years? My initial thought was that these students must have had really poor teachers in elementary school. Why else would they be consistently failing?

The students that I worked with that year taught me so much about how to teach students with learning disabilities. Two students from that first year stand out in my memory, Rosie and Sandra. Rosie was a bright and eager young lady who completed all of her classwork and homework, was almost always among the first to raise her hand to participate, and was often accurate and always thoughtful with her responses. As each unit came to a close, we would take our test, and she consistently got scores of 80 and above. Her fifth-grade MCAS score, though, was "warning," also known as failing. At first glance, this didn't make any sense, but it became clearer when we had to practice-MCAS days. Once every month and a half, we would take an assessment that pretty closely mirrored our state exam.

Each time I made the announcement about the next practice test, I would see Rosie's enthusiasm turn into anxiety. The first time this happened, I noticed her worried look and pulled her into the hallway, asking her if everything was okay.

"I hate these tests. I always do bad on them."

"You're not going to fail," I replied, as any encouraging and somewhat naïve first year teacher would. "You do so well on our class tests, and the questions are just like it."

She turned in her test, and I couldn't have been more excited to grade it to show her that she had gotten at least 65 or 70 percent, a mark that was supposed to be indicative of proficiency on the MCAS. Thirty-six percent. There it was. I didn't have the heart to tell her then. Instead, I told her that I wanted to give her feedback on all of the questions and that I'd show her the test the next day.

Now panic set in. What had I done wrong with my teaching? Maybe I wasn't teaching the right way, and that's why information wasn't sinking in. I returned the tests the next day, sweating in anticipation of the students' reactions, because the average score for my students with disabilities was in the 40s. Some weren't phased; others were visibly upset. I set them up on their next assignment and talked individually with some of the students. When I got to Rosie, she was still upset. I learned from her that she just "freaks out" when she gets a test and forgets what to do. There were too many things to remember.

Sandra had more difficulty on assessments. She even had trouble remembering material from day to day. Her learning disability affected her memory and her language. In class, she often had her head down. I would find any opportunity to call on her when I knew she could answer. She was more frustrated with school than most other students I had worked with. During the first week of school, when I made my beginning of the year phone calls, her mother had said that Sandra hated school because it made her "feel dumb." I made many calls to Sandra's mom that year and the following year. While Sandra had many moments of success in class, she couldn't do well on tests, and her grades were rarely higher than C on her report card.

As a first- and second-year classroom teacher, I never quite cracked the code for how best to help Sandra learn. I can partly attribute this to lack of experience and partly to the reality of her disability. A paper and pencil test was not how Sandra could show her knowledge. Unfortunately, with the pressures of testing, I felt the need to give my students that practice as frequently as I could, and that one mark is how her performance would be judged the following year.

The results of the MCAS from my first year of teaching came in August 2011. I was fully expecting that my students were going to do great. At least half of them should pass. We had worked so hard all year. Lo and behold, most were STILL failing. Failing? Really? My first thought was that there must have been something wrong with the scoring. They had made decent growth, measured in percentiles, but the bottom line is that most were still scoring in the warning range. I thought back to all of the days where we practiced for the MCAS. I thought of Rosie and Sandra. On those practice days, they made mistakes they never would have made in our regular classroom. I am now in my fourth year of teaching math and my eighth year of working with students with significant learning disabilities, and I still see the same patterns.

What I didn't think about that first year, and what these tests could not account for, was how a student with a learning disability actually learns. Students with learning disabilities are often unpredictable in their output, frequently making mistakes even if they understand the content they are being assessed on. Many of my students also have significant memory issues. Even if they can understand how to do a math problem, they may simply not remember all of the steps needed to complete it. All year we practice doing problems with resources to refer back to, and maybe three in every ten students use these resources on tests. When I ask them why they didn't use their references, the answer I get 95 percent of the time is, "I didn't even think to use them."

For the last three years, I have taught students with even more significant learning disabilities and mild intellectual impairments, students with IQs in the 55–70 range (80–120 being considered "average" intelligence). Many of these students struggle to remember daily routines and basic personal information like their address, family's phone number or job, or how to get to and from school. These students are still required to take and pass standardized tests in order to receive their high school diploma. They can attain functional literacy and math skills, but few are able to engage in any complex problem solving, language, or literary analysis. Yet these students are also expected to pass the MCAS in tenth grade, or at least by the end of twelfth grade, to receive a high school diploma. How were they and I going to meet this goal?

Each day I looked out into my first-period math classroom and saw twelve eager faces ready to learn. This particular group of students was so hard working, striving to do the best they could in math. Even the one or two that didn't always work their hardest, with the right kind of encouragement, showed moments of great success. And then came testing days. Their smiles left and their faces turned worried. Terror struck them, because it was yet again going to be another test where they would look at the questions and not know how to answer all of them. I tried to boost their confidence before these tests, reminding them that it's okay if they didn't know how to answer every question. They didn't need a perfect score to pass, and I was more concerned with how much they grew than the actual score (true for me, not necessarily true for how the state measures whether our school is a failing one, if my students will graduate, or if I am teaching well enough). To no avail. They so easily got stuck in a space of hopelessness: "I'm not going to know how to do anything on this test." Despite their frustration with these tests, this group outscored all of the general education classes in my school in terms of growth, scoring in the sixty-second percentile, considered a high mark. Even with this phenomenal progress, though, only two students passed the assessment.

Unfortunately for some of my students, I don't know if they have the cognitive skills to pass these high-level assessments. When you haven't mastered the third-grade math content, it's nearly impossible to get caught up on the material from fourth, fifth, sixth, and seventh grade, especially when your brain wiring requires more exposure to information to learn it and does not possess some of the memory or cognitive flexibility to do higher-level thinking problems. Sofia and Gina were two such students I had in class this past year. They were very organized, had good social skills, and worked hard at everything they did. Sofia was slow to learn to read and speak in English, so her vocabulary was still weak but was slowly improving with each passing day. Her memory, however, greatly stood in the way of her achievement. One day in math class, she became an expert in setting up proportion problems but could not remember all the steps for solving the problem. The next day, she needed to be retaught how to even set up the proportion that she had mastered the day before. Gina had memory issues as well, but was much better at finding and following patterns. Once she learned the pattern for solving a problem, she could solve that same type of problem with ease. As soon as the problem looked slightly different in either wording or layout, though, she would not know how to proceed.

I could have spent months teaching proportions to these young women. However, there are thirty-nine standards to cover by the beginning of May, when the math MCAS is administered. Do I teach them the functional skills to survive in the world or the academic skills needed to attain basic proficiency to receive a high school diploma? I haven't found a way to do both.

As part of the adoption of the Common Core State Standards, Massachusetts is developing a new and improved MCAS that includes elements from the Partnership for Assessment of Readiness for College and Careers (PARCC). The basic idea is to further increase the academic rigor that students, teachers and schools are accountable for. I look at sample items from this new assessment and wonder, how is this an assessment for readiness for college AND CAREER? Many of my students struggle in school because of their learning issues but will still achieve great things in this world. Some will go to college and will persevere through their learning challenges to achieve associate's, bachelor's, master's, and even doctoral degrees. Others are going to choose a less academic path, looking for work right out of high school.

I see so many of the strengths my students possess. Many of my students are more organized, mechanically inclined, or able to listen and respond thoughtfully to others than the average person in America. These skills are certainly invaluable to any number of careers that my students aspire to. Unfortunately, because of their learning challenges, they may not be afforded access to those careers based on the result of an assessment that does not evaluate the basic literacy and mathematics skills needed for some of these jobs. Many of my students' futures hang in the balance because of this one assessment. Simply put, they will not be able to get a high school diploma without passing it.

In any of the conversations I have had about new assessments and the Common Core State Standards, special education students are the last group to be considered, even though about 20 percent of American children have some type of disability. A calculator or read-aloud technology appears to be the solution that everyone has for students to pass these assessments. I can only speak for the students I have taught, but these accommodations have not been enough to date and will not suddenly be enough with the advent of another new test. There is certainly a subset of students with disabilities who can pass state assessments because they have more mild learning disabilities. I have worked with these students, and to help students unlock the code to their learning difficulties by teaching them strategies and skills is something remarkable. However, there is still a percentage of students with disabilities that lawmakers, education policy makers, and giant test producers are not considering, many of whom I teach today. Someone has to advocate for my students. Someone outside of the four walls of my classroom has to consider their academic and longer-term life needs.

Sean McAdam is in his eleventh year in the Boston Public Schools. He began his career as a speech-language pathologist and has been a special education classroom teacher for the past seven years. He has spent much of his career working with middle school students, and recently transitioned to working with students in the upper elementary grades.

Accept, Reject, Dismantle

The Life of a Testing Coordinator

LARISSA PAHOMOV

My name is Larissa.[53] Except when I'm working as testing coordinator at my school. Then you must call me Natasha.

I never expected to end up with an assumed name in my professional life. Of course, I didn't set out to become a testing coordinator, either. To be fair, it's a relatively limited part of my job. I work at Science Leadership Academy, a small public high school in Philadelphia that has been open for ten years with a curriculum that has been 100 percent project based from the start. Although we do give tests and quizzes, they are only used as formative assessments. There is no Scantron machine in the office. Instead, there is a framed t-shirt that hangs on the principal's wall. It reads: "Standardized Tests—Standardized Minds!"

In the regular life of my school—the world of my true teacher-self, Larissa—assessment is active, engaging, student centered, and measures higher-order thinking. We actively reject the idea that a numerical score can tell us more about our students than the work that we do together in our classrooms. So if we don't rely primarily on testing to assess student learning, what do we do instead? The more apt question might be, what *don't* we do? Our projects employ all kinds of methods and mediums. Students design prototypes, build models, write essays, make movies, and create public works of art. Our approach to teaching and learning reflects our belief that authentic education happens when you have the freedom and resources to pursue your own lines of inquiry, not when you are asked to memorize basic information and display it on an exam.

In any given subject, a new unit often opens with lessons that look like a more traditional classroom—assigned readings, analytical conversations, and the occasional quiz to check for mastery of basic content and skills. Those lessons become the foundation on which students then create a final product, which typically has both a real-world application and an authentic audience. In Spanish class, students might master new vocabulary about clothes and appearance before writing a script for a fashion show, with video of students modeling and narration recorded on top of the images. In algebra, students will be quizzed on the different components of parabolic functions before building trebuchets and catapults based on their independent calculations and then conducting multiple trials with their machines to verify their original equations. A 1:1 laptop program bolsters all of this creative work. Each student has a Chromebook that stays with them the whole school year. This combination of powerful tools and a generative mindset puts students in the driver's seat when it comes to their own education.

This incredible culture of teaching and learning also has a concrete, sophisticated system for assessing student mastery. The work of each quarter culminates with a benchmark project in each major subject, a nod to the multiple-choice "benchmark exams" given by many schools in our district. This project is graded via a rubric, with individual teachers giving specific criteria for assessment within five categories that are used schoolwide: design, knowledge, application, presentation, and process. Just as our unit plans provide a common baseline for students before they engage in more individualized exploration, our rubric gives teachers a scaffold for planning while still respecting their autonomy.

In addition to the rubric, each department has also developed criteria for standards-based grading. These standards describe the skills that students should master in sentence format, with teachers collecting multiple data points on each standard over the course of a school year. Online grade books make this tracking easy, and students can usually check their progress at any time. Each fall and spring, we also issue report cards with notes about student performance on each standard: exceeds, meets, approaching, does not meet. These standards-based reports live separately from the regular report cards issued by the school district and are discussed twice a year at advisor report card conferences along with long-form narratives written by the teachers. These are just a few strategies SLA uses to deemphasize the numerical grades the district requires us to give out. Each piece of the puzzle is designed to get students intrinsically motivated about their learning, to unshackle them from their previous notions about what school should be, in the hopes that their education will take flight as a result.

This environment may sound like a dreamland, and in many ways, it is. However, SLA was not built on a cloud; it exists in the real world. And that world includes the Keystones, a series of mandated standardized exams that seek to measure the academic proficiency of high school students in algebra, literature, and biology. There is no alternative assessment or exemption available. The tests are a sharp contrast to everyday life at SLA, an annual disruption to the learning environment we spend so much time cultivating. Without us saying a word, our students know that we don't place much value on these exams—our curriculum speaks for itself.

We do take time out for explicit test prep, but the approach is with a wink and a nod: it's a game, here are the rules, jump through the hoop, everybody. On the best days, the work feels novel and funny, not like we are drilling them to death. We also try to demystify exactly how standardized exams are built, essentially turning the prep into its own kind of project. When starting test prep in English class, I ask my students a multiple-choice question I wrote myself: Multiple-choice tests in reading comprehension best show . . . As a class, they have time to debate what they think the "best" answer is. I nudge them toward thinking critically about what the author of the question would say, and by the end of the discussion most of them have settled on "D. How well a student can take a multiple-choice test." We then review the different types of questions, pick apart sample items from previous years, write a few of our own, and do a collective brain dump of test-taking strategies they have learned in previous years and at previous schools. I ask students to explain their thought process as much as possible, as publicly as possible, supporting each other right up until the moment when they have to sit silently in that room and can't ask for help. We're also not afraid to get silly during these lessons. Sometimes the students turn into a ship full of pirates, throwing the less-than-best answer options overboard, or a band of ninjas, selectively assassinating them. If we're going to engage with the absurd, then we might as well have fun doing it.

In total, I'm fortunate to lose only about two weeks of teaching to the testing cycle—one for prep, one for the exams themselves. Then we're back to analytical performances of *Othello* in the blink of a fortnight. We don't see the results of the Keystones until sometime in the summer, and the kids eventually get a printed report on how they did, but those events don't get any fanfare—we're too busy preparing for the next year.

This take-it-with-a-grain-of-salt attitude at my school meant I could make my peace with the exams, at least as a classroom teacher. Then came the day when I was asked to become a testing coordinator alongside my colleague Michael. Becoming a testing coordinator means you are in charge of ensuring that every small detail of standardization is attended to by every student, teacher, and staff member in the building. It includes getting everyone to follow a set of rules that turn our school's environment from productively rambunctious to strict and silent. We didn't exactly jump at the opportunity, but at a small school like ours, there are only so many hands to go around, with looming budget shortfalls threatening who's left. We would have to figure out a way to navigate this role of compliance enforcer without losing our minds.

Fortunately, the very first testing coordinator at SLA had given us a path: become someone else. "From here on out, I am *not* going to be Zac when I am doing this work," he announced at the start of one of our proctor training sessions, somewhere back in the spring of 2009. "I don't want to be myself while I'm doing this job. Whenever you need to talk to me about testing, you need to talk to 'Rick.'" "Rick" was randomly selected, but subsequent testing coordinators leaned toward adopting celebrity names or fictional personas: Nurse Ratched, Marky Mark, Beach Dave. After a brief brainstorming session, we hit on an obvious choice: Boris and Natasha. We would play the villains, but they would be the loveable, cartoonish kind. The fact that one of us is Russian leant a vague air of legitimacy to the choice. The staff responded positively to the appearance of our cartoon personas in the training slide shows. But more than anything, the names were valuable because they gave us open license to be grumps. Teachers stopped asking me about testing matters without any warning. They developed the delightful habit of saying, "I have a question for Natasha"—to which I could reply, "Sorry, she's not available right now." Conversely, on a testing day, they would warn the (mildly confused) students: "Don't bother her. She's not Pahomov today."

The work is mundane at best and vexing at worst, but my situation is not as intense as it is in some buildings. In many schools and districts, the continued reliance on standardized test scores as a metric for both individual and community achievement encourages schools to do "whatever it takes" to meet their testing targets. Sometimes this results in the school culture revolving around the exams: pep rallies, t-shirts, extensive tracking of students. The children hear this message loud and clear: that their score is what defines them. Students from this kind of culture are easy to spot. When we ask them what they will contribute to SLA, their first response is, "I can bring your test scores up!"

Sometimes this mindset reflects educators who actually believe that the tests are a reasonable metric for students. Other times it's out of desperation, a response to the threat that the school will be closed or taken over if targets are not met. This desperation can take a dark turn if educators conclude that the situation is hopeless. In Philadelphia, several educators recently pleaded guilty to criminal conspiracy for cheating on the Pennsylvania System of School Assessment (PSSA) exams. In Atlanta, hundreds of educators were implicated by the district for cheating, and a group of teachers, administrators, and testing coordinators were eventually convicted in court. Many times these educators refuse to speak to the press, but those that do don't sound like criminal conspirators. They sound like dedicated teachers. Damany Lewis was the first teacher to be fired in Atlanta during the scandal. In an interview, his devotion to his students sounds like the same pep talks I give. "I'm not going to let the state slap them in the face and say they're failures," he said to reporters about his motivations for looking at copies of the state exam in advance of the testing window. "I'm going to do everything I can to prevent the why-try spirit."[54]

Reading about these cases as a newly minted testing coordinator both incensed and frightened me. I had no reason to expect misconduct at my school, but I fretted about the potential consequences of even an accidental misstep. Once, a previous testing coordinator forgot to send home an informational letter to families—an honest mistake—and eventually the district came calling about it. What detail might I be missing? At some point during every testing window, the district sends an observer to review all of our procedures and protocols, as well as to observe the testing rooms while teachers proctor. As Natasha, I sternly admonished my colleagues in advance of the exams: we never know when the monitor is going to show up. We also never know *who* is going to show up. Everybody fills out the same checklist, but the style of their inspection varies widely. One of them—I'll call her Susan—would follow me around sternly as I showed her our secure storage locations and answered her pop-quiz questions about proctor protocol. One time, I couldn't find the previous day's sign-out sheet, and had to frantically search every last testing room in the hopes that I had misplaced it while collecting calculators. Susan stood by, serious but patient. When I produced it, she was all smiles.

"I like this place," she said. "That's why I keep coming back. The kids here don't cause trouble. They're respectful."

I forced a smile. The tightness in my body would not unwind.

"I was at another school yesterday—elementary kids—and the students were so focused, all lined up outside the classroom. And I told them, 'You have integrity. Do you know what that means? It means that you respect adults and you know when to be quiet.'" I kept my smile plastered on my face and nodded, trying my hardest to look agreeable.

Do I have integrity as a testing coordinator? If Susan had told me to stand on my head in that moment, I would have done it. Is it possible to have any integrity when you actively support a practice that stands at pedagogical odds with what you believe to be best for children? In my darkest moments, I think: *throw the whole thing overboard.* The rabbit hole expands rapidly. *Forget these tests, forget the SAT, screw report cards and grades. I'm not helping them learn right now, I'm just getting in the way of their learning. Game over.*

Here's what gets me out of this downward spiral: the exams are, in their own way, a valuable learning experience for the students. At SLA, we have shown outsiders a school can be held accountable to outside metrics and bureaucracy without letting those elements pervade our culture, dampen our enthusiasm, suck away our joy. When they ask us hard questions about the Keystones and their purpose, we answer honestly. We stay up to date on the latest developments in state education politics, emphasizing to students that, for better and for worse, the rules of the game keep on changing, that we don't believe for a second that the tests are an objective yardstick, that they are much more of a malleable political tool than anything else. Underneath all of this, we are trying to not just say, but actually show our students: modern life requires a constant series of decisions about which systems you will accept, which you will reject, and which you will try to dismantle.

Some parties would love to see us, as members of a high-profile school in Philadelphia, ace all of the exams and then broadcast that fact, thereby proving the "value" of our school via traditional metrics. Others think it's our moral responsibility to reject the testing process wholesale because it would provide cover for schools that have less capital to do so. Ultimately, SLA teachers take a middle path. We reject the premise of the exams while still accepting its existence. We know we would be putting our jobs at risk if we took action as radical as refusing to administer the exam. And we're not blind to our own privilege—as we are a selective-admissions school, most of our students come to us already proficient at taking standardized exams and passing them. The threat of closure or takeover does not hang over our heads the way it does in some schools. However, our motivations are not merely practical. There's a pedagogical reason for our middle path as well: as an inquiry-based school, we don't force our own conclusions on our students. Instead, we ask them to assess each new situation on their own terms, consider their options, and act accordingly.

The good news is that when it comes to action around testing, students in Pennsylvania have the most powerful lever of all of us: they can legally opt out of exams. All it takes is a letter to the school district. Pennsylvania doesn't keep this a secret, but they don't trumpet it, either, and teachers at my school have been careful to make the process as easy as possible without pushing families toward any particular decision. Our own staff felt more comfortable with this process after teachers at the Feltonville School of Arts and Sciences made a dedicated effort to inform their families, especially those with children in the English for Speakers of Other Languages (ESOL) program, about how to opt out. And last year, after Pennsylvania decided to suspend the Keystones as a graduation requirement, Philadelphia high schools saw an uptick in students opting out. If the whole system is to come crashing down, there could be no more righteous and effective way than with students taking the lead.

In the meantime, Boris and Natasha will be sitting in a windowless room, putting scratch paper and collection bags for electronics into testing boxes, combing through a box of thousands of pencils to cull the ones with spent erasers, and properly labeling and setting aside the test booklets for students who have opted out. Thanks to the roles we have agreed to play for now, we cannot answer your academic questions until sometime next week.

Larissa Pahomov teaches students English and journalism at Science Leadership Academy, a public high school in Philadelphia, Pennsylvania. She has National Board Certification and is the author of Authentic Learning in the Digital Age, *a handbook designed to help teachers shift their practice to being more inquiry based and tech friendly.*

Alternatives to Standardized Tests

*How Performance-Based Assessments Supported a
Math Team's Journey Toward AP Calculus*

KARI KOKKA

"I'm going to go to college to become a math teacher, Kari,"[55] Reyna declared to me one day after Advisory. My eyes widened with excitement, "Ooooooh, really? You will be an amaaaaaazing teacher!" I started asking Reyna what type of school she wanted to teach in, what grade level, what type of projects she'd have students engage in. Her words were music to my math-teacher ears.

Reyna Echols had come to Vanguard High School on a safety transfer after getting into too many fights at her previous school. She had moved from Maryland to live with her grandmother in New York City because her mother had been picked up for her work as a "street pharmacist." At Vanguard, Reyna was a star mathematics student with whom I became very close through both math class and Advisory. I actually don't know why she had negative incidents in her previous school, because she and I always had a positive relationship. Perhaps the familial nature of Vanguard, the school's Advisory program, and our staff's efforts to build relationships with students fostered Reyna's growth. However, I attribute her accomplishments to her own tenacity and dedication to her education. She and I are still in touch these fourteen years later, and we recently copresented at a national education conference.[56]

Reyna was a student at Vanguard from 2002–2006, and during this time the math team at Vanguard embarked on a journey to increase the rigor of the mathematics program, with the ultimate goal of offering Advanced Placement (AP) Calculus. Vanguard High School is a Title I public school in New York City and a member of the New York Performance Standards Consortium, where students must present and pass four performance-based assessments, or PBAs, in English, history, math, and science in lieu of taking the New York State Regents standardized exams.[57] When Reyna was a freshman in 2002, the PBA in mathematics that seniors were supposed

to present as the expected graduation requirement addressed linear functions—a middle school topic! Clearly, we were not offering our students a
rigorous mathematics experience, nor holding them to high expectations
of what they were capable of. Around this time, in the early 2000s, several
math teachers joined the Vanguard community, and we committed ourselves to collaboratively transform the mathematics program as an equity
and social-justice endeavor.

PBAs offered a clear end goal, or target, for our work. We wanted to
develop a mathematics PBA project that challenged seniors to engage in
mathematics appropriate for a twelfth-grade mathematics course. A second, complementary goal was to introduce AP Calculus to our mathematics program while maintaining our commitment to students' enrollment in
untracked mathematics courses.

BENEFITS OF PBAS

PBAs helped us with our goal of increasing mathematical rigor by motivating teachers and students alike. Math PBAs consist of a project, written
report, and reflective essay coupled with a ninety-minute-long individual
dissertation-style oral defense to a committee of teachers, outside experts,
and student peers. Students must explain the mathematical concepts learned
in class and apply these concepts to real-world situations. PBAs radically
turn the tables on the student-teacher relationship. My students demanded
my help, in stark contrast to the typical scenario of the teacher coaxing students to come in after school to study. Students flooded my classroom after
school, asking how late I could stay to help them and if they could come in
on the weekend. Never in my teaching career had I experienced this level
of commitment to learning in helping students prepare for a standardized
exam or even for an end-of-unit test. In those cases, I was the one cajoling
students to come study with me.

I spoke with Reyna about her experience with PBAs at Vanguard while
she was in college and assigned to a student teaching placement in a school
without alternative assessments. Her reflections are powerful because they
reveal the perspective of a student and soon-to-be teacher:

> Now that I'm going to school for teaching, from PBAs I remember not just
> solving a problem and how to do it, but I can explain, why are we doing
> this math problem? I can relate it to real-world problems. What I'm learn-
> ing through my student teaching field placement in my program is that a

lot of what other teachers do is just teach because you have the test that you have to pass, and let's just teach toward the test. But at Vanguard, because of the PBAs, there was more attention to individual students. You weren't going to bypass one student and move too slow for others. Vanguard teachers took the time to interact with all of your students. And on top of that, these kids are urban children and go through issues at home and then get to school and it's hard to be the best student when you have issues going on at home. At Vanguard they worked with you and they cared about you.

Not only do PBAs encourage students to take ownership of their learning, but the extra time teachers and students spend together after school preparing for students' presentations fosters caring student-teacher relationships. These relationships were a necessary prerequisite to improve students' mathematics understanding. They fostered teachers' sense of responsibility for student learning and students' trust in their math teachers. Students with previous negative or traumatizing experiences with mathematics needed to believe that their teachers cared about them and truly wanted them to succeed. In addition to employing PBAs, Vanguard strives to personalize students' learning through an Advisory program, block scheduling (which reduces by half the number of students teachers are responsible for), and small school size.[58]

CHALLENGES AND STRATEGIES FOR SUCCESS

As a math team we encountered several challenges in our journey toward revamping the mathematics program at Vanguard. First, we needed to fill several gaps in students' mathematics skills.[59] Second, we needed to increase the rigor of our grades 9-11 math courses to prepare students for a twelfth-grade AP Calculus course while maintaining our commitment to untracked courses. Third, we needed to simultaneously prepare students for PBAs and standardized exams, such as the SAT, despite our belief that standardized exams are unreliable and unfair measures used to inequitably sort students.

To tackle the first challenge of filling students' gaps and bringing them "up to grade level" in their mathematics skills and understanding, we required students to take double-blocked math courses for their entire four years of high school, more than doubling the state's mathematics course-work requirement of three years of a single class period. We also offered a math elective class and instituted a Math Study Center staffed by math teachers and peer tutors for afterschool support for all students.

Second, to increase the rigor of the mathematics while preserving our untracked courses, we used a pedagogical strategy called Complex Instruction, an approach to group work specifically designed for academically heterogeneous classes.[60] Complex Instruction utilizes team roles, such as team captain, facilitator, resource manager, and recorder/reporter.[61] Using this in our math classes fostered a sense of community responsibility and support. Not only did students work together in class, they also helped each other at lunch, after school, and outside of school. The great heterogeneity of our untracked math classes, considered a tall hurdle by many math teachers, actually provided greater opportunities to collaborate. Students enjoyed helping others and felt empowered through their teachers' distribution of authority in the classroom.

These two strategies, double-blocked math classes and Complex Instruction, also helped us overcome the third challenge of preparing students for both performance tasks and tests. The extra time of double-blocked classes allowed us to develop students' critical-thinking skills necessary for PBAs while also addressing the breadth of knowledge needed for standardized gatekeeping exams. To further bolster students' test-taking skills, we offered an optional SAT preparation elective in students' junior and senior years.

AP CALCULUS

Introducing AP Calculus may have been a pipe dream when we first began this journey, but teamwork, administrative support, and students' commitment to their learning sustained us throughout the challenges. In 2007 we reached our goal of introducing AP Calculus to the mathematics program at Vanguard. We kept our untracked grades 9–11 math classes and decided to offer seniors the option of taking "twelfth-grade math" or "AP Calculus." The first AP Calculus class had twelve students, who completed a two-part PBA. Students presented on their project and taught their committee the concepts of calculus individually for the first portion. For the second portion, two students came together to engage in a "new and novel" calculus problem. The "new and novel" problems required students to use their conceptual understanding of calculus—different from questions on standardized exams, which often call on rote or procedural knowledge, which are lower-level thinking skills. AP Calculus students also took the AP exam at the end of the school year.

Leading up to the introduction of this new AP course, we worked collaboratively to design the PBA projects for the twelfth-grade math class and for the AP Calculus class. The weekly bell schedule was revised to include ample math team planning time during the school day.[62] We used our collaborative planning time to design the PBAs and to explicitly focus on improving our work as a team. If we expected our students to work together in our classes, we felt responsible to model our own behavior in the same manner. We even presented about our teamwork at the 2004 Coalition of Essential Schools Fall Forum, a national education conference. Our workshop was titled "Not Only Students Engage in Cooperative Learning! The Role of Lesson Study in Professional Development."[63] Lisa Gluckson, former Vanguard ninth-grade math teacher, describes how she felt empowered at Vanguard:

> I think a very unique aspect of Vanguard is that teachers had just as much say as the administration, and no decision was made in a bubble, which is what I find now in the suburbs in a much larger school. The size of the staff was small enough where everyone got involved in these meetings, and it wasn't just a presentation by administration of what we were supposed to do.

Lisa's perspective is particularly noteworthy because she was a first-year teacher who felt welcome and comfortable participating in the teacher-led decision-making process. I believe that our teamwork and the administrative support we received to make our own decisions were the keys to our successes.

Reyna graduated in 2006, the year before we offered AP Calculus, but the role of PBAs in her education and the changes we made to the math curriculum during her high school years left their mark. She continues her love of mathematics to this day and is working on her degree so she can become a math teacher. She and I copresented in March 2016 at the New York Collective of Radical Educators National Conference (NYCoRE). Our session was titled "Social Justice Mathematics: Sharing Power with Students." Reyna spoke about how Vanguard teachers' use of Complex Instruction group work in math classes distributed power to students. She shared with the audience the math PBA PowerPoint slides she had created back in 2006. As we prepared for the workshop, the tables were again turned on the traditional student-teacher relationship. Reyna gave me advice about my own career and life goals. She also shared that she wanted to become a math teacher because of my influence, and I was incredibly touched. But Reyna has also inspired me in my professional and personal endeavors. She has given me encouragement and words of wisdom from her time at Vanguard up until now, many years later. I could not feel any prouder of the young woman she's both always been and continues to become, and I feel extraordinarily blessed to have had the opportunity to learn from her.

Like Reyna, Vanguard students gain incredible confidence and pride through their ownership and commitment to their PBAs, lessons applicable to their academic and professional lives. PBAs supported the math team's goals of increasing the rigor of the mathematics program and realizing the introduction of the AP Calculus course. Other schools may also benefit from using alternatives to standardized tests like PBAs to empower students to be persistent, lifelong learners equipped for their future successes in the real world beyond high school.

Kari Kokka is a doctoral candidate at the Harvard Graduate School of Education studying urban STEM teacher retention and students' perspectives of social justice mathematics instruction. She was a math teacher and math coach for ten years in New York City at Vanguard High School, a member of the New York Performance Standards Consortium. At Vanguard she designed performance assessments and rubrics, prepared students, and conducted professional development for colleagues. She is also currently a math performance assessment development and research associate at the Stanford Center for Assessment, Learning, and Equity (SCALE). She completed her MA with the Stanford Teacher Education Program and her BS in mechanical engineering at Stanford University. She is cofounder and co-organizer of the Creating Balance in an Unjust World Conference on Math Education and Social Justice.

CHAPTER 2

QUALITY

Measuring a Teacher's Worth

Think back to your favorite teacher.

Get a picture of this person in your mind. What grade were you in? Did they teach your favorite subject, or one that you struggled with? Did she help guide you through the steps of the scientific process for your first-ever experiment or deliver an awe-inspiring lesson about the beauty of a geometric proof? Did he introduce you to the powerful speeches of Malcolm X or help you work through a passage in *King Lear*? Maybe she congratulated you on a hard-earned grade or pulled you aside to tell you how much better you could be doing. How would you describe this teacher? What made them great?

When politicians and reformers discuss their favorite teachers, they use many of the same descriptors that you probably just thought of. While they occasionally talk about a specific skill set they gained, they often discuss people who inspired or believed in them when no one else did. President Barack Obama has spoken about the teachers in his life who "opened the world up to me, who made me feel that maybe I had something to offer and maybe saw things in me before I saw them in myself."[1] Michelle Rhee, the former chancellor of Washington, DC, who became famous for her zeal to replace ineffective teachers, said her favorite high school English teacher made her "feel special" even when she struggled.[2] This language reflects how most Americans think about their favorite teachers. In a 2012 poll, teachers who had had a positive influence on one's life were most commonly described with words like caring, compassionate, motivating, and inspiring.[3]

There is a body of research on high-quality teaching from scholars and educators that explains the practices that can ignite these feelings within students. Strong teachers challenge students with difficult but attainable tasks and provide exemplar models of the kind of work they expect to see. They break down larger projects into structured steps and support student learning along the way. Rather than emphasize rote learning or memorization, they teach underlying concepts and encourage students to question, talk about their ideas, and share opinions. Good teachers assess student learning regularly, provide constant feedback, offer opportunities for revision, and adapt their teaching to meet students' needs. In classrooms of great teachers, you'll often find student work posted and celebrated on the walls. They'll visit different small groups to monitor and provide support, avoiding traditional rows of chairs. They are organized, so that students don't waste time looking for things like pencils and papers, and they help students monitor their own learning so they can become aware of their strengths, needs, and learning processes. These teachers value their students' backgrounds, experiences, and cultures and build strong relationships with their families.[4] Teachers make thousands of choices every day with their students in mind. It's complex work that often stretches well beyond regular school hours. And, as a starting point, pretty much everyone can agree: high-quality teaching matters.

The debates begin when this belief is translated into policy. In 2001, the No Child Left Behind Act (NCLB) brought this conversation to a national level by requiring a "high quality teacher in every classroom." "High quality" was defined by a set of minimum qualifications: teachers were required to have a bachelor's degree, state certification, and a "high level of competency" in the subject(s) in which they taught.[5] The expectation was that these requirements would result in "a talented teacher in every classroom," which, in turn, would give every student an opportunity to succeed.[6] States were mostly able to meet these goals by the time President George W. Bush was out of office, but subsequent research found that the quality requirements had little to no impact on the overall distribution of teachers or on student achievement.[7]

"EFFECTIVE" AND "EXCELLENT" TEACHING

Through the 2000s, the drumbeat about the critical importance of teachers shifted with a new wave of education reformers who zeroed in on teacher effectiveness rather than uniform qualifications. Epitomized by figures like Rhee, reformers used soaring language to describe what the best teachers could do. Bill Gates, the Microsoft billionaire turned public education philanthropist, claimed in a speech to the American Federation of Teachers, "The single most decisive factor in student achievement is excellent teaching."[8] Reformers looked for new ways to attract the "best and the brightest" to teaching, eschewing existing education programs in favor of alternative preparation. Organizations like Teach For America, which places recent college graduates from top colleges and universities in schools in low-income communities, grew in strength and size during this time, promising a corps of superior teachers who could produce incredible results. At the same time that alternative preparation programs sought to attract superstar teachers, others wanted to reward educators who could produce achievement-gap-obliterating gains. Looking to the business community's pay-for-performance model, merit pay programs popped up around the country, offering bonuses for high achievement in order to incentivize peak performance.[9]

This side of the teacher effectiveness movement was staked on finding and rewarding educators who could single-handedly produce significant gains in student outcomes. But there was a flip side to the reformers' argument about the power of teachers. If individual teachers can be the cause of achievement and success, then they are also individually accountable for failure.

In many reformers' minds, to get rid of the worst teachers—who researchers, pundits, and casual guessers estimate range from 1 to 10 percent of the total teaching force—meant that tenure must be destroyed.[10] Tenure is an employment classification that grants teachers legal protections from being fired. It is generally awarded after an evaluation that takes place between one to five years into a teacher's career, though the timing and substance of the evaluation varies widely across different states. The reformers' claim that tenure creates a system that works for educators, not kids, because it gives teachers a lifetime job no matter how poorly they perform in the classroom.[11]

The unions, for their part, have argued that tenure provides due process, not a lifetime guarantee, helping to ensure that teachers are not fired for the arbitrary and biased reasons that have been well documented throughout the history of public education in the United States and that continue to occur today.[12] Unions have recently been more open to modifications in tenure policies, including simplifying the process for removing ineffective teachers and lengthening the amount of time it takes before teachers are awarded tenure, but they stand by the policy as fair and necessary.[13] Union leaders also point to research that shows that states with strong teacher unions and tenure have higher academic outcomes, even when controlling for other factors.[14] The other major point unions make in response to education reformers is that decisions can't be made about hiring, firing, rewarding, and punishing teachers based on quality and effectiveness when we don't even have a reliable way to determine exactly who the good and bad teachers are, a surprisingly complicated task.[15]

MEASURING TEACHERS' WORTH

Traditionally, teacher evaluations have been based on observations. Two or three times a year, a principal or other administrator meets with a teacher ahead of time to discuss the lesson plan, comes into the class at a prescribed time, and shares observations and suggestions for improvement afterward. This system came increasingly under fire in the 2000s, in large part because too many teachers received high ratings.[16] If teachers were the cause of student failure, and students were failing, then how could so many teachers be doing their job well?

Creating a new teacher evaluation system was one of the central foci of education reform under President Obama and U.S. Secretary of Education Arne Duncan. In 2009, the U.S. Department of Education announced their first major federal education program, Race to the Top, which offered additional grants to states based on a competitive application process. States had to commit to specific changes, among them using test scores in teacher evaluation systems.[17] Two years later, the Department of Education began to offer waivers from No Child Left Behind, since the 2001 law unrealistically required that 100 percent of students in each state be proficient by 2014. In order to obtain a waiver, though, states had to develop new teacher evaluation systems with a "student growth component" that would rank teachers and make "personnel decisions." States that applied without the use of test scores in their teacher evaluations were denied the grant money or waivers associated with these programs.[18]

The growth component in these evaluations is otherwise known as value-added modeling, or VAM for short. VAM employs complicated algorithms to judge how much value a teacher has added to her students' academic progress for the year. These formulas compare a child's test scores to those of other students in the school or district and to their scores from previous years' tests. VAM formulas also attempt to set controls for characteristics of students, their classrooms, and their schools, including factors like race, poverty, or absences from school. There is no clear standard for how to calculate all of these variables, so different models select and measure different factors. Not surprisingly, depending on which model is used, the same teacher can get wildly divergent results.[19] In speeches and interviews, President Obama continued to talk about teachers who built self-esteem, imparted life lessons, and asked students to "dream," while the evaluations pushed by his administration focused on defined hard skills that could be measured by multiple-choice questions.[20] By 2016–2017, the end of his tenure, forty-four states had test scores in their teacher evaluation systems, compared to just four states in 2009.[21]

The problem with all of this "disruptive" change is that there's not much proof that all of these "hard choices" are the right ones. Leading up to the announcement of Race to the Top, the Board on Testing and Assessment, a group created as part of the National Research Council to provide scientific expertise and guidance to policy makers on these issues, pleaded with the Department of Education not to use test scores as part of their requirements for teacher evaluations. They wrote that not enough research had been done on the use of VAM, and that there were currently no reliable models for widespread implementation. They questioned the complicated algorithms that tried to control for the variability in students, calling them unreliable and too complicated to be understood by parents or teachers. In short, they wrote that while the idea of VAM was attractive, in its current state, it didn't work.[22]

The effects of these evaluation systems' quick implementations bore out many of these warnings. In New York, for example, where fifty thousand of sixty-seven thousand teachers were not leading classes that resulted in an exam, math exam results were included in art teachers' value-added scores, and literacy scores were included in the evaluations of physical education teachers.[23] Some states rushed to develop standardized tests for just about every class that students could take from kindergarten through twelfth grade. And even for those tests where teachers were evaluated on their own subjects, in many states, they did not receive the follow-up that would actually make the tests useful: results were not given out until the following year, if at all, with no question breakdown to guide instruction.[24] Pro-testing advocates regularly claim that the data from these exams can inform instruction and help improve teacher quality. As of yet, this is far from standard practice.

The new federal education law, the Every Student Succeeds Act (ESSA), does not require the use of testing data in evaluation systems. It will be up to each state to determine whether to keep the growth measures or revise their laws and find new ways to assess teacher effectiveness.

WHO WANTS TO BE A TEACHER?

The teacher effectiveness movement has, in many ways, attempted to focus on the factor that feels most controllable: whether or not teachers are doing a good job. But their approach has left many teachers feeling unfairly targeted, not only through new evaluations but through a series of polices that have limited what they're allowed to do within the classroom. While reformers have continued to look for ways to remove underperforming teachers, overall job satisfaction has sunk, teachers new and old are leaving for other jobs, and new recruits aren't showing up to take their place. By 2015 and 2016, teacher shortages were common in states all over the country.[25]

A MetLife survey to teachers in 2012 showed job satisfaction at its lowest rate in twenty-five years. At just 39 percent, it was 23 points lower than the 62 percent of teachers who were very satisfied with their jobs in 2008.[26] Young people deciding on their future have taken note. In a study of students taking the ACT college entrance exam, only 5 percent were interested in studying education, and of that number, 76 percent were white, despite making up only 56 percent of test takers.[27]

Dr. Richard Ingersoll at the University of Pennsylvania has been studying the character of the teaching force throughout his career. In one of his most recent reports for the Consortium for Policy Research in Education, Ingersoll found that, in comparison to recent decades, there are larger numbers of brand-new teachers, and that these beginners are less likely to stay in teaching. Thirteen percent of new teachers will leave after their first year, and 40 percent will leave within five years. Cities often see even higher turnover numbers.[28] In Washington, DC, for example, 55 percent of teachers leave after two years.[29] And despite some limited success in recruiting a more racially diverse pool of educators, schools are increasingly unable to retain teachers of color.[30]

Though some charter schools are touting short-lived teaching careers as a new and beneficial model of staffing, there is substantial evidence about the positive impact of experience and the negative effects of teacher turnover on student achievement.[31] Schools with high populations of low-income students and students of color have disproportionately high numbers of inexperienced, sometimes uncredentialed teachers who are more likely to quickly leave the profession.[32] Some schools in Chicago see 25 percent of their staff turn over every year, with disastrous effects.[33]

Fifteen years after No Child Left Behind established high-quality teachers as a necessary part of closing the achievement gap, we still don't have a reliable method for finding, measuring, and retaining good teachers. If we want to attract intelligent, passionate people to the field, keep strong educators in the classroom, and improve student learning across the board, states need to take a different approach to teacher quality than we saw under NCLB. Because teaching is complex work that requires constant critical thinking, the simple equation to a test score doesn't make sense, and the pay-for-performance merit pay reward system doesn't work.[34] When beginning teachers are just starting out, they should be paired with a strong mentor.[35] Beyond that, schools and districts need to help teachers build their skill set by providing them with extended and connected professional development.[36] When it comes to improving their performance, research has demonstrated that teachers work best in collaboration with other teachers.[37] This requires providing ample opportunity for teacher teams to meet, plan, and create inquiry groups and self-study programs.

Most teachers know they have more work to do. They're constantly thinking about how they can improve or brainstorming ways to better reach their students, because they know they can have an enormous impact on each young person that walks through their door. But they can't single-handedly change the world. The alternatives shared in the following essays speak to a broader vision, where teachers are engaged as coconspirators in the fight to achieve educational justice rather than as potential enemies to be rooted out in the process. It imagines a world where teachers aren't made to feel that their students' only opportunity for their future is dependent on raising their test scores by a few points. And it is hopeful for a time when we don't just give lip service to supporting teachers, but offer real feedback and guidance for how to improve their skills. At the end of all that, if you really want to reward and cherish teachers for all of this work, research also shows that a higher paycheck with good benefits helps too.[38] These kinds of reforms not only create environments that people want to work in, they also are proven to help students succeed.

TEACHERS' STORIES

In the first story in this section, "Why We Teach and Run," E.R. Santana reflects on her experience in an alternative certification program and how the reality of teaching collided with her expectations. Jacquelynn Charles also writes about her first years as a teacher, explaining how a new evaluation system and lack of support almost derailed her commitment to become a lifelong educator. The next two stories come from teachers with extensive experience in schools, who explain models of teacher-centered professional development. Veteran teacher Linda Bauld details her experiences with lesson study, National Board Certification, and Professional Learning Communities as ways to practice deep reflection and analysis of curriculum and student work. Aijeron Simmons, a science teacher based in Oakland, California, talks about a yearlong inquiry investigation she undertook with teachers from other schools and how their peer observations, feedback sessions, and brainstorming around implementation and support made her a stronger teacher. In the last story in this chapter, Boston teacher Riana Good shares how she turned to the people who were the biggest experts on her teaching—her students—and used both formal and informal surveys to guide her instruction.

Why We Teach and Run

Alternative Certification and the Two-Year Teacher

E. R. SANTANA

I probably matched the profile of a lot of new teachers these days: midt-wenties, Ivy League graduate, not initially intent on a career in teaching but compelled by a sense of civic duty to "check it out." It's a little more com-plicated than that, of course. But for me, as for many new teachers, it was a circuitous path paved with good, yet flawed intentions. And it ended not long after it began.

I taught for two years, entering the profession through New York City Teaching Fellows, an accelerated alternative certification program, and I probably would have left sooner had I not committed myself to two years when I signed on.

Alternative certification programs, such as the Fellows in various cit-ies and Teach for America, have ballooned in popularity over the past two decades. At first these programs were designed to fill legitimate teacher shortages. Then, as the economy shifted and shortage turned to glut, their purpose became that of addressing shortages of "quality" teachers.

In this case, I possessed the qualities that were desired by the teaching certification program—the diploma, the resume, the "look"—and as such was seen as fit to take on a pretty significant and potentially powerful role in at least a hundred or so young people's lives. And I enthusiastically took on that role, with only a vague and naive sense of the institution I was about to enter.

Many have debated the relative value of an enthusiastic but short-lived teacher. Some would argue that my brief tenure still had a positive impact on children's lives and educations. But I am of the conviction that becom-ing a classroom teacher is the closest professional equivalent to becoming a parent. You are taking responsibility for cultivating children's lives, and children need stable adult role models who stick around. For me, as hard as it is to swallow, I often think it would have been better had I never taught at all. Then, at least, I wouldn't have abandoned my students just when they were beginning to count on me.

I was set to be an academic from the ripe old age of 12. By the end of college, I had checked off all the boxes: prestigious high school internships, Ivy League education; but I had this nagging sense that academia was walled off from public service (i.e., the "ivory tower"), and so I delayed my fated entry into the academy, stalling grad school year after year in search of "meaningful" work that would "give back" to society, especially considering how much I had been given since birth. Rather than slog through a traditional teacher certification program, which seemed expensive and time-consuming, I applied for the NYC Teaching Fellows.

While some friends had warned me of the profound challenges of public school teaching, I heard nothing that convinced me that I couldn't do it or didn't want to at least try. Then again, I had never been faced with a true challenge in my life. I had no idea what couldn't be fixed—or at least completed decently—with thorough research, good intentions, and maybe a few all-nighters. Quality work had always come easily, with ample support from parents, bosses, and colleagues and few, if any, obstacles along the way. At worst, I figured I could teach for a few years and move on to something else. No harm done.

I received more heavily supervised training to become a supermarket cashier than I did to become a classroom teacher. Being in an alternative certification program, my "student teaching" was during a few weeks of summer school. My summer school mentor seemed thrilled I had some teaching experience, and assured me, "You'll be fine," with little to no critical feedback. In the last days leading up to the first day of the fall semester, I frantically tried to acquire the curriculum and textbooks for the classes I was assigned to teach. Some of the materials had magically disappeared since the prior school year; others consisted of binders full of lessons hand scrawled on loose-leaf paper and barely legible worksheets that had been copied on a Ditto machine in the 1980s and then photocopied every decade since.

That September I might have traded in my $100,000 diploma for a few weeks of prep time with my colleagues before the first day of school, but the first day came and went with nothing but the Wongs' seminal *The First Days of School* (a standard text for new teachers), to guide me. While my colleagues were nice and willing to help, from day one I had to proactively request any sort of support or assistance. It seemed odd, if not negligent, to train a new employee only when she asked for training. What if she didn't know what she was doing wrong?

It quickly became apparent that some of my veteran colleagues were struggling to stay afloat too, except that they had found inner resources to cope with the frustrations of working within a dysfunctional institution and were committed enough to the profession to ride the waves. They cared enough to help a good number of students, but accepted a base level of chaos and failure as inevitable. They scrawled notes on the board and on handouts in barely legible handwriting—these for students with dyslexia or other reading difficulties. They berated students, quipping that "even a caveman" could define "imperialism." They planned their lessons in the morning right before the bell rang, or when they "couldn't find" the materials from any of their past fifteen years of teaching. They showed me teaching strategies and then conceded, "This is how it should be done, but I don't do it like this anymore because I'm too lazy." Their expectations of quality had been shaped by years of being overworked, underresourced, and lightly supervised.

And then there were the veterans who regularly showed me the many ways the best teachers successfully reached students. Some of them were theatrical, running on batteries that enabled them to dramatically reenact Supreme Court cases at 7:30 in the morning. Others were teenagers at heart who could channel their inner recollections of angst and alienation toward some clever segue to whatever learning objective was at hand. And then there were the super-structured teachers, who managed to bring focus and discipline to an impressive percentage of their struggling students through routines: for group work, for collecting homework, for note taking, for everything. But nowhere in these models did I see a map to my own success. I was never a thespian (and certainly not one before noon), I had no memories of teen angst or alienation, and I hated routines. I envisioned a classroom where learning was self-directed, exploratory, and experiential. I tried to develop my own style, but doing so felt reckless without the constructive feedback of more experienced professionals. My supervisors barely had the time to schedule my minimum mandatory observations (a few a year), let alone to provide regular feedback.

Even the best teachers, the ones whom students came back from college to see, had an air of defeat around them, a melancholy, that to me transformed the entire school building into an emotional vacuum, draining me of my hope and optimism with each passing day. One afternoon, while chatting with a beloved veteran teacher, I joked about how much I dreaded my Sunday evenings when I had to prep for the coming week. She commiserated, "Oh yes, I've been dreading Sundays for forty years. It never goes away." My jaw dropped, filled with the dread of forty years of anxious Sundays. It never goes away?

Not only was there no time during the workweek to do our work, but we didn't have enough desks or enough computers, the printers rarely functioned, and there was no discretionary budget. I had worked for several nonprofits, which involved penny-pinching, but here there were no pennies to pinch. Dittos were handwritten because the computers were broken. Lessons were hastily planned Monday morning because of a weekend family emergency. There was nothing in place to prevent these occasional lapses of professional practice from becoming routine, and most everything was in place to encourage it. I was asked to change a student's grade from failing to passing so that he could graduate. Teachers helped students cheat on Regents exams. If these acts were part of some articulated strategy of resistance to tests and grading, I could have played along. But it was just educators frantically trying to fit round human students into square Department of Education holes, a bureaucratic task upon which both their jobs and the students' futures depended.

Many veterans frankly conceded that, were they starting their career again, they would probably avoid teaching. The emphasis on standardization was taking the joy and the art out of their practice. The pressure to mold every child into a uniform model of "proficiency" across all subject areas, regardless of their abilities, interests, or socioeconomic situation, felt like the ultimate industrialization of an already factory-like public education system. The teacher was no longer a craftsman, a shaper of lives, but rather, an assembly-line worker, charged with making sure the "product" came out consistently and on schedule. I could sense the veterans' ambivalence regarding the next generation of teachers: with one hand welcoming us into a career they had loved, with the other urging us to get out while we were still young enough to have options. For me, with my Ivy League degree and peers fast on their way to becoming highly respected doctors, lawyers, and academics, the options were alluring. The small, hard-won victories of student learning were not nearly enough to sate my appetite for achievement, autonomy, and action.

My graduate school classes were perhaps the ultimate disappointment. I went into them thinking: these are the master teachers, the teachers of teachers; they will show me the way. The classes were held at night, exclusively for fellows who taught full-time during the day. I hoped this would provide fodder for stimulating conversations that connected our day's work to our coursework. But alas, the courses were largely unfocused, slow moving, disconnected from our daily practice, and redundant. Over and over again I read in our assigned texts that students fail in school because of low/unclear expectations, lack of emotional and academic support structures, and lack of models of academic success around them. And here I was struggling because of low/unclear professional expectations, lack of emotional and professional support structures, and lack of models of professional success. The biggest difference between my students and me was that I had a choice—I could walk away from it all—and they (for the most part) didn't.

What I know now about teaching is this: Hard work is not enough. Caring is not enough. Good teaching is an act of both omnipotence and impotence. You must be comfortable establishing order, authority, and discipline, but accept that your orders can be thwarted a thousand ways by forces outside of your control. You must embrace the role you can have in young people's lives—from inspirational muse to disciplinarian—but concede that you are only one of a hundred role models, and your influence is calculated via the unknowable algorithm of human relationships. You must wake up early every morning, enthused at the possibility for young minds to grow, mature, and learn, but you must confront everyday hurdles that unjustly prevent you and your students from reaching their highest potential. Teaching is elation and despair, both hardness in a soft world and softness in a hard world. The teacher must bear this mane of contradiction and ambiguity, all the while presenting a face full of hope to her students.

I cannot be sure, had I been told these things, if it would have steered me on a different path, away from teaching. Hindsight is a fun-house mirror, irrevocably shaped by all that I've been through since my first day teaching. When I started out, I was passionate about the role of education in our democracy, and I loved engaging young people in interesting conversations about their observations and ideas. But these qualities were completely drowned in my despair at feeling powerless to control the terms of my work, and at hating more and more each day the society that had abandoned its children to such an insufficient institution. My anger was not productive, it was debilitating. Does this reflect a weakness of character on my part? The pathetic moans of a rich girl for whom everything has come easily in life? Or rather, the cruelty of teaching these days, in a climate where teachers are both blamed for and tasked with curing society's ills? Probably, as always, it is a bit of both.

In spite of it all, I still meet teachers who love what they do. It makes them come alive, and they pass this vitality and hope on to their students. It wasn't for me. Maybe, in a world where teachers were adequately trained and supported, and quality was more than a buzzword, I could have carved out a space for myself in teaching. Maybe not. I moved across the country to escape teaching, and I blamed it on my husband. I couldn't face the colleagues and students I had grown with for two years and simply say, "I can't do this anymore." On my last day, after fumbling to explain my decision to a group of students, one of them jeered, "You're leaving us to go on a road trip?" I can still envision the exact chair she was sitting in, the bulletin board behind her head filled with derelict staples, and the disgust in her face.

To those considering a career in teaching: Wanting educational equity to exist is not the same as wanting to do the painstaking work required to make it so; just as wanting universal health care is not the same as wanting to work for the department of health, and wanting safer streets is not the same as wanting to be a cop. If you are unsure that a true career in classroom teaching is for you, for god's sake, don't try it out for a year to find out. Don't indulge your curiosity on the backs of other people's children. Do your due diligence: volunteer, sub, work at an afterschool program or a tutoring center. Do a full year of student teaching. Get as close to the school and students as possible without becoming a full-fledged teacher. The system is chaotic enough as it is without your whimsical career exploration adding to it.

If you do choose to teach, drop your delusions of grandiosity and superhuman strength. There is no shortage of "quality" teachers, there is a shortage of resources, supervision, and support, and, if anything, a shortage of teachers who come from the communities they are teaching in and are best situated to serve as powerful role models for students experiencing similar circumstances.

And to those who teach the teachers: Be transparent about the rigors of the profession; celebrate them, even, and seek out those who thrive in challenging environments: not just the person who can teach, but the person who will teach for better or worse, who is committed to creating a stable empowering space for children in an often harsh world; not just the person who succeeds, but the person who has succeeded through struggle and can therefore persevere in a systemically unjust system and serve as a model of resilience for her students. Demand commitment, and then cultivate those who are committed with high expectations, support, and models of success. Inspire them to envision, explore, and fight for what quality teaching is and can be.

E. R. Santana is an educator and historian whose work explores how perceived boundaries in space and time artificially limit human consciousness and connection. She developed experiential curricula at museums and historical sites before her fateful two years as a classroom special educator. She currently oversees a team of youth advocates who support students at a transfer high school in East New York, Brooklyn.

Just Starting Out

Evaluating and Supporting New Teachers

JACQUELYNN CHARLES

My teaching career began in what felt like educational paradise. Despite having an overcrowded kindergarten class of twenty-seven, I felt prepared by my collegiate education program and supported by the teachers around me. I was hired by the new principal at the school where I completed my student teaching, and in the first weeks of school, I was happily exhausted. Veteran teachers warn how tough the first year of teaching is. I had always brushed them off before I started, but it's true. I worked twelve-hour days just to be prepared for the next day. I learned tricks and strategies on the fly with a class full of students who needed me to know them yesterday.

I eagerly anticipated the arrival of a mentor to provide feedback and direction and to help me improve, not just survive. Since I had attended the New Teacher Summer Academy, a two-day workshop for first-year teachers, a mentor should have been assigned to me. Shockingly, no one entered my class other than students and an occasional parent-volunteer until my first formal observation in December. In a way it was nice to be trusted to lead my class, but knowing the common errors rookie teachers make, I felt it was unfair to leave me alone for the first three months of school. This put a great deal of pressure on my first observation.

After a pilot year in selected schools, the new teacher evaluation system was implemented across the district in 2012–2013. Starting that year, teachers' ratings in Chicago were calculated using a combination of standardized tests, performance tasks, and classroom observations. The Illinois law requiring all school districts to update their evaluation protocols allowed five years for the new systems to take effect, but Chicago rushed ahead to implement a half-developed plan immediately. For grades 3–12, the standardized test portion of the teacher's rating would come from the growth of the teacher's own students on the exam. Instead of waiting to research or develop a reliable assessment for the primary grades, preK–2 teachers were evaluated through an average of third through eighth graders' scores.

It was argued that the use of third-grade scores to judge the previous year's teachers was justified because of the teamwork and accountability that should take place within a school. In reality, our district has a high transiency rate, which means that primary teachers would be assessed based on students we may have never had in our school. Additionally, teamwork and accountability are difficult when teachers have little, if any, time to meet to collaborate and create a coherent, comprehensive learning plan for the school. Administrators rarely set aside adequate time or provide resources devoted to making this a fully realized practice. And while collaboration among staff is critical, if my own job security is partially dependent on my rating, I want my own students' growth to be the measure used.

There were additional ambiguities about the evaluation system. Teachers and principals didn't know what the timeline for classroom observations would look like, how thoroughly paperwork should be filled out, what exactly was expected in preobservation and postobservation meetings, and how professional responsibilities would be assessed. The evaluations would only count for nontenured teachers during this first year. Our scores counted toward a summative rating that could be used to rehire or discontinue first-, second-, and third-year teachers. Ultimately, 561 nontenured teachers were not renewed at the end of the 2012–2013 school year. I was one of them.

My first formal evaluation took place in December. The assistant principal graciously walked me through the process and acknowledged that the new evaluation system would be a learning experience for everyone involved. A classroom observation begins with a preobservation meeting in which the teacher describes the current unit of study and prepares the observer to enter his or her classroom. Preparatory, prompting questions from the administrator help guide the discussion. It is suggested that the teacher type up responses to the questions, which usually brought me to a three-page document. After the observation, the teacher and observer meet to discuss. More guiding questions and another three-page document are typical.

It is important for teachers to be descriptive and thorough when explaining their planning process in order to obtain the highest score possible. Although I had taken all the right steps in planning for instruction, I needed support to explain my methods to another person. Instead of just giving me a lower score, the assistant principal asked probing questions to gain a deeper understanding of my planning process. After our discussion, she asked when I teach my literacy block and said she would be in to observe a language arts lesson sometime within the next five days. Instead of scheduling an observation so that the evaluator sees the lesson in its entirety, the evaluator is allowed to observe you at any point during instructional time within five days of the preobservation meeting. So for the next five days, I was a nervous wreck in anticipation of my first observation.

Thankfully, the observation went well. She watched me teach a mini lesson to the whole class, explain directions for learning centers, and conduct small-group instruction for reading skills. The assistant principal was impressed with my knowledge of the curriculum and the successful, research-based ways in which I delivered it. She complimented me on the relationships I built with my students. I received the highest score, "distinguished," for "creating an environment of respect and rapport."

"REACH Students," the name of the teacher evaluation system used by Chicago Public Schools, uses the Danielson rubric with a four-point scale: distinguished, proficient, basic, and unsatisfactory.[39] Teachers are assessed in four domains: planning and preparation, classroom environment, instruction, and professional responsibilities. Within each domain, there are various components like "designing student assessments, managing classroom procedures, engaging students in learning, and communicating with families." Between the preobservation conference, the observation, and the postobservation conference, the teacher is assessed by fifteen components and receives a rating for each. Four additional components are evaluated outside of classroom observations via teacher-submitted documents as evidence of professional responsibility. I felt relieved, since the first scores to count toward my summative rating were high for a first-year teacher. I received six basic ratings, eight proficient ratings, and one distinguished rating.

My second formal observation was less of a success. In January I met with the principal, and he asked me to talk through what I had written down in the preobservation paperwork while he typed notes on his laptop. He didn't really ask questions, although he did note my strong organizational skills. He didn't give feedback or coach me on what I had planned. On the day of the observation, he arrived late to my classroom. He missed me teach the actual lesson. The only thing he saw me do was assist students while they worked on an activity. It's hard to imagine how that gave him enough information to accurately rate me for each component of the rubric. I should have asked him to come another time, but I didn't know I could do that. With my job security partially dependent on his review of me, I didn't want to be difficult or pushy, so I didn't speak up for myself.

During that postobservation conference, the principal wasn't very help-ful. He listened to me talk through my written reflection and didn't con-tribute much to the conversation. Thinking back on the experience, I'm not sure if I knew what he was displeased about. The rubric didn't help me understand either. I could see my scores were considerably lower than my rating from the assistant principal, but I didn't know why, and he didn't take the time to explain. This time I received eleven basic ratings and four proficient ratings. There were no suggested strategies to try, resources to turn to, or next steps planned.

Two months later I was scheduled for another preobservation confer-ence with the assistant principal. She asked me to bring all my planning materials to the meeting so that she could observe my process firsthand. Again she was impressed, and I took the compliments to heart. She had taught kindergarten before and spent time engaging in conversation with me about teaching. Kindergarten is different from any other grade, because it is most Chicago students' first year in a full day of school. For many stu-dents, it's their first time in any type of school at all. I have to teach my students nearly everything about what it means to be in a classroom, and I have to do it in a way that is appropriate and interesting to five-year-olds. The assistant principal's specific experience with the grade that I taught was invaluable. I wished we could have talked more often, but we only had time during these short and infrequent observation meetings.

The observation itself was a disaster. After my mindful planning, the assistant principal pointed out that it was being wasted. My students were not all paying attention to me. She almost gave me my first "unsatisfac-tory" rating for "managing student behavior" because I had to make so many corrections and refocus the class so many times. Still, I received three basic ratings and twelve proficient ratings. I felt like an awful teacher for not realizing this problem sooner. I was only teaching to the kids who could sit still and listen, which in kindergarten isn't many. I often had to stop to remind students how to sit, to correct a behavior, or repeat myself in the middle of what I was saying. Without the continuous focus, their learning was disconnected, and they weren't internalizing as much as they could have. During the postobservation conference, the assistant princi-pal offered a few suggestions, including observing another kindergarten teacher, bringing that teacher into my class for peer observations, and fur-ther self-reflection.

Spring break was a week away. I used that last week to more closely observe myself, except I wasn't sure what to look for. I went to a workshop at the Chicago New Teacher Center and brought in another kindergarten teacher to help. After break, I got to work implementing some new classroom procedures and behavior management techniques. A kindergarten colleague came in to observe my class and offered some useful suggestions. Even though it was suggested, an arrangement was never made for me to observe her, because it would require someone to cover my classroom. As teachers, we model everything for our students before we expect them to do it on their own. Knowing what I needed to fix, the opportunity to see a teacher who excels in that area would have been incredibly helpful.

With a specific area of my teaching to tackle, I needed a mentor more than ever. Official classroom observations are intended to help me develop my practice, but the principal and assistant principal at my school had a staff of forty teachers they needed to work with in addition to their extensive administrative duties. Evaluations felt more like something that needed to get done to be in compliance with the contract rather than an opportunity to develop my skills as an educator. The organization responsible for mentoring new teachers in Chicago, The Chicago New Teacher Center, was ill equipped to handle the volume of new teachers that year. Hundreds of teachers retired after the 2011–2012 school year, so there were probably more first-year teachers during the 2012–2013 school year than usual. Only teachers who attended a New Teacher Summer Academy were even told about the mentorship program. Even teachers who went fell through the cracks: I never received a mentor.

The first day back from spring break, a mere six school days since my most recent postobservation conference, I got an email for another preobservation conference with the principal. I replied asking for more time. I knew if the principal came to observe my class again so soon after my last observation, he would end up giving me the same feedback and scores as the assistant principal. He was not pleased with my request. The district had just announced the deadline for finishing teacher observations, although the date was six weeks away. He finally relented and pushed back the observation a couple of weeks.

The preobservation conference was the same as my other meetings with him. He expected me to do all the talking and did not interject seeking to understand me more thoroughly or offer suggestions for improvement. The observation, though, was better than the previous one. This time he observed me teach a lesson in a unit about community helpers. I read my class a story about a baker, we added information to our chart that tracked details about various occupations, and then we labeled a picture of a baker and wrote a sentence about bakers. My students could now listen to an entire story without squirming or whispering to friends. When a student raised his or her hand to contribute to our discussion, the rest of the class respectfully listened. Their inventive spelling was becoming more logical and comprehensible. The principal sat off to the side typing notes and would occasionally ask a student about what we were doing. It was hard to tell if he was disengaged or trying to be inconspicuous.

Tired of walking into postobservation conferences not knowing what scores I was going to receive, I prepared myself well for this meeting. I looked through the "REACH Students" handbook and scored myself. I brought every piece of evidence of my practice I could think of. I was prepared to lead the conversation and defend or explain any of my actions. He was impressed with my reflection. His single suggestion during that meeting was that I should encourage students to write down their questions while working so they wouldn't waste class time waiting for me to help. I wanted to laugh at him! I certainly needed to address how students could spend that wait time, but my students couldn't write fluently yet. Most of their questions were about spelling a word or what letter makes what sound. If they could write down their questions they probably wouldn't have a question in the first place. Even the rigorous Common Core State Standards for writing state "with guidance and support from adults," or "use a combination of drawing, dictating, and writing." They aren't expected to be writing independently yet. The one suggestion I got from him all year highlighted that, with his background teaching high school history, he had no idea what it was like to teach kindergarten.

The different standards that teachers were supposed to use to guide instruction seemed similarly confused, out of touch, and often contradictory. Many of the Common Core State Standards for kindergarten start with "With prompting and support," but most of the "distinguished" descriptors in the REACH Students evaluation tool required that "students assume responsibility." It just doesn't match up. For literacy, the Common Core State Standards say that kindergartners should "follow words from left to right," sound out three-letter words, and "read common high-frequency words." In Chicago, kindergarten students were expected to be reading at a level C by the end of the year to be on track, which is much more involved than what the Common Core lays out. With all of these different directives, which are teachers expected to follow as the goal for their students' success?

At this late point in the school year, though, I could start to relax. Having finished our required formal observations for the year, the nontenured teachers rejoiced. All official scores for classroom observations had been accounted for, and we felt a considerable weight lifted. For me, however, that enchanted feeling was soon replaced by anxiety, fear, and near-constant nausea.

On May 10, 2013, an administrator knocked on my door saying the principal wanted to see me. It was 2:45 on a Friday afternoon. *Couldn't it wait until after school?* I walked into his office, and he handed me a large golden envelope and held out a typed letter. "The reason for your nonrenewal is that you are not on track to achieve proficiency as a teacher by the end of this school year," it read. I was speechless. There were no additional details to make sense of. I was especially confused because two pieces of my evaluation, my evidence of professional responsibility and standardized testing measures, had not yet been factored into my score. I asked if we could meet again next week, after I had time to process. He responded, "Sure, but there is only so much we can talk about, 'cause . . . ya know . . ." No, I didn't know what he meant, but I walked out the door to return to my classroom. I ended up crying in front of my students as they were getting ready to go home. Thankfully, kindergartners speak phenomenally encouraging words.

Talking with the union representative at my school during those weeks proved to be invaluable. We looked through the contract and found out I needed 100–209 points to be considered unsatisfactory, 210–284 to be rated developing, 285–339 points for a proficient score, and 340–400 points to be rated an excellent teacher. I couldn't believe that as a first-year teacher I needed to be rated proficient. The language for the "basic" category of the observation rubric, which generally translates into the "developing" rating in the total evaluation system, doesn't describe the world's greatest teacher, but getting there takes more than one year. The most difficult part for me to understand was that I didn't even receive mostly basic scores. I had more proficient ratings, yet I was still not on track to be rated proficient. After all factors were calculated, I scored 271.05 points, a developing teacher.

While my nonrenewal was being sorted out, the union representative sent dozens of emails on my behalf, a math teacher helped us crunch numbers to estimate my final rating, and we formulated a plan. A request to meet with the principal to discuss and clarify was denied. After the principal had been obviously avoiding us for a couple of days, the union representative approached him before school. The principal said he was being advised not to talk with nonrenewed teachers. At all. He had read me the scripted letter, and he wasn't allowed to stray from that message. This was the direction given to all principals and assistant principals. He informed the representative that if we had questions, we should call the human resources department. Perhaps I was feeling impatient, but it seemed like anyone at the union or in human resources took forever to get back to the representative and me. It seemed like nobody really knew the answers to my "so now what?" questions. I was starting to sense a theme within the district: enacting protocol before everything was thought through.

Since I was really only certain of one thing—that I needed a new job—I started updating my resume. The assistant principal offered to look at my resume and cover letter and conduct a mock interview with me. On the day of our meeting, she caught me in the hallway during my preparation period and canceled. Her face was so apologetic. I actually felt bad for her instead of being upset that she was backing out. She told me that, regrettably, she couldn't give me any advice or say anything to me that wasn't in the letter read to me on May 10. She promised to find another administrator who could review my documents, "because you're a good . . ." Teacher? She actually cut off her sentence, because she didn't want to get in trouble for straying from the May 10th script.

I carried on. The final piece of teachers' summative rating included submitting documents to prove a level of professional responsibility. This entailed compiling documents to demonstrate "maintaining accurate records, communicating with families, growing and developing professionally, and demonstrating professionalism." Knowing in the beginning of the year that I would need to submit documents would have been nice, so I could have saved them in a binder for months. Instead, nontenured teachers scrambled to gather parent letters, grade matrices, and evidence of professional development. Since I had worked so hard that year, I easily attained three proficient ratings and one basic rating for this evaluation piece.

Following the last day of attendance, I started mailing resumes to Chicago schools. Within days, a school called me for an interview. The interview went well until the principal informed me about the Teacher Quality Pool. Any nonrenewed, displaced, or laid-off teacher had to prequalify in order to be rehired in Chicago Public Schools. Tenured teachers with high ratings were automatically admitted into this rehiring pool. Nontenured teachers had to submit recommendation forms from two people who had officially observed us teach and pass a fifteen-minute screening via phone or in person. To be clear, the principal and assistant principal from my former school were not allowed to talk to me about literally anything, but I needed a recommendation form from them in order to teach again. Beyond this backwards logic, hundreds of teachers needed to go through this process, and the summer was only thirty-seven school days long.

On July 19, a *thousand* more teachers were laid off, in addition to the hundreds who had already lost their jobs due to nonrenewal and the fifty schools that had been closed. My original Teacher Quality Pool phone screening was canceled in order to accommodate this most recent batch of displaced teachers. I had to call human resources several times over two weeks before I finally found out I was admitted into the Teacher Quality Pool. Once that happened, my online application was visible to principals and I was eligible for hire. I went on ten interviews in three days and ended up with my choice in positions. I was offered my job the Friday before teachers were to report to school, and the paperwork went through that following Tuesday.

I am now teaching kindergarten at a smaller school with a lot of heart. The administrators are so much more supportive than I experienced last year. They have established a program with the local neighborhood association to pay parents to assist in classrooms, and they have set up a mentorship for me with a first-grade teacher. In a recent meeting with the principal and assistant principal, I cried tears of relief and appreciation for their understanding and commitment to my success. This year has presented new challenges that I didn't face last year, such as supporting students whose parents are incarcerated or teaching students with a wider range of reading abilities, but I don't have to tackle these challenges alone. I feel safe approaching my administrators for help, which is the complete opposite of what I experienced in my first year.

Day by day my stress and anxiety subside. At least for another year I won't have to worry about how I will make my student loan payments or that I will have to take a nonteaching job to pay my rent. I consider myself a strong, logical, optimistic person, but my first year of teaching left me feeling constantly fatigued and wary of the profession I care so much about. Teachers just want to teach and do our jobs well. Why do policy makers and school leaders find ways to make it so difficult?

Jacquelynn Charles grew up attending public schools in Milwaukee, Wisconsin, and knew early on she wanted to work with students in urban settings. She has taught kindergarten and fourth grade in Chicago Public Schools since 2011 and is her school's Chicago Teachers Union representative.

What Professional Development Looks Like When You Trust Teachers

LINDA BAULD

Education reform all starts from the same place: a desire to improve student achievement. While it seems everyone has an opinion, the actual experts in the field are rarely consulted. Decisions about what and how we teach involve politicians and academicians removed from classroom teaching. This diminishes and disrespects teachers. Adapting to new reforms such as the Common Core standards can be overwhelming. Often these new directions require substantial changes in practice, yet there is rarely professional development to support the teacher. In addition, the professional development opportunities lack follow-through and the monetary commitment to sustain efforts once they are started.

I have been an elementary classroom teacher for twenty-three years, and I have experienced many reform movements, but over the last ten years there has been a slow movement to honor the insights of teachers by allowing time for collaboration and self-reflection to discover the ways to permanently improve their practice. In my work, I have experienced lesson study, National Boards, self-study research, and, currently, professional learning communities as the best ways to make lasting changes in order to build effective, accomplished teachers.

To have an opportunity to collaborate and analyze student learning in order to become a better teacher may seem an obvious and common experience. Unfortunately, most professional development is decided by someone at the district level and doesn't change a teacher's practice. Often the material isn't relevant, or we aren't given the time needed to process and discuss. Traditionally, it has entailed bringing in an outside consultant, without utilizing the expertise of the staff. Teachers with twenty-plus years' experience sit with new teachers. For example, I attended a workshop on how to customize your teaching to fit the diverse needs in your class. Sounds great, right? The problem was, teachers weren't given any choice, and the presenter spoke to all 550 teachers in a lecture presentation! Ironic, isn't it? The following professional development experiences are fundamentally opposite and can make lasting and profound changes to an educator's practice.

Lesson study, as I experienced it, was based on the Japanese model of professional development. Teachers work in a small group to determine a topic/concept that needs an improved lesson based on student performance. They then craft a lesson that is taught by one teacher and observed by the rest of the group. Student data is collected based on the group's research questions and is analyzed. The lesson is then tweaked and taught to a new class by a different teacher. Sometimes a "knowledgeable other" who has expertise on the topic participates throughout the lesson study or during the observation lessons and debrief.

By working together and reflecting on the data, paradigm shifts can occur. In one lesson study group, we were investigating how to develop algebraic thinking in third graders. We used a lesson from a respected math organization and observed the students' understanding. After the first lesson, we realized we didn't know what the students actually understood. The worksheet that was provided with the lesson could be completed correctly *without* the student possessing the fundamental conceptual knowledge. This was a significant realization, and it had ramifications for the use of any premade worksheet. We discovered that any time students complete a worksheet in which the real thinking of how to set up the data has been done for them, we don't know what they actually can do on their own.

Lesson study empowers teachers to act as researchers, respects teachers' expertise, and allows them to observe colleagues and learn from them. Teachers are empowered when treated as professionals. Unfortunately, in the United States, teachers are often absent from the policy decisions that affect them. Oddly, it seems politicians consider themselves qualified to make these decisions. I experienced this with a lesson study observation. Our lesson was about developing the ability to observe and categorize mathematically by sorting the different types of triangles. Students could label the triangles through repeated practice, but we noticed they lacked the keen observational skills to classify them on their own. We invited community leaders to observe our lesson, including our school board members.

After the lesson, I reached out by email to one of our school board members who had arrived late and missed the observation briefing describing our purpose, goals, and data collection points. I was stunned by his comments. He was an engineer, and said, "I could have taught those kids what they needed to know in five minutes. You didn't need to spend an entire lesson on it." After calming down, I pointed out that he didn't know what we were trying to accomplish and had made a judgment without knowing all the facts. In addition, I said I would never presume to judge his building design without first discovering what his objectives were. He still didn't ask what we were trying to accomplish, yet responded with his opinion again. Unfortunately, many decision makers think they know how to teach, and it is amazingly difficult to open their minds.

Lesson study and its analytical examination of student learning became a natural bridge to my experiences in becoming a National Board Certified Teacher. The process involves more than a year of intense reflection and writing about the constant decisions behind a lesson or unit. Why did I group these children? Why did I start the lesson at this point? What were my goals, and how did I know they had been achieved? All the questions were based on showing how my teaching impacted student learning. This focus was the same for lesson study, so it became a natural next step.

Teaching can be an emotional roller-coaster ride. One minute you're on top of the world because students are understanding, and the next you're plummeting to the depths of self-doubt. I was tired of these ups and downs and wanted to learn about myself as a teacher so I could settle it once and for all. People who haven't taught don't understand how isolating it can feel. They don't understand that the more you care, the harder you can be on yourself. In addition, teachers receive very little constructive feedback from administrators. Often principals have only a few minutes to observe because of other time demands, or they lack the training and skills to be instructional leaders. I had asked several times for constructive feedback, but had never received any. So I pursued National Board Certification in order to work with fellow candidates in a support group at Stanford University. Through this collaboration, I not only was able to gain National Board Certification, but I came away with a clear idea of my strengths and weaknesses.

One weakness I discovered was in my literacy instruction. Working with colleagues helped me to see holes in my pedagogy and not enough high-level, meaningful projects. That resulted in my pursuing a master's in literacy at a local university. For my thesis project, I did a self-study on my teaching. My research question explored why some of my language learners were not progressing. By recording lessons and working with my advisor and colleagues, I discovered there were some simple things I could do to help my students. One was to explicitly state the lesson goal at the beginning of the lesson. Once I started writing "You will learn . . ." and "I am looking for . . ." on the board at the beginning of each lesson, students became much more focused and engaged. I saw an immediate improvement. Suddenly my students were with me from the beginning of the lesson and able to comprehend more of it. These students are struggling to learn in English, so having the goal written in front of them helped them process much more efficiently.

Self-study, like lesson study and board certification, involves reflection with colleagues over time. The feedback from a brief observation doesn't yield the deep insights that create permanent improvements. Through the process of reflecting on why and how I made the decisions in my lessons, I came to see what needed changing. That is the first step toward making solid improvements.

Now my school district is focused on the professional learning community (PLC) model to improve student learning. That process involves meeting as a small group (usually grade level) and looking at data to identify concepts needing improved student performance. Then the group agrees on a measurable goal (e.g., 90 percent of students will score 85 percent on the assessment) and determines the assessment. Hopefully there's still time to discuss instructional strategies that would actually help teachers find the best way to deliver content and build skills, but my experience is that we usually aren't given enough time for that. We gather again after giving the assessment and share results. Students are divided into groups based on their understanding, and new lessons are developed, both for those who didn't understand the first time and also as a second assessment. Students who have already demonstrated mastery are provided enrichment activities to push them to the next level. With this model, we are able to bring almost every student to mastery. Again, the answers for what needs to happen at each of these steps are discovered within the group of teachers.

All of these experiences require a significant amount of time. As is often the case in education, there is adequate funding to start the process, but that dries up a few years into the reform effort. The result is that teachers are left to accomplish this work on their own time. Our lesson study cycles were initially supported with release time and administrative support. Teachers were initially helped with the high cost of pursuing National Board Certification, but the state removed that funding in the years that followed. When we began our PLC work, we were supported with expert guidance, release time of several days to develop our assessments and review data, and were allowed to focus on two PLCs. Now we must complete five PLCs within our limited planning time after school.

In my work with lesson study I heard an interesting statement that compared the different teaching paradigms in Japan and in the United States. It was said that in the United States, we believe great teachers are born, but in Japan they believe great teachers are taught. Our approaches to professional development reflect this. Until we commit to building our profession from the teacher up, using the time, effort, and money required, teachers will be left to piece together their own professional development.

Linda Bauld is the director of the National Board Resource Center (NBRC) at Stanford University. In her role as director, she administers the National Board candidate support program, advocates for National Board certification throughout Northern California, develops online support programs, and acts as a resource for California's candidate support networks. Ms. Bauld retired as a classroom teacher in 2014 after teaching for twenty-three years in Title I schools in the Bay area. During her years of teaching, she received numerous awards and grants in the fields of math, science, and technology.

Using Teacher-Led Research to Improve Instruction

AIJERON SIMMONS

In early September, I was looking through the science notebooks of my fifth-grade students at the end of our third investigation. I pulled the notebooks of about six random students, focusing on how well students were able to write a final answer to the guiding question. Antonio's notebook stood out. What I believed he knew, based on my informal observations during science tasks, was in stark contrast to what his writing showed. His sentences were broken. They expressed ideas that made some sense and hinted at some understanding but were very difficult to decipher. This struck me as a glaring issue of inequity in how I was assessing my students. I realized that I needed to question how well my science lessons facilitated the learning of content in conjunction with the development of language. I also wondered how I could provide Antonio with more opportunities to share what he knew.

I closed Antonio's notebook as I contemplated these questions until his artistic cover captured my full attention. One of the first assignments we do in fifth-grade science class is answer the question, what is science? After a group discussion, we identify key terms and generate ideas for how to represent our ideas. Antonio's cover design depicted very detailed drawings of science tools—ideas from fourth-grade science concepts that he clearly remembered and understood. His attention to detail and the depth of the drawing in his cover art mirrored exactly what I wanted his writing to be. Spending time thinking through how I could meet his needs was the only way I could provide the educational opportunities Antonio and other students like him deserve.

Over the course of my eight years teaching elementary school, I have attended many professional trainings where I am taught "best practices" to engage students in rigorous content and to support language development. Many practices swing like a pendulum with whatever the educational trend of the day is. Most of these trainings involve learning instructional strategies and being told how my students will respond. Enthusiastically I press forward, excited to try something new with my students. Then I get into the classroom and it doesn't work like the training predicted. My students are missing some prerequisite from a different context. Or some students excel and others just glean bits and pieces. In most cases, the training is over and I won't get the opportunity to discuss how to deepen these practices so all my students receive equitable outcomes.

The same was initially true in this situation. My district science department began this push toward science notebooking in response to Common Core implementation. We received many wonderful training sessions on how to implement notebooking practices in the classroom. I could see how these trainings were deepening my practice and how some students were really thriving. I could also see a gap widening for some of my students, particularly for my classroom's large number of English language learners. Tailoring practices to support all students, looking critically at one's own ideas and lessons plans to ensure all students are being served, and thinking deeply about issues of equity are the real work of teaching. Most professional learning opportunities that I have encountered neglect to address these critical elements.

Among my district's many science initiatives was the CAL:BLAST (Collaborative Approach to Learning Bridging Language Acquisition and Science Teaching) program, a grant-based collaboration between the Lawrence Hall of Science at the University of California, Berkeley, the district, and elementary science teachers. Part of this grant project involved receiving coaching on using the content and language practices we were learning. In the third year of the project, the organizers began a critical inquiry group that met monthly to support teachers in grappling with difficult questions rooted in our real-world classrooms. This program involved identifying an issue of practice, observing each other teaching, and, most important, participating in critical conversations while looking at student work. This collaborative inquiry space gave me a place to figure out the dilemma that Antonio's notebook presented.

During a CAL:BLAST Saturday session, I shared an example of his notebooking during a science video and the content questions he answered afterward. Antonio was only able to capture a small amount of information in written form and needed a lot of scaffolding after the video to accurately answer the questions. I explained to my colleagues the difference between what I could understand from one-on-one conversations with him and what he was able to write. Then I showed them his detailed artistic representation of what science meant to him. One of my colleagues suggested that a graphic organizer would allow him to not just write notes, but to draw what he learned from the video. I immediately implemented this adjustment, and when I looked at his video notes after using the visual graphic organizer, I saw he had provided accurate drawings and labels for key ideas in the science video, along with short captions. This option had provided Antonio a chance to demonstrate his knowledge of science in a deeper way than by writing alone. It struck me that providing structured opportunities to create visual representations through sketching, diagramming, and labeling was an authentic scientific practice that could provide *all* of my students a chance to synthesize content knowledge while giving them more opportunities to engage with the content and develop language skills.

During a CAL:BLAST planning session, I mapped out the content of the living systems unit. This involved choosing the places where scientific concepts could be explored through poster making. After determining three places where students could make posters, I created an example poster to highlight the components students would need to consider, including a title, the focus question, drawings and/or diagrams, vocabulary, labels, directional cues, and captions to help the viewer understand the content presented in the poster. With my inquiry team's support, I planned our class activities to include an investigation of the focus question, analysis of the model, student-led discussions about poster design, and construction of their poster. This would be the beginning of a collaborative inquiry journey completely driven by student work and fueled by my desire to provide Antonio and English language learners like him a more equitable science classroom. At this point my inquiry question was, how would students demonstrate science content knowledge through poster making at the end of an investigation? This question deepened as my colleagues and I examined the students' work and refined the practice of poster making over the course of the year.

Our first poster-making session answered the question, how do living cells get the oxygen they need? The students needed to represent the connections between the respiratory system and the circulatory system. During this session, students worked for about forty-five minutes creating their poster. I walked around and observed students working and then chose to collect the same six students' notebooks at the end of the activity. After looking at the posters and their limited representations of how oxygen moves in the body, two things stood out. First, the language students generated during the conversation about what they should include in their posters was critical to surfacing key ideas and vocabulary, determining what should be represented in the poster. Second, the conversations between partners were richer than the actual posters. They understood the information, but it was coming out more clearly in the collaboration than in the final product.

Interestingly, I noticed that Antonio's poster and that of a redesignated English language learner, Julian, whose science writing was much clearer, seemed to reflect about the same level of understanding. Both students had drawn the heart, lungs, body cells, veins, and arteries. The higher-level student included no written explanation of the visual. Antonio, on the other hand, had two very unclear sentences that, in essence, translated to, "I think one reason is the cells get the oxygen while breathing. The last reason is the cells get the oxygen while we are running and we breathe more faster." He knew we get oxygen from breathing. He connected to our investigation, in which our heart rate increased as we ran, and he understood that we need to breathe faster as cells consume oxygen. His drawing showed the nose and included an arrow showing oxygen going into the nose. On this assignment he would actually score higher than the English-proficient student. Immediately I felt there had been a leveling of the playing field. I knew much more work needed to be done, but I was excited to see how this work could foster growth in both students.

At this point the value of having students collaborate while making their posters became apparent. I could see from our conversations that students could talk together to review the investigation and work together to problem-solve exactly what should be on their posters. Because we were in the middle of round two at the time of my analysis, I did not implement the collaborative poster making until round three. My inquiry question changed to, how would students demonstrate science content knowledge through collaborative poster making at the end of an investigation? I would bring this question to my inquiry group when we met again, along with the student work, and ask them to help me think about what supports both Antonio and Julian should receive to move them forward. I was also able to sign up to have the group of teachers observe the students during their poster-making session and help me collect data on the process.

The poster session for round three was our first collaborative session. Students used the content learned during two celery investigations, a video, and a science article on plant transport systems to help them answer the question, how do plants get water to all plant cells? During the session, students reviewed content, made a plan, and began the work of making the poster. My inquiry group came to observe the collaboration in action. They observed that in Antonio and Julian's group, the primary language spoken to discuss the content was English. The only Spanish spoken was to clarify issues that came up during the actual poster making. The group also noted that while Antonio wasn't the most outspoken member of the group, he readily took to drawing the group's diagrams and was at the center of the poster construction. Julian was able to support his group in synthesizing ideas that would go on the poster in the form of captions and vocabulary. As I debriefed the process with my inquiry team, we discussed the value of students working on how to represent the answer to a question visually. We realized students really needed to build the skills of summarizing main points and eliminating irrelevant information from their drawings. We also thought about how to interpret a collaborative poster in terms of individual contributions, places where students had to compromise on things they felt strongly about, and how students could use these posters as a place to revise their misconceptions. We had a deep conversation about how opportunities to enhance or revise the group poster could help students take their understanding of the content to the next level. Based on my evolving practice and their feedback, my inquiry shifted again so that my new question was, how will collaborative poster making and revision help students demonstrate and deepen science content knowledge?

For this, students would need a session like the many I had participated in through CAL:BLAST to give each other feedback on their content and presentation. Before moving to the next round, I devoted class time to this purpose. Students left feedback for each other's past posters and were given a chance to individually revise their group's poster by making their own version in their notebook. All these opportunities to review and recreate were exciting for the students. Looking at the revisions of poster three, I noted that all six of my focal students had made some change to the group's original poster. Antonio's poster after the revision eliminated unnecessary information, highlighted one key caption, and included a title and labels. The sentence states, "Plant get the water they need from the roots, from the leaf, and from the stem." This sentence really was a step forward from the previous captions, which were complete ramblings. Julian's work also showed significant growth. He revised the title, chose one very clear caption, highlighted key vocabulary, and eliminated some irrelevant information. My process in thinking about this project had allowed me to see why revision and peer reflection would help in their collaboration, and my students walked away with better comprehension of the content and improved visual and written explanations because of it.

Between the beginning of poster four and completing the cycle of poster sessions and revision, I met with the inquiry team. We looked at student work from the first poster session and the revision round. We examined the feedback on Post-it notes students had written to one another and looked at the changes in students' work. Our conversation centered around highlighting vocabulary for students, teaching how to give strategic feedback for revision, and the benefits of the work. After this conversation, I developed lessons to target feedback during the poster session. Our class went over how to ask critical questions that could lead to adding important information, eliminating unnecessary details, checking scientific facts, and strengthening organization.

Poster four would be a synthesis poster. This required students to bring together ideas from five different inquiry projects to answer the question, how does energy move from the sun to the cells of the human body? Students drew posters in collaboration, learned about types of questions that can lead to revision, and drew their revised versions of the poster. Antonio's attention to detail in his artwork began with the sun shining down on a tomato plant. It showed a young boy near the plant picking a tomato. He eats the tomato, and Antonio made a visual representation of the digestive system that showed the tomato moving through the various parts of the system. This poster for Antonio included a three-part caption. The same caption format appeared in Julian's final poster, but the captions read completely differently. Their collaboration had been mutually beneficial, allowing them to share ideas while holding on to their individuality. Antonio's captions read: "The energy from the sun comes to the tomato, then the energy is in the tomato. After the boy eats the tomato it's gonna go to the stomach. The boy eats the tomato and he gets the energy."

This was real growth for Antonio: he moved his writing to a paragraph written in several sections on his poster. Even here his writing stated that the tomato will go to the stomach; however, his drawing showed a tomato entering a labeled mouth, moving down a labeled esophagus, on to the stomach, into the small and large intestine, through the colon, and out the rectum, all of which are labeled. Julian's poster was drawn in a similar format to Antonio's. The writing component of Julian's poster was much more scientific and detailed in nature. It included the ideas of photosynthesis, the digestive system, food passing through the small intestine and being broken down into sugars, and then being transported to cells. He showed the digestive system, but did not show how the cherries traveled through the system. Although there was still work to be done here, these students were moving toward outcomes that were much more equitable than they were at the beginning of the year. They were talking, sharing ideas, highlighting vocabulary, synthesizing, and benefiting from each other's expertise.

My inquiry group continued to discuss strategies to help Antonio get to the level of vocabulary represented in Julian's poster, and to help Julian take more creative risks and learn to ask critical questions. I would think and think and adjust and adjust again to enhance learning for all parties involved. I would do the critical work of teaching for equity and social justice in collaboration with my colleagues. The practice of creation, collaboration, and revision that fuels the learning for my students also fuels my professional learning.

Aijeron Simmons taught fifth-grade sheltered English in Oakland Unified School District for nine years. She is currently associate director of Teacher Leadership with Mills Teacher Scholars and is Bay Area Writing Project codirector. She received a master's degree in elementary education from Mills College. Her master's research focused on the integration of science and literacy, particularly academic language development and writing. During her time in OUSD, she emphasized teaching fourth- and fifth-grade students to develop literacy through science. Currently she is coaching Bay Area teachers to develop leadership skills through facilitating teacher-inquiry sessions.

We Are the Ones in the Classroom— Ask Us!

Student Voice in Teacher Evaluations

RIANA GOOD

The slightly whiny query, "But why do we hafta . . .?" verbalizes many students' feelings of disempowerment in the classroom. Even in the most well-meaning schools, students are often faced with undemocratic authority and passive learning because their education is often structured with short classes, high student loads for teachers, little time for teachers to plan and collaborate, and few opportunities for young people to connect with each other and with adults. Add to that sometimes dull curricula and standardized testing, and the early spark in students can soon be extinguished. Learning is inherently pleasurable, but many of us instead associate it with criticism, fear, rigidity, and other harmful elements of schooling. While a critical, participatory classroom cannot single-handedly transform a multitude of oppressive forces in education, it can provide the basis for establishing positive feelings toward learning, critical analysis, and engagement with the world. In a democratic, participatory classroom, student input is encouraged and ultimately indispensable.

Student voice can span the range from Youth Participatory Action Research (YPAR) to input on class rules to rubric formation to feedback to the teacher. In Boston, youth have been at the forefront of incorporating student feedback into teacher evaluation, spearheaded by the Boston Student Advisory Council (BSAC) and Youth on Board. While some teachers are hesitant about the incorporation of student feedback into teacher evaluations, it is important to emphasize that it is not just another mandate from above, but rather a student-generated movement. Student perception data, when combined with observations and multiple measures of student achievement, provide a more reliable gauge of educator effectiveness and a stronger predictor of teacher impact on student learning.[40] Even more important, it empowers young people and offers educators meaningful insight, which they can use to modify and improve their practice.

When I first heard about the movement toward student input in teacher evaluation in the Boston Public Schools, the students in my seventh-grade Spanish class wouldn't be participating, as only input from high school students would be incorporated in the initial stages of implementation. In theory, I enthusiastically supported student input, but I was relieved to dodge the regulations as a K–8 teacher because I was not proud of my teaching that year and knew that would be reflected in their input. Surely the constant interruptions, the lack of respect, and the inadequate differentiation for their broad range of levels would be brazenly evident in their feedback. I was having a rough go of it with that group, and it was little solace to me, or to my students, that my colleagues were also struggling with that class. I was loathe to see in writing how dissatisfied they were, because I wanted to improve their classroom experience, and yet I didn't know what to do about it. I sought assistance, not further reinforcement of my shame. I thought that I would have faced feedback potentially so negative as to be overwhelming rather than informative, serving to discourage me rather than to serve as an impetus to change my practice.

While unfavorable feedback may cause discomfort or defeat, using a triangulation from multiple measures of evaluation can give a much better picture of our teaching than observations or test scores alone. Most states are looking to create teacher evaluation systems that combine classroom observations and student growth on tests. In many cases, this has required a significant increase in the overall number of observations, but already overworked administrators can't be expected to increase their load to such a degree. New national reforms require student achievement and improvement on high-stakes tests to be yet another measure, despite the fact that 83 percent of teachers in Massachusetts teach nontested grades and subjects.[41] Entire content areas—from music and art to foreign language and physical education—are not included, a testament to the inadequacy of test scores as an indicator. On top of this, the use of such value-added measures has been widely reported as unreliable and having wide margins of error. Some states have included other measures, such as portfolios, evidence of a teacher's professional goals and growth, and, to a lesser degree, student feedback.

The impulse to ask for students' input is not natural for the majority of people who grew up without any experience of it in their own education. Traditionally, adults decide and young people deal with the decisions. Even my own privileged education background didn't include that kind of student voice. Though I felt empowered and respected as a student in my suburban schools, we didn't have any say in the ways our classrooms were run. It was not until college that I was asked to give feedback on my courses, and even then it was an institutional formality rather than a sincere inquiry into learning and reflective teaching practice. I don't even know if any of my professors read our evaluations, let alone incorporated the feedback into future courses, or whether evaluations were routed right to the department chairs for quality control. If acquiring tenure depended more on research and published articles than on teaching undergraduate courses, I can't imagine that our evaluations held much weight, regardless. Even in graduate school, in classes specifically focused on the craft of teaching, this trend didn't shift. The professor predetermined everything and we followed along, ready to soak up this top-down process to recreate in our own classrooms someday. I have a distinct memory of the one exception to the top-down tendency: the evening our professor asked us to develop the rubric that she would use to evaluate our projects on navigating literacy for different media. We took a mere ten or fifteen minutes to decide on the categories and the weighting for the rubric, and yet that one episode in my seventeen years of formal schooling stands out as unique.

In my roles as teacher and advisor to our school's Student Government, I have heard similar sentiment from young people. When asked to rate their impact on our school's culture and policies, not a single student responded that he or she has a large impact, with the majority saying that they had no impact, and some stating that they had minimal or some impact through the Student Government. We had talked about being a rebel versus a revolutionary in response to dissatisfaction with the status quo, resisting for your own sake (or harm) versus changing policies to have a larger impact on the system as a whole. A student echoed that sentiment by saying, "Members of Student Government have common interests and care more, whereas our friends give more negative comments rather than be supportive with ideas." If students speak up without a collective movement, or when they are not asked, they are often seen as being disruptive, yet there are few formal avenues for student voices to be heard.

The experience of my students reflects the messages that I continue to receive: positive reinforcement for taking charge and for having tightly run classrooms of compliant students, a scenario where obedience is sometimes at odds with student engagement. It is hard to relinquish control, even as I, too, am exploring what it means to speak up in a system that discounts my worth and doesn't want to hear my opinions either. There are deep-seated parallels between the silencing of teachers' voices in education policy and reform and the silencing of young peoples' voices in the classroom. It is not tidy or convenient to seek input from others. It is even messier to apply it. It will likely go against the status quo. There will likely be dissenting opinions. It is all-around slower and harder to manage. I am seeking greater voice for both myself and for my students within my own school's decisions and in the greater education arena.

I've moved up to teaching high school since the student evaluations were first implemented and have made student input inherent to my classroom practice and pedagogical values, despite the challenges. I started with low-hanging fruit, seeking student input around changes to seating arrangements, balance of activities that address different modalities, grading policies, and the like, yet I still find it very hard to relinquish my conception of teacher control of the classroom. "But we only have forty-seven-minute classes!" I tell myself, "How will we get everything done if we decentralize and collaborate and ensure that I'm reaching every single student?!" Sometimes adults don't seem to notice that they are not getting valuable contributions, ideas, and creativity from young people—simply because we are not leaving enough space. If we keep teaching full steam ahead, it can feel that we're on a roll, that everyone's with us, that we've really hit our stride, and yet we are leaving some students behind. We are so far ahead that we haven't even looked back to notice. When I keep teaching new verb tenses and some students still haven't mastered present tense conjugation, or when I fear that slowing down will degrade my finely honed classroom flow into chaos, I am forgetting the purpose of a democratic education. It is a challenge for the active citizens that we want our students to become to emerge from an environment in which everything has been predetermined.

In my nine years of teaching, I have also used monthly student self-assessments, usually printed on the back of a vocabulary or grammar quiz, that ask:

- What were you proud of this month?
- What would you like to improve on for next month?
- What would you like to do more of (topics or activities)?

Students then rate themselves from 1 to 5 on measurements such as "I took risks to volunteer" and "I worked to the best of my abilities when given time in class." They are generally astute judges of their effort and participation. If students aren't taking risks or working to the best of their abilities, I ask myself—and often them—what can create an environment in which they are? Finally, I ask them to rate the pace of the class according to their perception as: way too slow, too slow, about right, too fast, way too fast. As this routine becomes more familiar, it takes just two to four minutes to complete. It counts toward their participation grade and gives me a solid sense of their perceived class pacing as well.

At the beginning of the year I was getting a lot of formal and informal feedback from students that input in the target language—Spanish—was a challenge, as this was a new experience for most of them. As such, I created a student-learning goal that stated, "Based on the fact that 60 percent of students currently assess the pace of the class to be about right, my goal is that by the end of April, at least 80 percent of students will assess the pace of the class to be about right." I linked this to my professional practice goal: "In order to ensure that the pace of the class is about right for the vast majority of my students, I will develop more take-home and website materials for scholars who are struggling, as well as check in with them via participation self-assessments that gauge their perception of their understanding and progress. I will monitor my progress toward this goal by documenting the materials that I have gathered on the class website and by collecting data from their self-assessments."

Some critics of democratic classrooms may offer disparaging comments about it being too "tolerant" or "touchy-feely," as if we wouldn't want tolerance or emotion in a place of learning. Yet democratic approaches can also translate to actionable data. Indeed, by monitoring student input on class pacing and taking the action steps of my professional practice goal, I exceeded my goal by March, with 92 percent of students assessing the pace of the class to be about right, leveling off at 87 percent of students in April and May. While I was able to use student input to modify my pacing, not all elements of student input are necessarily actionable. Seeking student input is also important for its own sake, for the sake of empowering young people, though that is not currently a primary focus of the regulations that require student input in educator evaluations.

At the end of the school year, I gave the joint Boston Public Schools/ Boston Student Advisory Council survey. Students completed it without comment, except for a student who asked unenthusiastically if they would be required in "*every single* class." I was able to assure him that this was just a trial run, though it would be required in the future. Survey fatigue— for both the surveyed and the surveyor—is real. Reading through more than 140 surveys didn't create the opportunity for reflection that I had anticipated, but the sparse narrative comments held some value. One student expressed feeling some discomfort when we got too silly, and another pleaded for less textbook time. Still, the anonymity didn't result in any big reveals. If anything, it meant that students knew I wouldn't know how much time they had put into their survey, and so their effort was somewhat diminished. Maybe as democratic classrooms take hold and students become more internally rather than externally motivated, that tendency will shift. Staggering the surveys throughout the year would be helpful, so that students don't get survey fatigue and will feel inspired to elaborate on the open-response questions, which have proven most useful for teacher feedback.

I am enthusiastic about young people's empowerment, and yet I still have some reservations about student feedback in the context of current education policy and reforms. Many people and institutions, both governmental and nongovernmental, are thinking about schools as if they are like businesses or corporation. When schools are conflated with businesses, young people are conflated with customers, and then their feedback is seen as yet another customer survey.

The nature of the feedback that we seek will determine the responses. The tone and spirit with which we seek feedback will determine its usefulness. Student feedback is like other elements of the educator evaluation system in that, if it is done in a climate of support and of valuing educators, it will be embraced and effective. If it is done in a climate of shaming and with a "gotcha" mentality, it will be met with resentment, avoidance, and excuses. An encouraging, respectful environment is a necessary underpinning for effective implementation of feedback.

What we measure as meaningful reflects what we value. Embracing young people's voices in the classroom raises up young people and gives us a better picture of teacher effectiveness.

Riana Good has taught Spanish in the Boston Public Schools for nine years, where she serves as an ally to young people in the classroom, as faculty advisor of the Gay/ Straight Alliance and the Student Government, and most recently as a supporter of their protests against budget cuts. She acts upon her vision of education for liberation through her union activism, leadership in Boston's Teacher Activist Group, and facilitation of a monthly support group for educators.

CHAPTER 3

CHOICE

Competition as the Path to Innovation

Many people see the freedom to choose is an essential part of what it means to be an American. Voting for our choice of candidates is seen as the foundation of our democracy. Picking our preferred products is the basis of our economic system. The idea of choice has also been applied to public education throughout the country's history, albeit selectively accessible. Private, independent, and parochial schools have existed as alternatives to the public common school since the 1800s.[1] In the 1950s and '60s, choice was used as a tool to both promote and fight against the desegregation of public schools.[2] Choice was advocated in the 1980s and '90s by progressive small-school educators and by conservatives arguing for public funding of private school vouchers.[3] In the past fifteen years, "choice" in education has become largely centered on charter schools.

Charter schools are publicly funded, privately operated schools. As independent entities, charters are not bound by many of the state, city, and district rules that traditional public schools have to follow. To start a charter school, a group of people, an organization, or a company can draw up a proposal, get approved by a charter school authorizer, receive start-up funding, and open. In traditional public schools, students are often assigned to a neighborhood school based on where they live; in charter schools, students are admitted through an application process that can reach across the traditional school zones.[4] Many charter schools combine public and private funding, receiving government funding per pupil and donations from companies and individuals. They are also by and large teacher union free and their teachers don't have collective bargaining rights.[5] In exchange for all of this freedom, most charter schools are expected to show student gains in a relatively short amount of time, heavily weighted by student performance on standardized tests.

THE RISE OF CHARTER SCHOOLS

The first charter school opened in Minnesota in 1992.[6] Today, there are about 6,700 charters across the United States serving about 2.9 million students, or almost 6 percent of the total public school student population.[7] The number of charter schools has grown over 300 percent since the 1999–2000 school year, and almost 2,000 new charter schools opened in the past five years alone.[8] Much of this recent expansion was spurred by the federal Race to the Top program, whose guidelines specifically favored states who lifted their cap on the number of charter schools allowed.[9]

Charter schools are often spoken about as one group, but they take on many forms. As reporter Nick Anderson described in *The Washington Post*, they include everything from "the Montessori method to what might be called the No-Method method, from math academies to arts academies, from distance learning to hands-on learning. They pop up in strip malls and abandoned churches. They compete for enrollment in suburbs and barrios and on Indian reservations."[10] Though their differences are important to keep in mind, there are some patterns that have come to characterize charter schools. They are more likely to be based in cities;[11] somewhat more likely to serve low-income students and to qualify as a high-poverty school; more likely to serve Black students and somewhat more likely to serve Latinx students than traditional public schools.[12] Charter schools as a whole enroll smaller numbers of English language learners and special education students.[13] The majority of charters are started by independent organizations or companies, though a growing number are led by charter management organizations (CMOs) or education management organizations (EMOs) that run chains of charter schools.[14]

The rapid growth of charter schools has occurred disproportionately in cities or districts with high concentrations of students of color that have also experienced a precipitous drop in the number of students attending traditional public schools. San Antonio School District, for example, saw a 483 percent increase in charter school enrollment from 2005 to 2012 at the same time that its overall public school enrollment dropped 22 percent. Ninety-eight percent of its student population are students of color. Gary, Indiana, where 99 percent of students are students of color, saw an increase of 197 percent in its charter school enrollment during that time period as its overall public school enrollment dropped 47 percent. Los Angeles: 91 percent students of color; 243 percent increase in charter school enrollment; 23 percent decline in total public school enrollment.[15] Charter schools are poised to continue their rapid growth under the new federal education law Every Student Succeeds Act (ESSA), which dedicates an entire section to the opening, replication, and expansion of charter schools.[16] ESSA offers charter schools a larger funding increase than any other program within the law and continues the role of the federal government as the biggest funder of their expansion.[17] And President Donald J. Trump has put charter school expansion at the top of his education agenda.[18]

The allure of charter schools is derived from a belief in the power of choice. Parents are free to choose whatever school in their area would be best for their kids; students can leave their neighborhood to choose a shot at a good life; teachers can choose to unburden themselves of union limitations that stop them from doing everything possible to help their students; schools can experiment with new structures that will solve the failure of our outdated education system; and business people, organizations and others usually on the outside of education can choose to invest in new school models that match their beliefs and interests. Early on, many charter proponents argued that, by being "mercifully free of red tape and bureaucratic rules," charter schools would be laboratories of research and development that would dramatically increase academic achievement as measured by standardized test scores.[19] These spotlights of high-impact reform would then spur improvement in all schools through a combination of idea sharing and competition.[20]

In the 2000s, some charter schools serving urban low-income students of color began receiving a large amount of media, political, and philanthropic attention. KIPP (Knowledge Is Power Program), Success Charter Network, YES Prep, Promise Academy, Achievement First, IDEA Public Schools, and Green Dot were among the charters schools lauded for their performance, particularly with low-income African American and Latinx students. Many of these schools were self-proclaimed "no excuses" charters, schools that pride themselves on setting very high expectations and that will do "whatever it takes" to ensure their students are college-bound.[21]

Documentaries like *Waiting for Superman* and *The Lottery* portrayed dramatic lottery admission days where students' fates seemed to be contingent on their number being drawn. Politicians and media commentators exclaimed that charter school leaders had created "one of the most profound changes in American education," teaching "lessons about what works and what doesn't in K–12" and offering a beacon of hope in an otherwise paralyzed system.[22] With heavy public and private financial backing, including donations in the millions of dollars from the Bill & Melinda Gates Foundation, the Walton Family Foundation, the Eli Broad Foundation, and many others, these golden children of the charter movement expanded into charter management organizations (CMOs) running multiple schools off of their original model.[23]

During this time, advocates reframed their procharter position. Charters were no longer "incubators of innovation" that needed to spread their best practices to improve the larger system of public education; they were now a preferred alternative to traditional schools, especially for traditionally underserved populations.[24] Expanding charter schools so that they serve a sizable portion—or a "market share"—of school-age children across the country has been recast as a matter of equity and justice, the only real option for these students to attain the American Dream.

WHAT THE NUMBERS SAY—AND DON'T SAY—ABOUT CHARTERS

Behind the bold claims about charter performance, the research is less satisfyingly clear. Most charter schools rely heavily on test scores as the measure of their success, yet, even based on those metrics, numerous reports and studies show that the results of charter schools vary, and that, overall, they perform no differently than traditional public schools.[25] The Center for Research on Education Outcomes (CREDO), one of the most widely heralded (and hotly contested) research institutions looking at charter achievement, released their latest national report in 2013 and found charter students had made miniscule gains over district schools in reading and math.[26] Another metastudy by the Center on Reinventing Public Education found no significant impact on reading scores and small positive impacts on math scores.[27] Studies pile up on either side of this back-and-forth, all of which land somewhere between small negative effects, small positive effects, or no effects at all.[28]

Many charter school supporters will readily accept that some charter schools are failing and others are mediocre, but they'll point to the superstar schools they've identified as raising students' test scores as evidence of what charter schools are capable of that traditional public schools are not. Many have also referred to studies that show students from select charter schools had higher high school graduation and college enrollment percentages and lower rates of teen pregnancy and incarceration compared to students from traditional public schools.[29]

Charter school critics contend these results obscure some glaring inequities. First, they point to the student populations at public versus charter schools, which, despite claims that charters are taking the same kids and making astonishing gains, have some critical differences. The clearest example of this is in the well-documented underenrollment of English language learners and special education students, something that many charters have pledged to improve, but whose numbers continue to be disproportionate.[30]

Charter schools also have a record of explicitly and implicitly screening students, from reviews of academic and discipline records to citizenship requirements. Stephanie Simon at Reuters documented a series of these practices, which included methods that would ensure that only the most motivated children and parents applied, including lengthy English-only applications, essay examinations, and mandatory family interviews. In addition to admissions hurdles, some charters also require parental time commitments and mandate that children get picked up during the day for misbehavior, including minor infractions. Parents who have less access to resources, have busy work schedules or multiple jobs, or who otherwise aren't involved in their kids' lives cannot equally apply to these schools.[31] So even when students are coming from disadvantaged backgrounds, the ability of charters to pool together the families who are highly supportive and able to contribute to their child's education gives them an advantage over traditional public schools, which by definition must accept everyone who comes to their doors.[32]

The charter school population is further shaped by students who are admitted but then forced out, counseled out, or who leave because the environment isn't right for them, all three of which have been reported regularly as charter schools expand, though this seems to be decreasing at some of the most well-known charter chains.[33] When students leave, these seats often go unfilled even when schools have long waiting lists, while traditional schools must accept students during whatever part of the school year they happen to arrive.[34] Combined, these factors create layers of nuance in the discussions comparing charter and traditional district school student populations and their results.

Critics also question claims about the success of charter schools that are based on dramatic increases in test scores because of the outsized role that tests play in charters' curriculum and pedagogy. A study by Dr. Will Dobbie and Dr. Roland G. Fryer Jr. on effective school practices analyzed the actual lessons teachers used at high-achieving charter schools. They found that the lessons were less likely to be at or above grade level or to include critical-thinking skills like analysis and synthesis. Their teachers' lessons were also less thoroughly designed and less differentiated to meet the needs of students with diverse needs and skill levels.[35] While a focus on basic skills has been effective for some charter schools in raising student test scores, the long-term effects are less clear. Another study by Dobbie and Fryer in 2016 sought to find if "no excuses" charter schools that raised test scores resulted in gains for their students later in life, but they found no effect on earnings. While they clarified that the design of their study could not pinpoint the causes for this mismatch, the authors worried about the possibility "that what it takes to increase achievement among the poor in charter schools deprives them of other skills that are important for labor markets."[36] While young people's education should not exclusively be linked to their future job prospects, the Dobbie and Fryer study opens up the conversation about charter school success beyond test score gains.

A number of newspapers, magazines, and blogs have covered test-prep culture within these schools, including multiple stories about Harlem Success Academy, one of the most lauded charter school networks. Exemplary of the tone described by these reports is an email sent by a leadership resident at one of the schools to her fourth-grade teachers ahead of the state tests. "We can NOT let up on them," she wrote. "This is serious business, and there has to be misery felt for the kids who are not doing what is expected of them." Studies analyzing trends across charter schools have found that an emphasis on testing has pushed many schools to replicate a routinized pedagogical approach rather than attempt creative, inspired teaching methods.[37]

There is increasing focus and pressure being brought to bear on charter schools around overly harsh discipline practices, a third element that critics claim impacts charter schools' test scores. Much of this criticism is directed at schools using the "no excuses" model. Many of these schools have exacting rules about behavior, from walking in single file lines to silent breakfast and lunch to specific instructions on how students are to sit in class. At KIPP, this is called SLANT: Sit Up, Listen, Ask and Answer Questions, Nod, and Track the Speaker.[38] At Success Academy, students have to keep their backs straight, their feet on the floor, and their hands clasped in front of them.[39] This approach has led to outsized suspension records for many of these schools. From 2011 to 2012, New York City charter schools suspended students almost three times as often as traditional public schools.[40] In Washington, DC, charter schools expelled 676 students over a three-year period, compared to 24 expulsions from district schools.[41]

Finally, critics argue that the test scores of some of the most widely heralded charter schools belie vast disparities in funding. In addition to the public funding that charter schools receive, some charter schools are able to attract large amounts in private donations. A study of school funding in New York City found that some charter schools receive as much as $10,000 more per pupil than traditional schools, even though, based on their students' special education and English language learner needs, they should receive about $2,500 less.[42] In Texas, some charter chains spend anywhere between 30 and 100 percent more per pupil than traditional schools in areas serving similar populations.[43]

As private entities become more entwined with public education, new questions arise about profit, transparency, and oversight. In 2011–2012, 42 percent of the nation's public charter school students were enrolled in privately operated charter schools, some of which include for-profit companies.[44] In addition, nonprofit charters often have for-profit companies that are contracted to do much of their work. These companies may handle everything from accounting to hiring teachers and managing finances, all without public oversight. Marian Wang documented a version of these deals—known as "sweeps" contracts—which give 95 to 100 percent of a school's public dollars to a management company, for the investigative journalism site ProPublica. In Buffalo and Brooklyn, New York, Washington, DC, Michigan, and Ohio, to name a few examples, millions of dollars have disappeared into private companies, and boards of education and regulatory agencies have had no authority to audit their records.[45] There are countless other examples of fraud and conflicts of interest in the management of public funds for charters. Combined, this has amounted to over $200 million in fraud, waste, and mismanagement.[46]

At the root of these critiques is a concern that charter schools are eroding the fundamental idea of a public education system that serves all students and is controlled by oversight from a democratically elected body. As charter schools are pushed to expand and serve more students, they divide the public schools into two increasingly unequal, separate systems.[47] In Chicago, for example, one month before the 2016–2017 school was set to start, one thousand teachers and school-based staff members were fired from district schools in what district administrators called a budget adjustment driven by decreasing enrollment largely attributable to the expansion of charter schools.[48] In the 2015 budget, neighborhood schools received almost $60 million less, while charter schools were set to get $30 million more.[49] As the overall number of school-age children in Chicago declines, the city continues to open new charter schools, further dividing resources.[50] Chicago is not an anomaly in this trend; similar patterns of school closures, increases in charter school enrollment, and public school budget shortfalls are being seen in other cities across the country.[51]

WHY CHARTERS?

One of the early proponents of charter schools was Albert Shanker, then president of the American Federation of Teachers (AFT). In Shanker's vision, charter schools could exist outside the mainstream system, providing a space for teachers to lead in experimenting and cultivating practices for students who were often left behind by traditional schools. He also imagined charters would be a tool for integration in a way that neighborhood schools never could. Without zoning restrictions, these schools could bring together racially and economically diverse students from around a city or district.[52] Drawing from the lessons of the earlier small-schools movement, these schools were often conceived as community-based, teacher-run institutions where professional educators and families could work together to most effectively provide for their students.[53] There are charter schools working to fulfill many of these original goals. Blackstone Valley Prep Mayoral Academy in Rhode Island and Community Roots Charter School in Brooklyn are intentionally creating diverse and integrated student bodies, and the Avalon School in St. Paul uses a teacher-cooperative model to run the school, to name a few examples.[54] But charter schools as a whole have not embodied those ideals.

For many, the question still remains: why are two separate systems needed for these kinds of schools to exist, particularly given some of the far-reaching negative implications? Researchers who have analyzed successful charter schools often point to governance innovations, not pedagogy, as making the difference for students, and many of these governance innovations are things that people working in traditional schools would love to have the freedom to do too.[55] One strategy that is often highlighted is the use of frequent feedback to teachers.[56] Principals in most charter school networks have the time to observe and coach their teachers because they don't have to deal with the day-to-day management of the school; staff at the management organization handles that for them. Charter schools' flexibility in hiring additional staff to respond to school or student needs has also been linked to increased achievement.[57] In both cases, resources for staffing provides the kind of time for real, meaningful work that most principals and teachers can only dream of but would readily welcome in their schools.[58]

Another oft-cited charter governance method associated with improved student outcomes is an extended school day and/or longer school year, something that district schools are increasingly adopting.[59] Studies that have connected specific charter school curricula to achievement have pinpointed the skill and content coherence between grades and subjects along with a clear alignment with the school mission, a practice that has been proven in decades of research on school effectiveness.[60] In short, none of these elements needs to be linked to just one kind of school, and many of them have a long history within education research on what makes schools successful.

Charter schools arose from the idea that continuing along with business as usual was not working for all students, and that schools should be able to respond to the needs of local communities and students. These are values that most educators can rally behind. The question for a public education system that is increasingly divided between different kinds of schools is whether we can provide this equitably for all students.

TEACHERS' STORIES

The differences between student populations and funding levels between charters, magnet and district schools can become particularly glaring when the two are in the same building. Los Angeles teacher Ruth Luevanos shares her experiences with co-location, detailing how students at her district school were impacted when a charter school moved in. In her story, "If This Isn't the Solution, What Is?," Radha Radkar explains the evolution of a "no excuses" charter school in Brooklyn, where an obsession with meeting test score requirements created a learning environment that relied on excessive suspensions and a curriculum focused on isolated skill building. In her portrait of a successful public Montessori school in Milwaukee, Stephanie Schneider questions reformers' commitment to choice and innovation. In her case, education policy has consistently pushed to standardize the unique education provided by her school, removing a high-quality option for families. Brandon Ligon takes readers into another unique school, a charter school started by a teacher union that was created with a full vote from the community. In the last story, Virginia Rhodes challenges the idea that innovation can only take place in charter schools by sharing an example of a STEM high school in Cincinnati, Ohio, founded and operated by a team of teachers.

Socially Inequitable Education

Co-Locations and the Widening of the Achievement Gap

RUTH LUEVANOS

As a veteran middle school teacher working in an inner-city school, I see more and more charter schools, pilot schools, and "academies" every year, yet the achievement gap for at-risk students continues to increase. Why? In my experience, I see that these schools siphon off the students who have higher test scores while not accepting students who are English language learners, have special needs, or have discipline issues. A fellow social studies teacher expressed her frustration to me about one of the "academies" for at-risk, disadvantaged students that was recently formed at her school. This school weeded out students by requiring parents to pay $500 entrance fees to get into the academy. Parents who wanted their children to go to this academy but could not afford the $500 could still have their child attend if they volunteered to work in the school during school hours. This, of course, was an impossible requirement for parents who worked two or three jobs or who had little ones at home.

This, in effect, screened out the students whom this very academy was meant to help. The "best" students went to the academy, while the remainder of the students went to the resident school. The result: a shift in the population whereby more students with special needs, English language learners, and students with discipline issues went to the resident school. This is exactly what happens at many schools across the country when charter schools, pilot schools, and academies are able to pick and choose who attends their school. This further exacerbates the problem, because there are more and more students with high academic, emotional and social needs left at the resident school, which does not receive the economic resources, staff, or educational opportunities such as field trips, that the charter, pilot, or academy schools receive.

At the school where I teach, there is great disparity between the magnet and resident schools that share the campus and the resources that students have access to on a regular basis. The only electives offered at my resident school are those offered by the one drama teacher and one band teacher that we have for the entire population of 1200 students. The only students who have a remote possibility of going on field trips are sixth graders. In the two years since they have rebuilt the school's auditorium that burned down six years ago, I have taken my resident students there only once for one assembly, which happened to be on antibullying. In fact, so much preference is shown to the magnet school that when I scheduled a parent workshop with a guest speaker coming from Arizona to speak on his experiences of being Latino and going to Harvard, I was told that there was no room in the auditorium or social hall for my guest speaker because the magnet drama and choir teachers were rehearsing and their sets could not be disturbed. This year the only field trips scheduled are for students in the magnet school who are in drama, choir, dance, or film classes. This causes low morale for the students at the resident school, who had looked forward to field trips that would expand their application of academic concepts in real-life experiences and other hands-on experiences.

EDUCATIONAL ANGST AND UNCERTAINTY: PLAYING THE NUMBERS GAME

Every spring for the past five years, our principal has called the staff into the library to let us know that yet another charter school has applied to co-locate onto our campus. It is a way to make us feel as if we are to blame for this "takeover." We are asked to reach out to parents, even though the administrators frown on authentic partnerships with parents the whole year long by making it very difficult to have workshops, speakers, or sessions for parents. We are told to ask them to call the school district to let them know that they don't want a charter school on our campus. We are told of the horrors that other schools have faced, of co-located campuses where some students wear uniforms and others don't, where there are four different bells for each period, and where students have to share access to the music room, theater, gym, cafeteria, auditorium, and social hall with the charter school. We all talk about how awful it would be to have a charter, and how they are going to steal all of the "good" kids until eventually they take over the whole school. But deep down, we know that they will never take over the whole school. Why? Because they need some public schools to take all of the kids that do not fit their elite definition of a successful student. They need public schools to take all of the students that will not increase their test scores or Academic Performance Indexes. They need a place to dump the "misfit" students that do not fit their mold of productive or successful—students that do not help them simulate a measure of academic success at their school.

PARENTS' PERCEPTIONS OF CHARTER SCHOOLS

As a former high school teacher at a continuation school for five years prior to teaching at Partridge Middle School, I had already witnessed the great disservice that charter schools had done to at-risk high school students in my community. Continuation schools exist in order to help students who have failed classes, been out of school, or have other problems that have kept them from gaining class credits get back on track in order to graduate from high school. I had students who had transferred from charter schools, and I wondered how they had fallen behind on credits when charter schools were supposed to have more resources, better accountability, and more student support. However, what I encountered in my five years of teaching at a continuation high school were students who lost anywhere from 15 to 65 credits in as little as one year at their charter school. I had one student, Natalie, who had come from a recently formed local charter high school with 65 credits of advisory class. I asked her what exactly advisory was, and she told me that they "advised her on how to study." She said, "It was basically study hall." When I called the school district to see how many of those "advisory" credits would actually count toward her graduation, they stated that only 5 of the 65 credits would count. Natalie was devastated to find out that she had basically lost a whole year of high school credits. Her mother was equally upset. Natalie was admitted as a freshman, even though she should have been a junior. She ended up taking the California High School Proficiency Exam in English language arts, which she passed. When we enrolled her at my continuation school, I helped her study for the math portion of the California High School Proficiency Exam, noting that her eighteenth birthday was coming up, and there was no way she could catch up on a whole year's worth of lost credits from the charter school she attended. She eventually passed and received her high school diploma from the state of California. Other students who left charter schools to come to our continuation high school told stories of being left to learn on their own, or of other types of independent-study classes with no support from teachers providing actual direct instruction. They mentioned having "new teachers who really didn't know what they were doing" teaching algebra, geometry, or physics.

I thought that these negative experiences with charter schools were limited to high school students until I went to Partridge Middle School and more and more parents came up to me during parent workshops or conferences and told me about their own children's bad experiences at pilot middle and charter elementary schools in the community. Many parents talked about how they were unable to donate forty hours of volunteer service a month to their charter school because they were working two full-time jobs. Other parents said they were unable to fulfill the fund-raising commitment that the pilot or charter schools required of them. During one parent workshop, one parent got up and announced to other parents that they "should not fall for the expensive and nice computers that the charter schools are offering, because as soon as your kid gets into trouble or falls behind, they will kick them out." These parents felt abandoned by the charter schools and pilot schools, who had promised a better education for their children but then discovered that their children did not meet the standards of the "model" student or "model" parent that the charter and pilot schools demanded. What they discovered in returning to Partridge Middle School is that public schools would accept their children no matter what academic, social, emotional, and economic challenges they faced and would provide support for their children to succeed academically.

My experience in K–12 public schools over the past sixteen years has led me to the conclusion that charter schools, co-locations, magnet schools, and pilot schools are not necessarily the answer for our most vulnerable students. In fact, it seems that these types of schools have only widened the achievement gap for underserved students by changing public school demographics and taking away precious resources and educational experiences that they need to succeed academically.

Ruth Luevanos is a social studies teacher who has taught students in K–12 schools in the Los Angeles area for seventeen years. She is a National Board certified teacher in social studies who works to promote civic education, college and career preparation skills, and parental involvement at the Title I elementary, middle, and high schools where she has worked. She was honored as the Middle School Teacher of the Year by the National Council for Geography Education in 2011. She was a TeachPlus Fellow in Los Angeles from 2014–2015. She is on the board of directors for the California Council for Social Studies, where she chairs the Committee for Diversity and Social Justice. Ruth graduated from George Washington University with a BA in criminal justice, earned her JD from Loyola Law School, and a MA in instructional leadership from Argosy University. She is currently a full-time social studies teacher, department chair, and lead teacher at a Title I public middle school in Los Angeles.

"If This Isn't the Solution, What Is?"

RADHA RADKAR

Three years after opening, the charter school where I taught was put on probation by the New York City Department of Education. When I handed in my resignation letter, the assistant principal spent forty-five minutes defending the priorities and policies of the school. I tried to be polite in explaining how I could not justify going along with what the school was doing as it struggled to stay afloat, because they were acting without regard to what was actually good for students or for the community that it was a part of. Toward the end of our conversation, he posed a question that seemed odd considering the school's current status, yet encapsulated the administration's firm yet unfounded belief in what they were doing: "If you don't believe that this is the solution, then what is?"

The school, opened in Brooklyn, New York, was named with a word from an East African language that signified community. Its mission was to serve the local underserved community and provide a stellar alternative education based on five values: perseverance, respect, independence, discipline, and excellence. I started working there as a teaching assistant, writing lesson plans and units of study, creating worksheets, calling parents, and fulfilling every other responsibility typical of a full-time teacher. I had completed undergraduate and graduate work in English, focusing heavily on the relationship between privilege, schooling, and vernacular forms of English. I saw education as a critical process of democracy that has been historically withheld from the disenfranchised, and I wanted to do something about it. I also wanted to find an opportunity to serve my community in my city rather than become a transplant in a community alien to me. As such, I accepted this job with the understanding that responsibilities would be gradually released and that I would learn in an apprenticeship teaching model. This was a position designed specifically as an alternative to, according to the principal at the time, "ineffective" student-teacher training models.

The stated goals of the charter school and the emphasis on high expectations for students and teachers were not as clear in practice as they had been on paper. Prior to my arrival, four or five staff members hired during that academic year either were fired or had quit. Multiple members of the leadership team were shuffling between vaguely defined and arbitrarily assigned roles. The principal was eventually forced to step down after the board of directors responded to complaints from the recently formed teacher union, though she remained in her other position as executive director of the school for the rest of the year. Many classes had no permanent teachers and were taught instead by substitutes and teaching assistants. The main office and school leadership were understaffed as well. The responsibilities of teachers were ever expanding, and my role as teaching assistant was constantly stretched and redefined, making what was supposed to be a gradual release of responsibility a stressful, confusing, and demoralizing experience because of how vicious the politics of the school had become.

The founding principal had a background in criminal justice and, interestingly, became involved in teaching and founding a school because she believed the justice system failed to provide early adolescent students of color necessary academic and community support. Her solution, however, mirrored the strict discipline systems seen in many "no excuses" charter and parochial schools. Students were given demerits—notes identifying specific negative infractions—for talking, chewing gum, or coming to class without school supplies. If a child was out of uniform, they were sent home and not allowed back in school. One day, a few students in one of my classes walked up to the principal to ask her a question. She merely held up her hand and said, "I can't hear you until you fix your uniform," and repeated this several times until they tucked in their shirts and stood in one straight line facing her. These rules were disastrous for students with legitimate social and emotional needs, which were never addressed by the school counselor, who was known for yelling at the majority of the school during school assemblies as a means of reprimanding them for behavior. Teachers were not exactly enthusiastic about those bland assemblies singing old chants either. The small school had a large number of in- and out-of-school suspensions and one of the highest attrition rates in the city.

All of this in-house toxicity did not go unnoticed, and the Department of Education eventually provided the school with a warning for possible probation, outlining concerns after reviewing two years of its performance. As part of the city's regulatory process, a warning letter precedes a formal site visit. In anticipation of the visit, school administrators are required to submit a self-evaluation document that outlines the school's plans for curriculum and organizational growth, along with reflections on their weaknesses and their proposed solutions. Shared among staff members and administrators at a board meeting, the document promised further alignment of the curriculum with state standardized tests, to be built with the help of outside consultants. What the document did not address—and was apparently not a concern of the Department of Education—was the lack of any purpose for the school's curriculum beyond testing, a significantly reduced staff of full-time teachers and substitutes, and no permanent school leader who could support daily functioning of the school and development of the staff. To put it bluntly, there was nothing addressing the regular chaos that was happening around us.

That summer, we were placed on probation. This document outlined breaches from the school's charter as well as violations of state law. It focused on the extremely high attrition and suspension rates alongside the charter's inability to achieve 75 percent proficiency goals on the state exams in math and English. While these were major issues that needed to be addressed by the school, there were other problems that the DOE never mentioned. The mismanagement of special education was a glaring one. Many students at our school were classified as needing special education services and were not receiving appropriate services or were not receiving them in the correct settings in accordance with their Individualized Education Programs (IEP), a legal document that under federal law outlines the specific learning needs of a special education student. Keeping these students enrolled ensured the school higher per-pupil funding while jeopardizing the students' education.

If the letter was meant to send a stern message, it appeared to work: my next period at our school had a marked emphasis on a major institutional "change." By the summer of 2012, we were all very excited about the new direction of what many had begun to feel was a seriously misguided school. I was asked to be a full-time sixth-grade English language arts teacher, and I wanted to take the opportunity to support the turnaround of our school. I ignored the consternation of family and friends and signed a contract for one more year of employment. We had some hopeful signs once a new principal had filled in temporarily. Our new school leader, a doctor of literacy with years of consulting experience, was portrayed as a reformer within the mostly militaristic, no-exceptions world of charter schools.

Our original curriculum had been poorly designed, and exposed the first administration's lack of experience. Now, we were promised a new methodology that would follow the reading and writing workshop models developed and popularized in the mid-1980s through the Teachers' College Reading and Writing Project. The model prioritizes reading regularly and independently both in school and at home. Contemporary proponents had also begun to consider the impact of different languages, cultures, and learning styles in classrooms by incorporating a diversity of materials. This seemed especially helpful for our school, located in a primarily Caribbean community where students grew up speaking many languages, certainly different from the American Standard English taught in our classrooms.

In reality, the curriculum that was implemented at my school did not recognize difference anywhere, culturally or linguistically. The version of the reading workshop model they used was deeply monolingual and monocultural, but the principal, literacy coaches, and administrators of my school did not recognize this as a problem. As a progressive teacher of color, I felt that intentionally ignoring the backgrounds of my students was harmful and caused them to be detached from what they were learning. I wanted to argue for acknowledging racial, ethnic, and linguistic diversity, but was baffled when so many of the people supporting this more formalistic model were people of color themselves. Their point, which I sympathized with, was that the most important thing to focus on was that our students' reading skills were two to three grade levels below where they should be. Because our school's goal required that 75 percent of our students score a three or above on the state exams, meeting this dictated the majority our curriculum and became the focus of our survival as a school. Under these stark terms, an emphasis on a select set of literacy skills was seen as more important than anything else.

What this model did very well was accentuate deficit thinking about our students. I had a lot of information on what they could *not* do, but very few suggestions on what they did well and what interested them. We knew they misunderstood differences in form, especially fiction and nonfiction; confused elements within fiction and their relationship to character development; struggled to develop their own narratives and creative writing pieces; couldn't determine differences between facts and opinions; and had difficulty articulating their own ideas. The curriculum provided opportunities to address these issues, because in the eyes of Common Core and standardized testing, these were priority skills. Arguably our most successful unit was one in which students read and wrote biographies about popular musicians, athletes, celebrities, politicians, and historical figures. The irony was that, while this ended up becoming a mutated argument for the success of our curriculum, it also marked the only time that students were allowed to engage in acts of literacy about content they cared about very deeply. Its success inspired teachers to pursue other topics that might engage students in similar ways. They were all summarily shut down.

Another flaw in the implementation of this curriculum was that I never received the level of support I would need as a novice teacher using this model. I was told to send lesson plans to members of leadership for support in differentiation, both for students with documented special education needs as well as students who were tracked as struggling in reading or writing. For a system that requires rigorous and purposeful documentation of information, teachers were never instructed on the best ways to go about using this information. This "data" proved useless, anyway—tracking students by skills they struggle in, number of pages and words read, and noting which words they were struggling to decode simply was not enough to support strong literacy teaching. Instead of thinking about ways our curriculum could meaningfully revisit concepts and skills we believed students were struggling with—defining literacy as an act that students work through and return to regularly in every subject area—teachers focused on isolated sets of skills to repeatedly teach in the hopes of having more and more students demonstrate "mastery." We all found ourselves repeating concepts between poorly connected units.

This misstep articulated a primary issue of this school: misunderstanding our students, further exacerbated through the creation of uninspired and deeply flawed curricula and school models. Our curriculum worked within a definition of literacy as intrinsically alien and unattainable. Teachers and students alike were miserable and frustrated by how little we had to contribute to the curriculum. For my students, many of whom already felt they were without language to express their social and emotional lives, and given little opportunity to do so in our classes, this left them feeling further divorced from what they were learning. Even while many school administrators would argue their intentions were ultimately good, from one administration to the next, the school mission and vision were changing so rapidly and haphazardly that no one could effectively wrap their head around addressing the problems at our school.

By the time state tests were near, most students and staff were beginning to feel some level of panic. A new, Common Core–aligned ELA test was being administered that spring. At a planning meeting with other department members present, I listened to the interim principal describe how instruction was going to be impacted by the impending exams. Rather than continue to focus on providing support for our struggling and learning-disabled students, we were told that literacy specialists and teachers should instead focus conferencing time during class for students we believed had the best chances of receiving at least a passing score. Our school was already struggling to adequately support students who had come to us from public schools that supposedly could not meet their needs, and our intense focus on testing through selective support for students made this worse. I witnessed several students have severe panic attacks and hysterically cry over the three days exams were administered. They did not feel confident in even trying to take a test they believed they were inevitably going to fail. Our students became linchpins in a larger process of securing renewal for the school. Establishing what we continued to call (but really wasn't) a curriculum and a model of teaching was not about improving the quality of education and teaching in the school, but a blanket solution for problems in teaching literacy no one seemed ready and willing to meaningfully resolve. Our school's entire goal centered on students hitting certain scores, and the Department of Education had approved that as a worthwhile and meaningful reason to start a new school in this community.

Over my two-year tenure at my charter school, I occupied two diametrically opposed identities as a teacher: one an activist who was firmly against standardized testing and a proponent of progressive education, and another who performed acts that contradicted my philosophy of teaching. I eventually recognized this was an issue of ideological differences in education between this ever-changing, chaotic school and myself. When the newly appointed and permanent principal of our school indicated moves would be made toward a new literacy model—different from the workshop model and signifying yet another year of work in reading and writing to prepare students for tests—and pushed for instructional methods I felt were still avoiding the needs of our students and only designed to ostracize teachers, I realized my time at this school needed to come to an end.

Charter schools like the one that I worked in often implement popular strategies of the education reform movement in neighborhoods that they declare need fixing. When they don't work, or when the reliance on testing to prove their worth becomes the sole purpose of the school, it should serve as a clarion call about the impacts of these policies across our public school education system. Our school's emphasis on resolving surface-level issues rather than deep-rooted, systemic inequalities avoided complicated, interlocking relationships between race, poverty, and literacy. The rhetoric around choice seemed impressive enough: providing an alternative to traditional public schools would allow people a chance to envision new possibilities of a universal education system. But in the movement's effort to prove its success or expand to the next location, charter schools have often produced normalized, systematized learning still incapable of addressing racial and social inequities.

Radha Radkar has worked in a variety of learning contexts, including writing centers, afterschool programs, charter schools, and colleges. She also serves as a curriculum developer, workshop facilitator, and as an organizer with the New York Collective of Radical Educators. Currently, she works at the Bard Prison Initiative.

What Choice?

How Education Reform Is Crushing Our Montessori School

STEPHANIE SCHNEIDER

"This question comes up every year," said my trainer to the group of eager Montessori teachers-to-be. "What does folding napkins have to do with world peace?"

A number of us sitting in that classroom had already shared that part of our attraction to the Montessori method was its focus on the relationship between education and peace. This method, developed by Dr. Maria Montessori over a hundred years ago, aims to develop the intrinsic learner through didactic materials as opposed to direct instruction and focuses on the total development of the child—both physical and psychological needs—as it allows the child to exercise choice and independence while engaging in activities in the classroom. As Dr. Maria Montessori wrote, "Establishing lasting *peace* is the work of education; all politics can do is keep us out of war."

Establishing peace through your classroom practice is quite the charge. As we learned about the first lessons we would give, what we call the exercises of practical life, it was only natural to wonder how such a task would be accomplished by showing the children how to wash their hands, polish a mirror, or peel a carrot.

Though the connection isn't necessarily obvious, I trusted this method. I had faith in this pedagogy because I was a Montessori child. I started school when I was a year and a half old at a private Montessori school, and from my earliest memories, I always loved it. I can still picture the classroom I had from ages three to six. I can remember all the beautiful materials I was able to work with and which ones were my favorites. I remember having the freedom to follow my interests, doing "research," and planning field trips with my fellow students. I hated having to miss school, because it never was a place I dreaded. It was a place where I could chart my day, decide what it was I wanted to learn about, and feel empowered and excited.

I think about my Montessori education as a great gift, and one that has served me throughout life. It's not the content of what I learned, necessarily, that I cherish, but rather the opportunity to exercise my curiosity and to have cultivated an insatiable drive to learn and seek experience. This is what has stayed with me and given my life an indelible richness.

Because of this profound effect, I knew that when I decided to become a teacher I wanted to become a Montessori teacher. I had had such a great relationship with school; I wanted my future students to have the same. When I received the call letting me know I was hired to teach in Milwaukee, I was thrilled. Most Montessori schools in the United States are private schools. These are the schools I spent my weeks student teaching in. The materials were impeccable, class sizes were small, and resources were plentiful. This type of school, as wonderful as it was, seemed to confirm the stereotype that Montessori schools are for the elite. But in Milwaukee exists the oldest and largest collection of public Montessori schools—not charters, not vouchers, but straight-up public schools. In a large bureaucratic school system, the Montessori method has thrived for almost forty years.

A serious threat to that success was growing. The first blow was financial. When I began my teaching career nine years ago, my school had about one hundred fewer students but several more teachers, including nonclassroom support positions. From what I heard from others, in the recent past the schools had cut even more resources—the shrinking a result of cumulative budget cuts over previous years. In Milwaukee, such cuts are due to both shrinking of state funding and, both directly and consequently, the expansion of the voucher and charter systems, which deflects public dollars that otherwise would be going to public schools.

I learned quickly that the way schools secured their budgets was through enrollment. More students equaled more money. As per-pupil spending was going down, our class sizes were rising. This led schools to make difficult decisions as to whether or not to reduce staffing or increase class sizes (and in many cases, schools were forced to do both). The days of a class size under thirty seemed long ago and far away. And although Dr. Montessori didn't advocate for small class sizes, what she did advocate was for the children to have enough space. The Association Montessori International (AMI), the worldwide Montessori training body, recommends 40 square feet per child. Of course, as our class sizes grew, that recommendation became almost laughable. Our classrooms were situated in school buildings that were designed and built in the early twentieth century, which certainly subscribed to a different model of schooling. To have the room for thirty-plus children to move about freely and to work at individual tables and to have adequate floor space requires rooms twice the size of the ones we had.

With these limitations, it became even more important to stay consistent with the other tenets of a Montessori education. To establish a functioning community of thirty-plus students, the Montessori practice of phase-in became more important than ever. Phase-in is the thoughtful system of having children new to the school at the beginning of the year stagger their start, with only a few new three-year-olds starting for the first few days of school instead of having all students come on the first day.

When I first started in MPS, we were able to do just that. In fact, on the first day of school, only our new students would come, along with their parents. The parents went to the auditorium for an orientation, and the new three-year-olds would stay in their classrooms for their first introduction to school. It lasted only an hour, but its short time was intentional, and was effective at getting students acclimated to their room and school in a calm and peaceful manner. I spent this day introducing myself to the students, showing them a few activities, and going over important information like how to get to the bathroom. If someone had a difficult separation from their parent, the assistant or I could attend to them. It was a gradual and nonthreatening start to this idea that they would be coming to this room every day.

With the last change of superintendents, this valid and recognized practice was eliminated. The new leadership wanted every student in school the first day, and wanted them to be learning from the first minute they walked in. No time to build community, no time to develop trust with the teacher or dry the tears (of both student and parent). With a limited sense of what rigor means and what it takes to achieve it, they wanted students to get right to work. We were a "District in Need of Improvement," and were told we had no time to waste on practices like phase-in. The teacher union has been fighting back since this change, and we're making incremental gains as we continue to push to regain the entirety of the practice.

This idea of uniformity, of the ability of someone to walk into any classroom at any time and see the teacher teaching the same thing as someone in another classroom across the city, appeared to be the goal of the district. Franchising has been good in business, so why not in schools? Yet this idea seems to run completely against another strain of education reform: choice. Of course, choice in Milwaukee is a loaded word when it comes to education. The rhetoric around vouchers and charter schools is that parents should be able to choose a school, as if there was an educational marketplace. The problem is that one side becomes drained of resources while the other is lauded and supported, creating huge inequities and making any kind of real choice a fabrication. Choice in public schools, because of certain reform efforts, has actually become very minimal, only offering more scripted curricula and a bunch of tests. There's no flexibility to explore pedagogies that have been shown to be developmentally appropriate and scientifically sound outside of those mandates. As the district moves toward uniformity, it leaves parents with fewer and fewer choices and teachers with less ability to practice skills and methods they've spent years and thousands of dollars studying in order to discover what is most successful.

This uniformity is especially harmful to the Montessori method because of its increasing reliance on technology and testing, and in my experience the two come hand in hand. Both the tests and their resulting prescribed interventions are being delivered through a computer. Having children use more technology gives the illusion that schools are "cutting edge" and that we're preparing our children for an increasingly digital world, but in my classroom of three- to six-year-olds, I want to keep screen time to a minimum. For the children I work with, spending time staring at a computer, clicking a mouse, or fiddling with an iPad means less time putting their hands on materials. The interaction of the child and these didactic materials is the core of the Montessori method. Their sense of touch or hearing or smell or sight developed in these experiences is how they learn and understand the world.

If a child needs to count apples on the plate, he or she needs to feel their smooth skin, examine their color, see them sliced open, taste their crisp sweetness, and share a slice with a friend. They don't need to click and drag with a mouse. Education for those so new to our world needs to be experiential, for this will serve them better than any test score because it leads to a greater quality of life. This is such an important idea behind many of the Montessori activities. I show children how to grade and sort color tablets not so they learn the names and I can quiz them later, but so they can really get to know yellow. And when that child gets older and visits the art museum and looks at a painting, that intimate knowledge of the various grades of yellow will make that interaction all the more special. These early interactions, these early "first experiences" will give the child something great—an awesome appreciation for our world and universe. That to me seems a much greater gift than any high score or "college or career readiness." We are impacting children's quality of life. That is the work I signed up for but am increasingly unable to accomplish.

I haven't forgotten this motivation. There are studies that show that, yes, a Montessori education can make a difference in improving test scores, if we want to value that. Having children in kindergarten be fluent readers and mathematicians is certainly important, but for me that's just the gravy. The real work of education, as Dr. Montessori puts it, is as "an aid to life." And so we must ask ourselves, what kind of life do we want our children to have? Is it more important to have our children be college and career ready from the minute they begin school, or for the child to be ready to be five? The more we disregard the present moment for the child and only look to how that child will function as a consumer or producer in the future, the more we dehumanize education.

The heart of the Montessori method is about creating human beings who are not only independent, but who see themselves as interdependent. I often explain this transformation to parents of three- to six-year-olds. First, your child will wash the table because of the enjoyment of the activity. There's something personally satisfying for that young child to do this activity. As the child grows in the classroom and becomes more aware of belonging to a community, that desire to wash the table shifts. The child of five now washes the table because it's messy, and not because the teacher tells him to. Children wash the table because they are able to recognize a need in the community and respond to it. And as the child grows older in the Montessori method, that recognition of needs of the community expands to more abstract notions of fairness and social justice.

Guiding the child to interdependence—to caring for the community, to being able to navigate social conflict and have an innate sense of social justice—this is the revolution that Dr. Montessori described. This is how learning to fold napkins can lead to world peace. This is a choice that our society deserves.

Stephanie Schneider is a Milwaukee Public Schools teacher and for the last ten years has taught three- to six-year-olds in a public Montessori school. She is involved with the Educators Network for Social Justice, a group of teacher activists in the Milwaukee area organizing around issues of educational justice. Stephanie is also active in her union and has served on the executive board of the Milwaukee Teachers Education Association (MTEA) the past four years.

Not an Oxymoron

Our Union-Led, Community-Based Charter School

BRANDON LIGON

In a world, where standardized testing ruled every teachers' talents, skills, and well-being . . .

Pardon the dramatics, I need to set the stage for my experience, and it sounded fitting, based on the state of our campus, to open up with a dreary statement. It was true. Our school had just been hit with the news that, based on our test scores, we were named "academically unacceptable." Our school had very unique qualities. We had an extremely diverse population. We were a Title I elementary school, grades preK–5, which basically means we received financial assistance due to our high number of children from low-income families. We also had a large number of wealthy families, whose professions ranged from musicians to engineers to lawyers. We were located in the heart of Austin, Texas, and were the absolute definition of "Keep Austin weird!" So it was a huge blow to our little gem of a school when we received the shattering news of our new discouraging status.

As if that label wasn't tough enough, a dark cloud had swept over our campus due to the overwhelming amount of intense, strict curriculum requirements. Morale was at an all-time low. Teachers began to feel "academically incapable," and their drive to teach seemed to be fading. I've always loved teaching and have made it my mission never to let this kind of stuff destroy my vibe. This mantra made it easier for me to see the amount of distress my fellow colleagues were in. The teacher's lounge became a pit of misery and never-ending venting. All eyes were on our campus. Multiple visitors with clipboards and permanent frowns on their faces walked in and out of our classrooms, ripping instruction apart. Nothing seemed right. Just when you thought you had cooked up a powerful, rigorous lesson, the big chefs found everything wrong with your recipe and offered no suggestions for seasonings.

This was our lives, teaching under the watchful eye of district kings and queens. They enforced elaborate instructions about what you had to teach, when you had to teach it, and what should be up on the walls in your room. There were even scripts to follow word for word to ensure lessons were taught "correctly." It was almost like we were performing in a Broadway play called *Teach the Test*. We rehearsed our lines daily, designed the set, and performed our hearts out every "show," aka observation. But what were our students learning? Did it mean anything to them? I personally began to feel like I was providing my students the biggest disservice. I wasn't catering to their needs, attempting to create lifelong learners. I had become a high-stakes testing cyborg whose only mission was to get his students to pass a test so the big bosses would get off our backs. Well . . . Mission accomplished. But now what?

A couple years later, things went semiback to normal. We were still frightened by the fact that any time our test scores dropped the infamous "walk-through monsters" would return to devour the flesh of our hard working teachers. We never wanted to end up in that horrible predicament again. Our safest bet was to continue teaching in the good old restricted, specific, boring, scripted, not really relevant, boring way . . . did I mention boring? We added a new meaning to the saying "If it ain't broke, don't fix it." But something was broken. Our spirits were broken. We were in desperate need of a change.

Members of Education Austin, our local teacher union, began to pop up at our school to talk to us about how we were feeling about being teachers. They set up times to pick our brains on the climate of our campus and our hopes for the future. See, we had just been chosen to receive this Innovation Grant, a national grant awarded through Education Austin and Austin Interfaith. This grant provided funding for our community to engage in conversations and research to create a vision for the future of our school. I'm not going to lie, I didn't quite understand all of this at first. Many of us, myself included, were extremely hesitant to open up to these people. What would really be the repercussions of my comments and feelings? What could they do to me? Most important, what could they do *for* me?

As I slowly began to let my guard down and revealed the scars of the prior years under the microscope, I realized my love for teaching had been damaged. Many teachers on our campus came to that same conclusion. That's when we were made aware of a magical land where teachers could be respected for their craft and trusted to control their curriculum. Students could have meaningful and relevant learning experiences that would mold them into strong thinkers and productive citizens. In other words, we could create a school that trusted professional educators and families to partner together in serving students. We could use this grant to help fund these new changes in our school. Extensive research went into planning. Our school was known to be a diverse school, reflecting the Greater Austin area demographics. The plan prioritized ways to meet the needs of the students in our neighborhood while keeping alive our tradition of providing a warm, welcoming environment for all learners.

In collaboration with our teacher union, we decided that the best way to do this would be to become a charter school. A charter school would grant us what we called "The Five Freedoms," including how we teach and spend our money, the freedom to change the cafeteria menu and our school schedule, and the freedom to add more art, music, PE, technology, and foreign language classes. Becoming an in-district charter school seemed like a dream that our school would never be able to see to fruition. There had to be a catch. All this glitter could not be gold!

The chatter around the campus became all about this "charter school" idea. Was this real? I kept having visions of the movie *From Dusk till Dawn*. George Clooney and Quentin Tarantino are robbers that stumble into a club in Mexico. It's swarmed with beautiful women and unlimited cocktails for all the guests. That is, until they all turn into blood-thirsty vampires and feed on everyone in sight! Was this charter school mumbo-jumbo just presented to lure us in when we were at our most vulnerable state, only to feast on our blood and leave us empty inside? Again, vivid and dramatic, but only to make a point. I wasn't sure if we could pull this off, but this concept got me excited about teaching again. I definitely wasn't jumping up and down about the way we were doing things now. Why not entertain this?

So that's exactly what I did. I joined a team of teachers, administrators, parents, and Education Austin representatives, including the president, Ken Zarifus, and started doing some research. We explored different schools and their curricula. We looked into programs, methods, and technology. The union supported our journey the entire way. They facilitated conversations between staff and the community. They helped parents and teachers explore their visions of an ideal school they would want to be part of. So much of what was explored fit my teaching style. Yes, please! We ventured into the realms of expeditionary and project-based learning, which both focus on working in teams and using real-world scenarios to learn concepts across disciplines. I fell in love with service learning, an empowering program where students recognize a need in their community and develop and provide a service around it. All of these programs call for the same skills we had been teaching like certified robots in the past, but these approaches appeal to all types of learners.

Learning has never been a "one-size-fits-all" thing. I felt like many of our students never knew the feeling of success because they were led to believe that the definition of success was passing a test. Programs that allow the artist to shine, the musician to jam, and the engineer to build ultimately develop problem solvers. I wanted to be a part of that! Having the autonomy to make decisions at the campus-level based on the school's needs year to year was a key factor for our new school. Instead of being forced to take on district-mandated programs and policies—the cookie-cutter approach across all elementary schools—ours would be a school that considered what would benefit the needs of our campus. It included changes in our schedule to provide teachers with more planning time, opportunities for team building, and meaningful professional development. We could incorporate physical activity into the school day and have the opportunity to assess which programs benefited our children and added value. Our school community wanted the chance to choose.

The next challenge was to get the rest of the staff on board, identify and receive training on all the programs we decided to use, and ultimately implement what we had designed. Anyone that thought taking the route of becoming a charter school was going to be easier and less work was sadly mistaken. It was completely the opposite! It took crazy collaboration and time to pull off the vision. That's the beauty of teachers, though. If the purpose is clear and it's for the greater good of our students, we'll move mountains to make it happen. Several mistakes were made along the way. Teachers feared standards would not be met due to all the innovations and lack of emphasis on standardized testing. Some decided that this was a road they didn't want to drive on and took other paths.

The payoff was what made it all worth it to me. Teachers' instruction strengthened, causing students to become actively engaged, pushing their limits. So many skills were involved in every lesson and project and students were able to see the relevance of their work. I fell in love with teaching again. And I don't think I was the only one. Even the most skeptical teacher pushed himself or herself to the limit and became stronger. After many discussions, planning sessions, reports and meetings, and trial and error implementation, a schoolwide vote was held in October 2012. Volunteers worked to get input from every family in our school, as the district noted the plan for the first campus-based, in-district charter would only be able to move forward if at least 80 percent of parents, teachers, and staff supported it. In the end, more than 95 percent of families, teachers, and staff supported the plan. The AISD School Board voted unanimously to approve our petition. The dream was a now a reality. The fantasy was now nonfiction. We did it! Together. Teachers. Administrators. Parents.

So that's how we went from being a regular school to being a charter school, no longer tied to the demands of our district. With the end in mind, we were able to create our own school with our own rules. I've never worked harder in my life, but it was totally worth it. Teachers and parents collaborate to ensure students get the best learning experiences. Students own their learning through projects that encourage teamwork and critical thinking. You can hear the sounds of students' feet as they participate in physical activities throughout their daily instruction. And that dark cloud that once followed every teacher around and rained on his or her morale and drive? It's faded away to reveal a rainbow that's as bright as our students.

Brandon "B. Liggy" Ligon is a passionate, energetic, and creative educator whose true mission in life is to motivate students and teachers to strive for success. He's an educational rapper and motivational speaker who shares his talents on You-Tube and in speaking engagements and learning conferences throughout the state of Texas. He taught fourth grade for ten years in Austin, Texas, and is currently an assistant principal at Lee Middle School in San Angelo, Texas.

Districts Innovate Too!

A Teacher-Led STEM School Offers a New Model

VIRGINIA RHODES

Do schools need principals to start or "run" them? Maybe, maybe not. I was lucky enough to be hired as principal of the biggest teacher-led school in Ohio. Driven by a group of teachers who were inspired to teach and collaborate in an innovative way for their students, primarily low-income, African American teenagers, this project was crackling and sizzling with creativity, dynamic ideas, and high performers. Superman (a terrific principal under whom we all had worked) had left the building, and Godot wasn't coming. This new school idea felt like it was going to be the most significant project of my career, and it turned out to be just that.

When the planning group of teachers initially brought the idea of a teacher-led school to the district for approval, the response was lukewarm, to put it mildly. The administrative work culture of the district was not conducive to this kind of innovation. Instead, their message to administrators was to follow orders and get your teachers to obey the district initiatives; improve and transform your school, but don't rock the boat; and don't expect the district to accommodate any differences in scheduling, training, curriculum, or leadership models. As a principal, the result of just doing everything the district way was that, in the poorest schools, your kids and teachers would fail to thrive and your ranking would stay in the toilet. But as an administrator, you would eventually be richly rewarded with a *real* school: one with middle-class kids, private foundation support, and magnet status. It was kind of like the Joe Hill song where conforming and suffering will get you rewarded with "pie in the sky when you die." Or a little like the Cold War mentality: if you're doing anything really different, for God's sake, don't talk about it.

The teachers redoubled their efforts and were able to secure high interest from the National Science Foundation, winning a $3 million STEM grant. When they returned to the district again, they focused their pitch on STEM and the related awards they had received. They included some information about teamwork, collaboration, social-emotional learning (SEL), and project-based learning (PBL). But since we got either blank looks, raised eye-brows, or quizzical frowns when we talked about "teacher led," we didn't exactly advertise just how different that model would be, since it was clear there would be no resources available for *that*. The district praised the teachers for their initiative and approved the project, but once the Memo-randum of Understanding was signed, there was no official mention of the teacher-led aspect of the school.

Moving forward with the planning for the school, we armed ourselves with a small group of STEM and other "innovation" allies who could promote our ideas with the superintendent and district leadership. These included the local university, prominent community organizations, the local Museum Center and the school's alumni organization. Other teacher-lead-ers within the city also provided necessary support and guidance in shaping how the teacher team planned to run the school. The teacher union presi-dent at the time was a champion of this concept and an advocate for a "prin-cipal-less" school. He knew that many European schools embraced more of a master-teacher model of decision making, and had thought through how teacher leadership could be structurally accomplished within a school.

Teachers expected a principal to come on board to assist with the remain-der of their planning in late September of 2008. But the installation of a new superintendent in August resulted in a new administration with a full plate of other matters. As a result, hiring of the STEM principal was put to the side, creating the school's first major practical crisis. The planning team, while organizing the basic structures of the school, had no champion within the district to approve and advance its design and operational pro-posals. They sometimes could not identify the central office structure and resources well enough to pursue their ideas, or couldn't get answers from those in charge.

The original STEM grant provided for a full-time principal released from other duties. In February 2009, when the hiring process finally came to an end, I was named principal of both the STEM and the existing school on the same campus, which was then scheduled to be phased out. This deci-sion was made in February, but it was not effective until June 1, leaving the committee without the help they needed. The STEM start-up required intense, immediate, and frequent contact with the Ohio STEM Learning Network (OSLN) and many people in business and university communi-ties. These partners were already highly involved in initiating STEM proj-ects at the school and had developed relationships with the planning team. Coordinating all of these pieces required a serious investment of administrative time that the district, by delaying the hiring and physical assignment, did not support.

The founding teachers had established many components to address the values, principles, and tone of the school. These were done so well, there was little more to contribute. But they hadn't figured out ways to codify, communicate, and promulgate these ideas, and that's where I could lend my expertise. I also knew that we would collectively need to broaden the group's communication and involvement with other constituencies, particularly the families of our students and other community stakeholders. So policy ideas got written up and foundational understandings were put into documents used for trainings, discussions, publicity, and to develop the full staff for the first year. It all felt like an intense whirlwind at the time, but it moved the founding teachers' initial policies toward usable products.

One of the areas in which we had to do this kind of idea-to-reality translation was figuring out how the school's vision of teacher leadership could fit into the teachers' contract, which we knew contained many progressive structures. Many of us had been involved as union activists in this AFT-affiliated district and had helped design some of the clauses that we could lean on now. Although many administrators saw these policies as impediments to their control, we were excited to prove how bolstering the role of the teacher actually extended a principal's success rather than diminished it. Most significant were the decision-making structures, including the Instructional Leadership Team (ILT) and the Local School Decision-Making Committee (LSDMC). The ILT was composed primarily of teacher representatives, with a few community/parent slots. The LSDMC was primarily community/parent/partner representatives with some staff as well. The committees worked in tandem to gain resources for the school, choose the school's program and schedule, give final approval of the budget, and recommend candidates for staffing. All positions in both bodies were elected democratically by their own constituencies. We developed and used these structures faithfully, and they gave us a powerful way to fix problems, try out new ideas, and unify to pressure the district.

I was at a district meeting toward the end of our third year in which my principal colleagues challenged me about this transparency, certain that there would be lots of grievances if they tried this. How many grievances had we had in the three years, one guy asked. Everyone knew that with as many positions as we had filled (hiring forty-five teachers) and the long hours we were known for, the typical answer might have been a dozen, or even two dozen. I told them we'd had two, both by disappointed candidates who believed that they should have been hired in spite of terrible interview performances.

As time went on, we built other structures, like our team-task hiring process (T2), the unique interactive hiring process we designed. The interview had two parts. The first part was an interview with the committee (with questions, of course, that were very deliberately designed to reveal specific skills and beliefs about how teachers should do their work). We stressed an "all business" demeanor in these interviews, not sending overly positive signals to candidates and taking copious notes to compare later. This enabled us to more objectively discuss in detail both positives and negatives rather than come to the table with polarized arguments between those that had gotten on that candidate's bandwagon and those that had reservations. This put initial, sometimes implicitly biased, impressions of "liking" the person in perspective. In the second part, we paired two candidates from different subject areas for a team task that they had only twenty minutes to perform. After we established this process, the word went out: STEM's new hiring process is no joke. With an emphasis on creating a diverse and highly skilled staff, we were able to make our message clear: the new STEM school was going to be very exciting, fast paced, and full of interesting and talented colleagues.

Other systems we used were borrowed from other schools and adapted to our needs, like Intersession, flex scheduling, a student voice project, and student-led conferencing. My role was to take the great, sometimes casual ideas that teachers had and make a sustainable structure out of them that could continue and become part of the culture of the school. Two teachers started what we called "Tech Café" in a storage closet between their two classrooms. One liked to cook, and the other brought in his wife's cooking. We also started a faculty writing group, "DAGG!!" (Data Acquisition/Generating Group), born in late fall 2009. The name of the group was in honor of several staff members who, like myself, were from Southern roots and used that expression, as in, "DAGG!! We ran out of time on our project today!" or "DAGG!! When is the board going to approve these positions? We can't wait any longer!" Our writing group met on Saturday mornings at the coffee shop of the church across the street from the school. Participation varied from four to fourteen a week, and not always the same people. It was a crack-up, relieved stress, and created a deep camaraderie and support among those who came.

I was the one in our group who had done research on school structure, while the teachers tended to be experts in their instructional areas. This meant that I was able to connect their vision with emerging best practice. For everything we did, I asked four questions: Is it engaging? Is it consistent with our core values? Does it develop skills of collaboration and teamwork? Does it teach students how to go about learning anything that they will need to know about in the future? For us this meant developing an aggressive program of social-emotional learning that would enable students to truly replace their fears with trust and confidence alongside our academic rigorous instruction.

With all of these pieces in place, we opened our doors. It was an exciting fall. We had our first fall Intersession, in which all students spent a week on a local college campus, leading to a buzz from students around the school and an increased focus on studying. The semester was very intense, high energy, and wearing on the staff. The long hours beyond the contract were given voluntarily, but the teachers had such high goals for themselves that they worked many, many hours. I knew it was causing stress, though nobody complained, because everyone was committed to the outcomes, saw this initial investment of energy as critical, and figured they would find the right balance later.

By January, teachers were seriously tired. I was painfully conscious of how easy our teachers could make things for themselves and their families just by transferring to a more "normal" school. As our ILT was faced with budgeting and staffing decisions and the district began hiring rounds for the next fall, I had to train myself to not "lose it" when I began to get wind of this or that teacher was thinking about transferring. Lots of kids said the same thing: this was the hardest school most had ever been to. As we recruited prospective teachers and students, however, current teachers and students described feelings of excitement and success that were very close to the vision of the founding group. We came through the winter with gritted teeth.

Then something happened as a result of our design that turned out to be culture changing. It was spring Intersession. Unlike the fall session, this one was designed to be an SEL "Take all 1,000 kids out of school, out of the box, blow all their minds at once" type of experience. It was ambitious. The teachers had designed each session, recruited parents and outside partners, and led learning experiences in the community and outdoors that exposed kids to new things and ideas. It reenergized staff and kids and significantly shifted the culture of the school. Students and teachers got to know each other in a deeper and more informal way, which reduced conflict for the remainder of the year, and for subsequent years as well. It changed the dialogue, too. Talk in the lunchroom among kids was no longer limited to griping about the hard work and how bad somebody's hair looked. Kids talked about the secret idea their team in math had to win a roller-coaster competition and which of their friends they were trying to get to come to our school. Teachers talked about colleagues they'd like to see as the next teachers.

In the end, we lost no teachers the first year, and only one the next, a teacher who turned out not to be comfortable with his decision-making role. As for students, recruitment surged, and we overfilled the incoming fall class. This sealed our funding, as we could go through the "no-show" period knowing that we had enough to avoid disruptive cuts that the district often made even as late as September.

I stayed on as principal until 2012. Fulfilling this role in a teacher-led school was the pinnacle of my career. I could not have asked for a more talented group of teachers, with whom I felt privileged to work. And it gave me a post-retirement mission: to continue the fight to replace "factory-model schooling" with vibrant models and high student engagement. My conference activities convince me each time that this is the time for teacher leadership to be propelled forward, not squelched. Charter schools are being permitted unfettered experimentation; it's now time for excellent teachers in public schools, and the new models they are designing, to be given access to state and federal monies and freedom for innovative school design as well. Their experience and insights are just what's needed to break through the tangle of private interests promoting strategies that do much for profits, but little for kids.

As a high school principal in Cincinnati, Ohio, Dr. Virginia Rhodes led collaborative projects that established Ohio's first public environmental school and Hughes STEM High School, Ohio's largest and most ambitious STEM project, as well as the largest teacher-led public high school in the United States. Rhodes now researches and consults on student mobility, school climate, innovative teacher hiring, twenty-first-century collaborative administrative strategies, teacher-led school models, white privilege, STEM, SEL, de facto Learning Theory, and school security.

CHAPTER 4

FAILURE

When Schools Don't Pass the Test

In many ways, the neighborhood school is the core of American public education. In its most idyllic form, it's a trusted local institution, a place where communities come together and where parents, students, and teachers build strong relationships. But neighborhood schools have also been shaped by a history of discriminatory housing policies, urban renewal programs, and real estate development that have left a legacy of segregation and unequal resources in their wake. Largely ignoring this broader context, federal and state governments have increasingly concerned themselves with the business of school improvement. No Child Left Behind included one of the first references to the idea of a school "turnaround"[1] and mandated that state and local education agencies identify and reform low-performing schools.[2] Reformers throughout the Bush and Obama administrations argued that methods such as school closures were the kind of bold action necessary to improve young people's lives. From 2001 to 2013, 21,010 schools were closed in the United States.[3]

In 2014, community organizations in Newark, New Orleans, and Chicago filed civil rights complaints in each of their cities, arguing that the overwhelming concentration of school closures in communities of color in the name of accountability violated the Civil Rights Act of 1964. Activists connected school closures to the dismantling of public housing and the rise of gentrification in their cities as yet another way they were being pushed out. And they decried education reformers who used the language of the Civil Rights Movement to press for "the racial injustice of school closings . . . Neighborhood schools are the hearts of our communities, and the harm caused by just one school closure is deep and devastating. This is death by a thousand cuts."[4]

TARGETING STRUGGLING SCHOOLS

Under NCLB, schools were judged on whether they met Adequate Yearly Progress, or AYP. Because the ultimate goal of NCLB was for students to demonstrate 100 percent proficiency on state standards by 2014, states determined test-score benchmarks for every year from 2001 to 2014. If schools' test scores matched that year's goal, they met AYP; if they didn't, they were put on the state's list of failing schools. The Obama reforms, including Race to the Top, School Improvement Grants (SIG), and the NCLB waivers, also relied on standardized tests, asking states to identify the bottom 5 to 15 percent of schools by looking both at absolute scores and growth in test scores over time.

While these policies were enacted with the justification that they would make schools equal, the reality is that some schools were expected to do much more for students than others. Rich white kids will generally score well on these tests, no matter what happens in their schools. Schools that serve low-income, high-needs students, however, must do a lot more. And certain schools face a confluence of critical circumstances, including foster care, homelessness, abuse, and more that make their jobs exceedingly difficult, and that research on school improvement shows significantly narrow the possibility of academic gains without intensive support.[5] *New York Times* reporter Elizabeth A. Harris documented one such school, where 47 percent of students are homeless and many of the other students come from three housing projects in the surrounding neighborhood. The school gives out deodorant, toothbrushes, uniforms, and shoes alongside pens and paper, and is installing a washer and dryer to help families that don't have access to regular laundry facilities. The building is open every weekday until 6 p.m., on Saturdays, and during the summer, and English classes and immigration legal services are provided for parents. Judging by their test scores, this school is failing: 9 percent of students met state standards in English and 14 percent met standards in math in 2015. Principal Suany Ramos, though, refuses that label: "We have so many families who come in with so many issues. Success is how much we have done for the family, not just the child."[6]

One thing has remained pretty consistent about which schools are being labeled failing and targeted for intervention: they serve low-income communities of color. In the over two thousand schools targeted under SIG, 81 percent of students were students of color and 69 percent were poor. Eighty-five percent of the most urgently targeted schools had high concentrations of poverty, where more than 90 percent of students are eligible for free or reduced-price lunch.[7] This is not inconsistent with national data on test scores and the so-called achievement gap. A 2006 study by Tulane professor Dr. Doug Harris found that only 1.1 percent of schools with a high concentration of low-income students of color consistently achieved at high levels in multiple subjects on standardized tests.[8] A recent preliminary study by Dr. Sean Reardon of Stanford analyzed 215 million test scores from 40 million third through eighth graders in every public school district in the country. He found that almost every school district enrolling large numbers of low-income students had testing outcomes below the national average. Furthermore, of the 946 school districts nationwide who serve at least one hundred Black students per grade, there were only 18 districts where Black students had test scores at or above the national average. These districts serve just one half of one percent of all Black students in the United States.[9] It's hard to look at those numbers, see the correlations with race and class, and still conclude that these trends are the result of individual failing schools.

"FIXING" THE "FAILURES"

Whether accurately or not, NCLB and the subsequent policies brought the question of failing schools to the center of the nation's conversation around education reform. The rhetoric in the 1980s and 1990s had been largely focused on the failure of the entire education system to make America competitive, stoked in large part by the 1983 report *A Nation At Risk*. In the 2000s, we had both the policy and data capabilities to target specific schools as the culprits. The idea became popularized in the media as well. In an analysis of mainstream news outlets' use of the term "failing schools," journalist Paul Farhi found 544 news stories in a one-month span in 2012. Twenty years earlier, it appeared just thirteen times.[10]

In particular, the drumbeat for reform focused on the disproportionate number of these schools serving low-income students of color, and fixing failing schools became folded into a broader civil rights narrative. The idea that these students should have access to a higher quality education was not news to the communities of color, who had been fighting throughout United States history for better schools,[11] but failing schools were now part of the mainstream consciousness, taken up under the mantle of education reform. Former Secretary of State Condeleezza Rice echoed many other reformers' views when she said, "Poor black kids trapped in failing neighborhoods schools, that's the biggest race problem of today. That's the biggest civil rights issue of today . . . Anybody who isn't in favor of educational reform, anybody who defends the status quo in the educational system, that's racist to me."[12]

Of course, the tests only pinpointed a problem, and the problem kept growing. In 2010, almost thirty thousand schools failed to make adequate yearly progress, or one in three schools in the United States.[13] One in five schools in the country at that point had been "failing" for two or more years and were mandated to be in one of the five stages of improvement.[14] Without the time to build capacity on any level, much of school improvement efforts under NCLB were characterized by piecemeal efforts—alterations to programs, removal of a principal, or more coaching to improve instruction. Districts looked for "silver bullet" strategies like a longer school day or quick implementation of smaller learning communities,[15] but state and district support of schools didn't go much further. During a speech following the signing of NCLB, President George W. Bush explained that the law "says that we're never going to give up on a school that's performing poorly, that when we find poor performance, a school will be given time and incentives and resources to correct their problems."[16] Yet 42 percent of schools under restructuring did not receive the district support that they were entitled to,[17] and very few states had the capacity to fully take on turnaround schools either.[18] On all levels, people were clear that more needed to be done, but no one seemed sure of what to do or how it could actually happen on such a large scale.

That was not the story being told, though. Feature articles about individual schools and speeches from politicians made it seem like the answer was obvious, as if everyone had been sitting on the right way to improve schools but just didn't want to put in the work to make it happen. President Obama was among those in this camp. In his State of the Union speech in 2010, he said, "The idea here is simple: Instead of rewarding failure, we only reward success. Instead of funding the status quo, we only invest in reform—reform that raises student achievement. . . and turns around failing schools that steal the future of too many young Americans. In the 21st century, one of the best anti-poverty programs is a world-class education."[19]

But Obama also believed school turnaround required resources, and he regularly criticized NCLB for "leav[ing] the money behind."[20] To rectify this, part of the economic stimulus package passed in response to the deep recession that hit in 2008 included billions of dollars for school improvement efforts. One large chunk of this funding came in the form of School Improvement Grants (SIG). SIGs were initially introduced through NCLB, though the program wasn't funded until 2007, when it received $125 million.[21] The SIG budget dramatically increased to $3.5 billion for the 2010–2011 school year, and almost the same amount went to funding statewide reform through Race to the Top (RTTT). In both SIG and RTTT, states were awarded money depending on their alignment with a tightly controlled set of school improvement strategies outlined by the U.S. Department of Education: transformation, turnaround, restart, or closure.

Transformation requires the replacement of the principal, the use of an evaluation system based on growth in students' test scores to reward and fire teachers, and increased professional development. Turnaround also demanded the principal to be removed, in addition to firing all of the staff and rehiring at most 50 percent. This approach also asked schools to implement a new governance structure, increase their use of student data, extend the learning day, and provide socioemotional services and supports. The final two options, restart and closure, both involved closing the school, with the former reopening it as a charter school and the latter sending students to other schools in the area.[22]

These policies targeted current teachers and principals as the cause for school failure. As detailed in the Quality chapter, the much larger problem for many failing schools is high teacher turnover and lack of qualified teacher candidates, problems that are made worse under policies that identify schools as struggling or failing.[23] In many high-poverty schools, this means a high percentage of substitutes staffing classes on a regular basis,[24] and only half of districts in the United States require that substitutes have a bachelor's degree.[25]

Although SIG and RTTT offered substantially more resources than NCLB, they ultimately relied on many of the same premises and were built on poorly conceived implementation plans. None of these policies has made significant impact on student achievement.[26] Rather than focus on improving processes of teaching and learning, work with educators to build skills and capacity, or address systemic problems affecting schools such as the distribution of resources and teacher placement, the Obama-era reforms sought to remove the "bad elements" by taking out leaders and teachers or shutting down schools altogether. But despite the lofty rhetorical claims, many of the practices mandated by these policies were not supported by research.[27] The options under NCLB, RTTT, SIG, and the NCLB waivers were essentially experiments in school improvement, tried out on some of our country's most vulnerable kids.

A CLOSER LOOK: SCHOOL CLOSURES

The restart and closure options under SIG and RTTT offer clear examples of these trials with school improvement. Shutting down a school is seen by many reformers as necessary if schools repeatedly demonstrate that they cannot improve students' outcomes. Andy Smarick, president of the Maryland State Board of Education and resident scholar at the American Enterprise Institute, has written that some schools are essentially reform proof. Reformers like Smarick argue that these schools represent a kind of moral imperative, because while we wait for improvements that never come, young people's lives are destroyed. The desire for such dramatic action can be strong, particularly for schools that have a long history of violence and safety concerns, low test scores, high dropout rates, and buildings that sometimes are literally falling apart.[28] As Arne Duncan remarked on the school closures he oversaw in Chicago as then-superintendent, "It gives you hope that anything is possible with enough effort and determination and the right people."[29]

Presented as an option by both NCLB and the Obama-era reforms, school closures have become a widespread tool of education reform.[30] True to form, these policies have hit low-income communities of color the hardest. The Schott Foundation released an analysis of the students and communities most affected by school closures in three cities during the 2010–2011 school year. In Chicago, forty-nine schools were closed. Eighty-seven percent of the students affected were Black, 94 percent were from low-income families. One percent of students affected were white. In New York, twenty-two schools were closed. Fifty-three percent of affected students were Black; 41 percent were Latinx; 2 percent were white. And in Philadelphia, where twenty-three schools were closed in one year, 81 percent of students affected were Black and 93 percent of students were from low-income families.[31]

Overall, while there are standout examples, school closures have failed to achieve the goals that reformers claimed. When a school is shut down, it usually changes from a zoned community school to an unzoned school that can accept students from all over the district or city. Many of the schools that open in place of the former neighborhood schools are charter schools. This is meant to offer the new school the opportunity and flexibility to establish a school culture that can achieve results.[32] While some of the schools opened in the wake of school closures have shown higher test scores, many of them are not serving the same population of students who were there before. In a rigorous analysis of school closures in Chicago, the University of Chicago Consortium on School Research found that students in the new schools were from less disadvantaged neighborhoods, had higher prior achievement, and were less likely to be overage.[33]

New York City witnessed a clear example of this kind of student shuffling under Mayor Michael Bloomberg. From 2002 to 2012, the New York City Department of Education closed 140 schools.[34] Large schools were shut down in favor of small, themed schools throughout the city, a move supported and funded by the Bill & Melinda Gates Foundation.[35] But reports by the New York City–based Urban Youth Collaborative, the Center for New York City Affairs, and Advocates for Children of New York found that students who attended the closed high schools were not admitted to the small schools that literally moved into the same building. In fact, many of these students were placed in other large comprehensive high schools that had yet to be shut down, soon overwhelming those schools and making them next in line for closure.[36] This was exacerbated by a citywide policy that allowed the new small schools to not provide special education and English language learner services for the first two years to help the schools get started.[37] A domino effect ensued: disproportionate numbers of high-needs students, including those who were undercredited, overage, homeless, in foster care, and were classified as special education or English language learners, were placed in struggling schools without any additional resources or help. Those schools were then deemed failures and marked for closure. During the phase-out, resources were continually taken away as the school shrank, including the teachers, social workers, and other support staff most needed to support a student population that essentially was thrown to the wolves. Subsequently, attendance and graduation rates decreased, and the city could point to those numbers as justification for closing down the school.[38]

Most students leave closed schools to attend schools in other parts of the district or city. Once there, these students often do not perform better than they did at their old school, usually experiencing negative short-term effects and no consistent long-term gains.[39] This should not be particularly surprising, given a large body of research that shows that mobility is not good for student outcomes.[40] If students leave closed schools for schools that are markedly higher quality, they are more likely to show positive effects; however, that is rare. Students are much more likely to go from one low performing school to another. In Chicago, only 6 percent of students from closed schools were then enrolled in high performing schools. A study of school closures in North Carolina found that only 14 percent of students transferred to schools *not* considered to be low performing after their original school was closed.[41]

School closures also disperse kids who used to attend school within their neighborhoods throughout the city or district. This can result in wildly increased transportation times, with daily commutes as long as two to three hours for kids as young as nine.[42] For some students, it has also meant that going to school is a risk to their safety. In Chicago, the closing of dozens of schools has been connected to an increase in violence among teenagers as students from different neighborhoods and gang affiliations were suddenly mixed together in new campuses, and schools were ill informed, ill prepared, or not supported to handle the new dynamics. A heartbreaking and shocking example of this was seen by millions in 2009 when the murder of Derrion Albert was filmed by a cell phone camera. Albert was beaten to death by a group of teenagers, apparently caught in a long-running fight between young people from two different neighborhoods who had recently been pushed together in Fenger High School after one of the neighborhood's schools was converted to a military academy.[43] Fenger was also taking in students from other closed schools around the city and had been named a "turnaround" school, firing large numbers of teachers, which some claimed had only further destabilized the school.[44]

In most of these cases, the decision to close schools is made by politicians acting *for* the community, who claim they are attempting to give families choice in their children's education; however, the plans themselves are rarely created or implemented *with* the community. A stark example of this interplay can be seen in the public hearings or school board meetings that have been held around the country when a district decides to close a school. In Newark, New Jersey, then Superintendent Cami Anderson and her team stopped attending these meetings because the public opposition to her plan to close a number of schools and convert them to charter schools was "no longer focused on achieving educational outcomes for children."[45] As brilliantly detailed by reporter Dale Russakoff in the book *The Prize: Who's in Charge of America's Schools?*, the decisions to remake Newark's public school system were largely made behind closed doors by Newark Mayor Cory Booker, New Jersey Governor Chris Christie, and, due to a donation of $100 million, Facebook CEO Mark Zuckerberg. Similarly, Philadelphia started its process of school closures to charter conversions by holding public votes. But after two communities rejected the charterization of their schools, district leaders removed the community vote from the process, authorizing the charters on their own.[46] The lack of community input has also been cited in Washington, DC, Chicago, and New York among other cities where closures have been widely used, and amounts to what the Alliance to Reclaim Our Schools has called "the systematic disenfranchisement of African American and Latino communities."[47]

Reform districts are the latest iteration of the school closure policy. Under this policy, states can create cohorts of schools that can be closed, restarted, or converted to charter schools all at once. This model first appeared in New Orleans. In 2003, the Louisiana State legislature created a Recovery School District (RSD). Initially, five schools in New Orleans were taken from local control and converted to charter schools because their students scored below a state-determined minimum on their standardized tests. When Hurricane Katrina hit in 2005, the legislature quickly established a new, higher minimum achievement score just for New Orleans, and all but four of the city's public schools were usurped into the RSD, which used a combination of school closures and conversions to create the first all-charter school district in the United States.[48]

Reformers spent the next ten years glowing about the new district. Indeed, some journalists went so far as to wish their own cities could be wiped clean by a hurricane like Katrina so they could do the same.[49] Many of these articles failed to mention the seven thousand teachers who were laid off, a significant number of whom were Black women. Similar to the trends seen in school closures and other turnaround efforts elsewhere, these educators were then replaced by newer, whiter out-of-towners from alternative certification programs, who made up 30 percent of the teaching force by 2012.[50] In total, the percent of Black teachers in New Orleans dropped from 71 percent to 49 percent from 2004 to 2014.[51]

An outgrowth of the fanfare over New Orleans' Recovery School District has been the portfolio district.[52] Rather than take over an entire city's public school system, states select a group of low performing schools and either take over operations themselves or, as is more often the case, hand them over to a charter management organization. Tennessee was the first major adopter of this model with their Achievement School District (ASD) in Memphis and Nashville,[53] followed by Michigan's takeover of schools in Detroit[54] and Wisconsin's "Opportunity Schools and Partnership Program" in Milwaukee.[55] A number of other states lined up to join the team in 2015 and 2016, including Nevada, Pennsylvania, Georgia, Arkansas, Missouri, South Carolina, Texas, and Utah.[56] The rapid spread of legislation around the formation of these districts has been funded by many of the big names in educational philanthropy, including the Walton Family Foundation, whose lobbyists wrote a bill to take over a group of schools in Little Rock.[57] Thus far, there has been little evidence of a strong link to increased student achievement.[58] In the case of Detroit, the state district has had a spectacularly depressing fallout that included an FBI corruption investigation[59] and a civil rights lawsuit.[60]

WHEN SCHOOL IMPROVEMENT WORKS AND WHAT'S AHEAD

Caitlin Emma, writing for *POLITICO*, tracked the story of two schools that received SIG funding and their drastically different results. The successful one, Miami's Edison Senior High School, made gains where other schools didn't because the school district thoughtfully prepared and supported the school and community. They held open meetings to inform parents of upcoming changes and got their input on next steps, created a partnership with the teachers' union around the school-based reforms, and designed a districtwide system to bring strong teachers into the school. At the school level, teachers were thoroughly involved in the improvement plan and invested in its success. As one teacher at the school, Danielle Boyer, said, "When you feel empowered to do your job, who wouldn't get results?"[61] The changes at Edison High School highlight the implementation of a number of practices for school improvement that have been repeatedly demonstrated in research and yet run counter to much of what has been at the core of federal and state turnaround policy.

Researchers at the University of Chicago's Consortium on School Research undertook one of the most extensive studies on school reform ever completed when they looked at the performance of over two hundred schools over a seven-year period to understand why one hundred of these schools made gains while the other one hundred did not. They found five essential elements of school improvement: collaborative teachers, ambitious instruction, effective leaders, involved families, and a safe and supportive environment. When schools had three or more of these elements, they were ten times more likely to show achievement gains, in an era before NCLB made test scores a focal point for reform. These schools also had stronger attendance, higher levels of student engagement, and more positive perceptions of school climate.[62] Each of these elements is rooted in building and sustaining capacity as an organization. The operations of a school—particularly the teaching and learning parts—are ultimately dependent on the individual skills and knowledge of every person in the building and how they work together to build community and improve their practice.

Organizations like Journey for Justice and the Schott Foundation have advocated for a model of reform that incorporates these elements and more, called the Sustainable School Success Model, developed by Communities for Excellent Public Schools. They offer another option for how to turn schools around, premised on the idea that, from the very beginning, families, students, communities, and school staff should work together to plan each stage of improvement. Through this process, teams plan how to improve their school's culture, curriculum, and the quality of teaching, and implement wraparound supports for students that include health care, social-emotional services, guidance counselors, and mentoring programs within a positive youth development framework.[63]

Their proposal mirrors many of the elements of the Community Schools movement, which advocates for school-community partnerships, often integrating a traditional focus on academics with health and social services, youth and community development, and community engagement. Schools are recognized as central institutions within a community and are treated as such, providing an open and supportive space for students, their families, and their neighbors. Community Schools have a strong track record of success[64] and, increasingly, are being advocated as a tool for school improvement.[65]

Under the Every Student Succeeds Act, states have the opportunity to develop such a holistic, inclusive approach. Annual Yearly Progress, the measure of school worth under NCLB, is gone. States are still required to intervene in schools, using measurements that include test scores, but they can also include a nonacademic indicator, like levels of student or family engagement, school climate, or socioemotional learning. And instead of a prescriptive list of options for school turnaround, states are left to determine the course of action they'd like to take. The language to justify a new direction is there: we've moved from calling schools failing to emphasizing support. The policy decisions that follow will determine the future of schools and communities in the next era of education reform.

TEACHERS' STORIES

The stories in this chapter bring you into so-called failing schools: those that have been marked for closure, those that scramble to find quick fixes to avoid being labeled, those going through the process of being shut down, and those that have been "turned around." K. Jennifer Oki, a founding teacher at a small school that later would be marked as failing, provides a complex picture about what causes schools to struggle. Reflecting on NCLB's Adequate Yearly Progress policy, Alex Diamond's story is a warning about measuring school quality through a series of numerical targets. He explains how the pressure to avoid being called a "failure" pushed his school to attempt a series of short term measures that further eroded educational quality rather than develop long-term schoolwide improvements. Megan Behrent describes what happened when her school was targeted for closure, and Tim Bernier brings us into the culture of a school taken over by a turnaround management organization. Finally, Liz Sullivan offers an example of what community-based school improvement can be like with her story of the transformation of Whittier Elementary School in Oakland, California.

On Dissonance and Light

How to Tell a Story of Success or Failure

K. JENNIFER OKI

Not long ago I found myself seated in a small cafe near my house, laptop on the table, second cup of coffee drained, sobbing. If I'd been able to pay attention to those around me, I imagine they may have been alarmed, conjuring up any number of potential reasons why this stranger was crying so publicly in such a small space. I doubt any of them would have guessed that the trigger for my tears, and the deep, aching belly-full sobs, was reading, in full, the transcript of the public hearing on the closing of our school. "Our school"—the first, and only, school I had taught at, where I had been a founding teacher years before. At the peak of the New York City small-schools movement, our school, a nascent grade 6–12 community and justice-oriented traditional public school, was a dream come true in my new teaching life. Under the leadership of a Black woman from the same Harlem neighborhood our school was in, led by a team of Black women administrators who'd worked in the same schools that would feed our new one, and staffed by a mix of veteran district teachers and bright young talented alumni of an alternative teaching program, this school would be a model for what was possible in NYC public schools in the reform-heavy era of Mayor Michael Bloomberg and School Chancellor Joel Klein.

Yet six years later, in a hearing transcript like many I had read before, the dream was tarnished. The proposal: truncate the school and replace it with the latest outgrowth of a well-known and rapidly expanding charter management organization. In proposing both actions together, the hearing engendered a confusing scene, with the charter expansion a clear flashpoint—it requested more space, more access, and less responsibility to share than any of the other four schools in the building. I read line after line of teachers, parents, and administrators asking, advocating, pleading in turn for the school to remain open and for the charter to stay far away, not always linking the asks; the two issues are closely connected, but not the same. I read, eyes welling up, the deputy chancellor's acknowledgment of the "feelings" in the space and clarity that the district "sees it differently."

What exactly are those "feelings"? From everything I read in the transcript—and from everything I had seen in my years teaching—this was about much more than feelings. What my colleagues and I had observed, along with the parents of hundreds of our students, was concrete and tactile: our school had many tangible successes, and it could have had far more. A piece of testimony from a parent proves the point:

> I'm all choked up because I think it's ridiculous. We've just started to turn the corner. We have plans in place. We've taken corrective action where it needed to be taken, and I just think we're letting this thing go away before the sunset arrives. I think we're giving up, and it's important to tell my kids, to tell the kids in this building . . . that they've done nothing wrong.

I choked up with her as I read the assertion between the lines of the transcript that the school was an irredeemable failure. I cannot reconcile this with the school I knew; I do not recognize it. I *do* recognize the teachers that parents describe going above and beyond for their children. I recognize the colleagues that teachers reference as they explain how their peers make do with little, work within burdensome constraints, handle oversized classes and undersized classrooms. I remember our SETSS[66] room in a converted closet, our special education pull-out students literally relegated to a place where we tuck things away, and the converted "classrooms" in the basement when we were stretched for space.

I believe that there are many ways our school failed. We failed to become what we'd envisioned, failed to meet the standard we held for our students and community. But this has little to do with the Department of Education's notion of abject *failure*—an assessment backed up with quantitative measures shorn of context, with little connection to broader concepts like purpose, vision, or even quality—all crucial aspects of the model of liberatory education we worked toward. I wasn't at the hearing, but I couldn't help but picture an actual, literal divide. Maybe the deputy chancellor and his team were seated on a dais; maybe the microphone for public comment was off to the side. This image, which came from nowhere but felt so convincing, was a projection of the dissonance I experienced as I read the transcript. All of us—the school's teachers, parents, and administrators—had in mind a very different vision of success for our students than those with the power to deem us a failure.

The memory of this dissonance was and remains painful, yet when I think back to my time at the school, I realize that dissonance was present almost from the very beginning of my time as a teacher. As soon as the school had an academic and social vision for its students, it had to confront another vision—a bureaucratic and seemingly arbitrary approach that would, in the end, win out. I remember an especially vivid confrontation with this about halfway through my third year of teaching, when I found myself listening to a smiling, confident stranger chastising our staff for our high academic expectations.

On professional development days the students left at 2 p.m., most of them clambering out after one another to leave the building as quickly as possible and spill out into the light of day. Years later, standing in a bright, airy school in Oklahoma marveling at the high ceilings and wide hallways, I would wonder how we ever allowed a school environment so dark and constraining. I would remember the controlled movements, from the dark hallways of our fourth-floor space, down the dark stairwells, to our dark, shared basement cafeteria or our dark, barebones auditorium. I would remember the front entrance with its heavy metal doors. Students would come through those doors before our school's staggered start time—set up to accommodate the other three schools in our building, and so late that students were frequently harassed by truancy cops on their way to school— walk past surly police officers, through metal detectors, and away from the sun that they would not see again until 4:30 p.m. It is a marvel how easily one adjusts to constraints. How did we ever allow that to happen?

On professional development days, and this one in particular, I watched the students run toward the light. I'd chat with and reassure the few students who didn't want to leave, who rarely wanted to leave right away, or ever, who would volunteer to grade, to clear or decorate, to just hang out, to do anything to stay a little longer in my room. Most days I'd let them stay as long as they needed to, some leaving the building with me if I left by 6 p.m., sometimes taking the M100 up the hill together for those who lived near me. On professional development days, I'd apologetically shuffle them out before making my way down to our branded hallways to the largest and brightest classroom on the floor.

> *"Education is the passport to the future; tomorrow belongs to those who prepare for it today."*   —Malcolm X

Malcolm X spoke to us daily, in our bold blue school color, our social justice logo confidently placed next to his words, and Baldwin's words, and Gandhi's words, and Mary McLeod Bethune's. I read every word every time I walked the empty hallways; I wonder now if the bright blue and white letters did anything to lift my students' spirits in their daily walk.

An empowerment school, given a modicum of autonomy by the district due to assessed principal strength, our school had frequent professional development days, hours upon hours dedicated to teacher collaboration and growth. Like most schools I knew, the relative utility of the hours varied widely. Over the years, as I went from first-year teacher with resources dripping from my ears to the longest-serving high school teacher with just three years under my belt, I'd led some of these afternoons myself, my professional development responsibilities reflecting the growth trajectory of my practice and the rapidly shifting landscape of New York City school reform. I'd spent time teaching my colleagues how to use spreadsheets to track quantitative growth by students using multiple assessments; I'd led vertical alignment trainings for subject teams on planning backwards, twelfth to sixth grade, for curricular synchronicity; I'd led trainings on facilitating effective advisories for adolescents, using a curriculum I designed. Somehow, a teacher in years one through three of proficiency— as gifted and creative as my mama always told me I was—held a significant amount of responsibility. We all did; a group of just over twenty committed educators, we led inquiry circles, led professional development sessions, worked late and came early, supported each other without question. It seemed a hallmark of our culture at the time, but as much as it was done out of passion (our advisory program was my baby and our pride), it was also done out of necessity. There were top-down impositions, such as the requirement to track formative assessment data, but limited direct support. It is a marvel how easily one adjusts to constraints. We did what we could with what we had.

But on this day we were welcomed by two faces. Verónica, a familiar face from our organizational partner, and a new one, a tall white woman with a suit, a smile, and the kind of confidence I read as coming from being overpaid to deliver advice to teachers one doesn't know in schools one has never set foot in before. After an effusive introduction from our familiar face, new face—Heather, let's call her—delivered the first resounding announcement that our school, empowered though it was, branded though it was, and despite our lauded contributions to other schools in our empowerment network,[67] was doing a disservice to students. Now halfway through our third year of existence as it was, we had one formal review under our belts and another on the way. We knew clearly what the district said about our AYP, our progress report grade, our credit accumulation and pass rate on the Regents[68] in the high school, our test scores in the middle school, how many students moved from our eighth grade into our ninth, how many transferred or went to charters. We *knew* what the district expected to see in our binders, we knew our quantitatively assessable strengths and shortcomings, and we knew too well the pressures our school was under. What was news this professional-development Friday, delivered with a smile I recall with perhaps more condescension than it actually held, was that we were doing a disservice to students.

"I've been looking at the grades in your AP U.S. history class," Heather said, shoulders rounded in a physical demonstration of disappointment. My eyes scanned the room for my friend—Ms. Kelly, the AP U.S. history teacher, my partner in social studies crime, pioneer of our first-offered AP course, and current teacher under the microscope—and remembered she wasn't there that day. "I noticed that the students in the AP U.S. history class have markedly lower grade percentages than the students in the Regents class." Heather frowned, I remember, her face—her never before seen in the hallways of our three-year-old school face—was a stark contrast to the still beaming, always bright face of Verónica. She allowed for a dramatic pause, long enough for the high school teachers in the room to squirm a bit and lob confused looks at each other, before continuing: "It's as if you all don't know what your students go through. Don't you want them to succeed?"

Heather would go on to explain to us that our students—this particular cohort of our founding students, whom I'd taught history for two years, who achieved the highest Regents scores and pass rates in our building—were at a disadvantage because of our actions. When she looked across all the other schools in our comparison group, across the other schools in our empowerment network, their students had much higher grades in their APs; they would graduate competitive, with strong GPAs in high-level classes, and our students would be left in the dust, unable to get into college. What was happening, Heather wondered, that we weren't working together to set our students up for success? What didn't we understand and how could she help?

Setting aside the anger beginning to rise in my throat—they *had known for months* Ms. Kelly was going to be out today, why would we ever have this conversation without her?—I composed myself enough to be part of our collegial inquiry:

- "To clarify, you are concerned about the percentage grade on this last quarter's progress reports, not their final grade?"
- "Have you looked at their growth from the start of the course to now?"
- "Just so I understand, you're saying that you are surprised that there is a difference in the raw percentage grade in the first semester of the first AP course, compared to the standard U.S. history Regents class?"
- "If the AP standard is variable by school, how do the students do when they get to college? Do you know?"
- "What do you mean when you say 'what our students go through?' What do you think we are missing?"

Heather was on message and didn't miss a beat. Yes, the grade matters; not the AP test score or pass rate, she didn't know those numbers. No, she wasn't sure that the schools enrolled their students in the exam; the exam was superfluous for our students. Yes, she would expect to see similar 80 percent and 90 percent grade range of our "top" students, even in a more challenging class—don't we control the grading? Our students deal with challenges, you know—they are living in poverty, they have to go through a lot just to get to school. They have responsibilities we can't imagine, the least we could do is invest in and support their success.

In retrospect, I know I didn't hate Heather, despite the bile in my throat; I didn't know her and would never see her again. In the moment, however, Heather—and Verónica, by virtue of having brought this stranger into our school—stood as an agent of doom, describing such a narrow, deficit-based view of what our students could and should do, that I was driven to rage. Our goal, to build strong, capable, curious, and college-ready students, was doing our students a disservice; we were oriented in the wrong direction, and, if we continued in this way, we would be marked because of it. There was no actual development that day, no offer of support. Heather and Verónica, whose smile I could never quite return the same way after that, just came to tell us: *these kids can't do that; stop trying.*

There are so many things I did not know at twenty-five years old, in my third year of teaching, in the third year of our school, and I am sure there were likely some things Heather could have taught me. Here, however, are some things I did know, as "chair" of the social studies department, comprising four teachers in a three-year-old school, as a teacher who was there for its founding and who had watched it morph over the years:

The year we opened, our district had a 54 percent graduation rate, with a 36 percent global history Regents pass rate. As a new teacher, a founding teacher, and the global history teacher, I knew the weight of our responsibility to the progress measures that control access for our students' post-secondary success. As someone with immense educational privilege and a recent college graduate, I knew that the Regents, graduation gatekeepers as they were, did not indicate college readiness. As a scholar of ethnic studies and a believer in our school's mission, I knew the potential power of our history curriculum: it could prepare our students to be active and engaged participants in making a more just world, or it could perpetuate half-truths and narratives of power, keep my students isolated, relegate their peoples' histories to the margins, and subsequently ask them to live their lives in the margins, taking up no space. That opening year, a prominent and highly regarded charter school had, with little fanfare, dismissed an entire group of students whose cohort "strength" wasn't quite strong enough to be the charter's first high school class. Many of those students would come to us, with varied emotional responses to being "kicked out" of the school they'd known and loved for years, with its multimillion-dollar facilities, monetary stipends, and abundant wraparound services and extracurricular activities.

In the first years of our school, guided by a vision for college preparation and social justice, we worked to build a middle school and high school that felt connected, that used AP high school courses as our anchor for backward vertical planning, and, in our social studies department, held a bar for success much higher than the New York State standardized exam. That test, though, that broad and shallow test, was a behemoth; my first parent-teacher conferences featured multiple parents telling me how they knew from stories or experience that global history might be the exam that kept their child from graduation. My students came with their own global history fears and varied preparation in the things that might set them up for success in history—strong reading and writing skills, exposure to historical texts and primary sources, experience with rigorous critical-thinking-based curricula. They also came, as Heather was eager to "remind" us, with the acute challenges that living in a racist, capitalist, nativist, and segregated society can bring. And the adults in the building? We came with hope, with an investment in our students and our community, with content expertise, with a vision for education that led to real options for our students, and with a commitment to doing what it took to get there. For some of us, like Ms. Washington, who had grown up in the neighborhood, that commitment looked like driving her car around looking for students who weren't in school after the first bell and bringing them to our building instead of to the truancy police. For others it looked like fund-raising and planning and scheming to get our students the kind of immersive educational experiences—like our history trip through Europe—that can make content pop off the page and into their lives. For yet others, it was digging up textbooks and leading afterschool classes for science subjects we couldn't find a teacher for. For all, it looked like long hours and investment, extra tasks, extra energy, extra creativity.

In the first years of our school, with a 36 percent district global history pass rate, every single one of our students passed their global history Regents—*That is not our bar, historians. It's the floor*—many with flying colors. That cohort we were doing such a disservice to went far beyond the quantitative measure laid before us and moved on to tackle AP U.S. history.

On that day, however, that knowledge seemed to matter little; on the days that would follow, it would matter less and less. What our students were capable of, what we envisioned for their lives, what we wanted to work toward—was not the goal. The goal was whatever Heather said it was . . . and Derrick after her, and Jessica the time next, and maybe Andrea months later. We accepted their goals; slowly but surely we shifted our vision to whatever moving target was placed in front of us, and we suffered the consequences. Our administrators, our Black women leaders from our community with a passion for our children and our work, moved their goal and changed the way they led us. It is a marvel how easily one adjusts to constraints, how the absurd becomes normal. Our teachers, still pushing, pushing, pushing, started to wonder what we were pushing for; our lights dimmed, we burned out, we left. The school got a little bit darker. By the end of that school year, many of our longer-serving teachers were gone. Not long after, our founding administrators would be gone.

The guilt I hold from leaving our school is palpable, unceasing, and specific. If I went to a regular therapist, I imagine they might tell me that the burden I place on myself as solely responsible for everything and everyone I'm proximate to is outsized and pathological. The guilt is a theme in my life, but my guilt around our school is acute. I wonder almost every day in the years since I left what could have been if I had stayed. But years later, upon reading the hearing transcript, I knew that guilt was not the only cause for the unceasing tears. My deep emotional reaction is tied to the astounding dissonance between what I know to be true of the place we built and the people who sustained it, and the narrative of failure that has unfolded. When others read of what happened, what will they make of the space between the lines of this transcript? Where is the data that captures what we did? How do we reconcile the two visions of this school? What do they know about who was there, of the love and commitment that held that place? What do they know about our kids (the charter didn't absorb the students outright)? What do our kids think about themselves?

I want to tell a story of a school that built and lost a vision of what was possible. To explore the ways we allowed—as we chased our survival in the public education system—desperation to drive us. To articulate what it means for smart, committed, invested people to accept the rules of a rigged game while trying to pull our kids out of it. I want to tell that story, but I don't know how to fit it within the confines of our debate about school success and failure.

Neither Heather nor Verónica was at the hearing about the closing of the school. In 2013 the school was far past its empowerment days, two principals past in fact, and our network partner was no more. I would read later that the charter that "replaced" the school asked the students and teachers who remained to use the back door entrance so the front could be reserved as their exclusive entryway. In an imperfect recollection I think about the light—the shadows cast by the building on its own courtyard in the rear, the way the narrow back entrance is just that much darker than the double front doors. I wonder if the blues and whites still brand the hallways of the remaining half of our school; if the colors, the quotes, are bright enough to lift our students' spirits every day. I wonder if they're used to this new normal; it really is a marvel how easily one adjusts to constraints.

I hear the parent's voice from the hearing, I imagine I know her, though I'm years removed at this point: *"It's important to tell my kids, to tell the kids in this building . . . that they've done nothing wrong."*

K. Jennifer Oki taught global history and geography and ethnic studies in New York City. A Black Japanese American raised in multiple countries and educational contexts, she bridges her academic rooting and political investments to support the professional development of aspiring social justice educators. She currently serves as the educational editor for The Microaggressions Project and as one half of Ukhululiwe, and holds a BA from Columbia University and a MST from Pace University School of Education.

Under Pressure

The Unintended Consequences of Education Reform

ALEX DIAMOND

"If we don't handle our business, they're going to roll up the buses and ship all of us on out of here."

My principal was speaking, invoking the collaboration, hard work, and acquiescence to new policies that would be required of us, the staff of an inner-city Memphis high school, to meet certain benchmarks mandated by education reform policies. Also, he was threatening us. Not in an "I'm-going-to-fire-you" sort of way. Rather, it was the rallying cry of the besieged, a description of a shared menace, a challenge to be confronted together as a staff facing the reality of a low-achieving school in a low-income community. And aside from the fact that laid-off teachers are seldom provided with a bus to the unemployment office, this was not an idle threat. We were a "failing" school and could be closed if we didn't meet particular statistical measures of effectiveness or, more accurately, if our students fell short of certain standards of achievement.

Our principal trotted out this vision of education reformers pulling up in a Greyhound at nearly every staff meeting as he introduced multiple policies we were expected to follow. He was a hard-working man, new as the principal but well liked and respected after many years as coach, teacher, and vice-principal at the school. When he imposed these often unpopular new policies, he defended them as administrative or districtwide decisions necessitated by a brave new world of public education. The policies he implemented were the kind of logical responses made by well-meaning educators to the reforms sweeping across American public schools. But they were counterproductive, bad ideas—changes that decreased the effectiveness of our school as an institution of learning.

Memphis at that time was at the forefront of education reform, in a way that put the squeeze on teachers and administrators. In 2009, the Bill & Melinda Gates Foundation awarded the city $90 million for a new Teacher Effectiveness Initiative. The grant was to fund the use of teacher evaluations, measured by several factors including student growth on state exams, to make decisions around hiring and retention. At the same time, Tennessee was competing for federal education funding through Race to the Top. In order to receive a piece of the $4.35 billion pie, the state passed measures to meet federal requirements for the funding, including permitting districts to use student test scores to decide which teachers would be granted tenure. They also passed a law stating that student achievement data would make up 50 percent of a teacher's evaluation. Tennessee lawmakers raised the cap on the number of charter schools and increased the number of students eligible for charter schools. Finally, they included plans to expand the number of Teach For America corps members in Tennessee from one hundred to five hundred. When Tennessee was awarded $500 million in Race to the Top money in 2010, the money was earmarked in part for the expansion of teacher evaluation and the creation of an Achievement School District to allow for yet more charter schools and state takeover of lowest performing schools.

My school had a demographic makeup typical of the schools that tend to be taken over. The student population was more than 99 percent Black, and more than 90 percent of students were classified as economically disadvantaged. Students entered every day through metal detectors, and we received training on how to recognize gang signals. A majority of teachers had been at the school long enough to have taught their students' brothers and sisters, mentor students from freshman to senior year, and become familiar with the strengths and challenges present in the surrounding community. I heard my students' stories about their family members' struggles to find jobs or stay out of jail and witnessed too many of my students end up arrested, pregnant, or shot. These events make English homework seem pretty inconsequential, and it stands to reason that students who lack supportive family structures, worry about getting enough to eat, and live in communities riddled with joblessness and criminality have a harder time achieving the same levels of academic performance as their more privileged peers. Between the evaluations of our school and the new metrics for grading teachers, it seemed like none of those factors was considered. Instead, it felt like we were under siege.

As we were pressed to meet high expectations without adequate time or necessary resources, policies were enacted to keep our school afloat, including a mandate for how many students were allowed to fail each class: 10 percent or less. Never mind that the 90 percent we were required to pass was significantly higher than the number of students who completed their work, passed their exams, or attended even half the classes. Unfortunately, many students knew it, and depended on grade leniency to get through. "Just give me that 70" (the lowest passing grade) became a common refrain from unmotivated students. While plenty of motivated, intelligent, hardworking kids were shooting for more than a 70, those less inclined would look at the class roll of thirty people, identify three students doing worse, and know they were safe.

So why did my high school's administrators limit teachers' power to assign grades and instead push along students with grades they didn't deserve in subjects they didn't understand? In 2009, my school had been identified as a "target" school after one year of not making Adequate Yearly Progress (AYP) under the No Child Left Behind Act (NCLB). The benchmark graduation rate was 90 percent. We'd achieved 66.7 percent. With each subsequent year our students fell short, we would skid further down a slippery slope of escalating penalties. According to the Tennessee Accountability Chart, after the second year of missing AYP, students would have the right to attend other schools in the district (and falling enrollment, of course, means a reduction in school staff). After the fourth year, replacing staff was one of several potential corrective actions, and after the fifth, the whole school could be restructured as a charter school (i.e., roll up the buses and ship everyone out).

In the face of such consequences, what could an administrator do? If our administration had tried to do an exhaustive analysis, they likely would have found a number of causes behind each individual student who failed to graduate: lack of motivation, family troubles, suspensions due to disciplinary problems, inadequate academic skills, and broader systemic inequality are a few I can think of. But such an analysis, interesting though it may be, likely wouldn't get them from two-thirds to nine-tenths. So they looked at the situation practically: we needed to achieve a 90 percent graduation rate, so that was the number of students that had to pass our classes. Teachers, not surprisingly, hated this policy, feeling disempowered and handcuffed in their ability to manage difficult students. Even more important, it had a significant effect on the already poor academic culture of the school as it ran headfirst into even lower expectations and requirements.

I discovered early on that pushing students along had already been a problem in the school. I entered the first days of my world history class with a well-thought-out plan to motivate my students and demonstrate the power and importance of history in the modern world. I introduced my unit by asking my students why we celebrate Columbus Day. "Because he discovered America" is the standard answer. I gave them short excerpts from historians Howard Zinn and Hans Koning with a simple assignment: find three reasons why we honor Columbus with his own holiday. It's a trick. The readings describe Columbus's reign as governor of the Caribbean island of Hispaniola, in particular the systems of slavery and punishment that included cutting off the hands of Taíno Indians who failed to bring him the gold he demanded. We would then compare Columbus to Nathan Bedford Forrest, a noted slave trader, slave owner, general in the Confederate Army, and early leader of the Ku Klux Klan, who had both a park and a statue in his honor near downtown Memphis.[69] I hoped to inspire my students, have them draw parallels between world history and something closer to home, and understand that there is power in how history is told.

The problem with my plan? Many of my students couldn't read. They could make the sounds of words on a page, but were unable to sit down with a text and comprehend the main ideas. When I gave them the readings, many students resorted to a coping mechanism I referred to (un)affectionately as "the seek and copy." Faced with a basic comprehension question, they would search in the text for the sentence that shared the most keywords with the question. They would then copy down the sentence verbatim, assuming the answer was held within. They weren't trying to cheat; they were trying to get the right answer and make a good impression on their new teacher. But "the seek and copy" was no way to actually learn anything—and besides, Koning and Zinn's readings were completely bereft of reasons to honor Columbus.

I knew about the achievement gap on a theoretical level but didn't understand what it looked like in the classroom, the curricular choices that it forced teachers to make. I soon found that I was making questionable choices too. I avoided all but the simplest reading assignments, only exacerbating the problem and doing a major disservice to students with higher-level skills who should have been preparing for college-level reading. In the same vein, math teachers complained that students entered algebra II unable to solve basic equations from algebra I. With test scores based on an algebra II curriculum that students were unprepared to study, many teachers felt they had no option other than to teach strategies to beat the test.

The fact that students lacked some of the basic skills needed to be successful in high school classes was undoubtedly a large part of the reason many were failing to graduate. This unfortunate state of affairs made the classification of my high school as a "target" perfectly appropriate. Something did need to change. But rather than attempting to help students develop these skills, we were told to play a numbers game, ensuring that they could graduate in an attempt to meet AYP benchmarks. As a result, teachers were faced with a series of damned-if-you-do, damned-if-you-don't alternatives. We could try to bring unprepared students up to speed at the expense of those who were ready for the "real" course material; we could teach according to the state standards for a given subject and leave large groups of students behind; or we could focus on test-taking strategies instead of the actual course material in an attempt to get a decent evaluation and keep our jobs.

One day our principal gave us a presentation that at the outset seemed to address this exact problem: a major skills gap that left students across the city ill prepared for college-level courses. Based on an empirical observation of our students, this was a valid criticism. A guidance counselor had told me that of the students who did make it to college from my high school, the majority dropped out before finishing a degree. I suspected that a lack of preparedness for the pressures and requirements of college-level curriculum was part of the reason for this. Also, low homework completion rates discouraged many teachers from assigning the outside-of-class work that might instill the effective study habits that students need to succeed in a college setting.

But the district-prepared PowerPoint presentation he delivered didn't seek to explain why students were ill prepared for college. Instead it spelled out the district's statistical definition of college readiness based on an empirical analysis of the ACT test and announced this would be the newest measure added to our evaluation. In order to be deemed college ready for each of four first-year college courses—English composition, college algebra, biology, and an introductory social science course—students had to achieve a certain ACT score in English, mathematics, science, and reading, respectively. Our students from the class of 2010 had an average ACT composite score of 15.3, compared with 21 in Shelby County Schools (the more affluent suburban school district), 19.5 across the state, and 21 nationwide.

Like all district schools, we would immediately be expected to meet a particular percentage growth benchmark in the number of college-ready students. The year before, my school had graduated exactly zero college-ready students. A college-ready mathematics student can probably tell you that regardless of the target percentage growth, zero is a number better suited to grow by addition than multiplication. Whether it be 10 percent growth or 700 percent growth, zero stays right at zero (I think this was also one of the rejected slogans for the college-readiness initiative). But we had to show growth. So in order to satisfy the district's college readiness initiative, from a school with roughly one thousand students we needed to produce a grand total of one college-ready student the next year. With that goal in mind, the principal outlined the plan. Every single day, every single class in all subjects was to begin with ACT practice. The hope was that out of this relentless barrage of ACT prep, one brave student would emerge able to churn out the necessary scores.

As with many education reform policies, the college-readiness initiative began with a real problem. In order to get a clear picture of the problem (and in order to hold schools, administrators, and teachers accountable), it sought to define the problem in measurable, concrete terms. Once defined, the numbers became the goal, replacing the resolution of the actual problem and creating classroom outcomes that were often counterproductive—even if they improved the numbers. An appropriate analogy from the sports world would be recognizing that heavier high school football players are more likely to succeed, and then, in high schools with sub-.500 football teams, mandate that the first fifteen minutes of every practice be a fried-chicken-eating contest, no vomiting allowed.

Among rationales I've used with students to explain why they should care about a particular lesson, "because it's going to be on the test" has come in second only to "because I said so" in its ineffectiveness. My most successful and motivating lessons were the most personalized (read: least standardized), those that tapped into my students' attitudes, sensibilities, and real-life concerns. In class, my students compared the exploitation of the Taíno Indians by Columbus from the beginning of the year with the exploitation of the Indonesian factory workers who make the Air Jordans that graced my students' feet; the effects of inequality on the victims of Hurricane Katrina with the effects of inequality that prompted the Third Estate to rise up against the French Church and nobility during the French Revolution. The reason we could do that was because, somehow, world history had slipped through the cracks in Tennessee's End of Course Testing. Without a test to teach to, I had the freedom to develop my own evaluation and to tailor my curriculum to what I thought would motivate and interest my students while developing useful academic skills. Additionally, like at least a few other teachers at the school, I defied our college-readiness initiative in order to teach the lessons I wanted. The same ACT practice questions stayed written on my board for weeks (after an administrator visited my classroom, I would change to a new question). Additionally, I knew I wasn't going to continue teaching in Memphis, so it was easier to defy some of the policies handed down in the name of education reform. The teachers I saw that did not have these luxuries felt inordinate pressure to improve students' test grades while having to follow other arbitrary policies, leaving little room for creativity and personalization.

A basic tenet of economics—a statistics-driven field if ever there was one—is that humans attempt to maximize outcomes based on their preferences and certain given limitations. For the vast majority of teachers, their career choice is not a profit-maximizing decision. We can talk all we want about teacher salaries and even vacation time, but the teachers I met at my school left me with no doubt that the vast majority of people enter the teaching profession out of a preference to connect with and help young people. These new systems of accountability and evaluation combine with waves of new and often short-term teachers to put pressure on experienced educators and administrators in all kinds of undesirable ways. Faced with the loss of their livelihood under new district and national policies, educators make rational adjustments. Principals will institute policies that go against their values. Teachers will follow such policies, teach to tests, and even begin to see their students as numbers because they are made to feel there are no other realistic options.

The discourse around education reform at my school was focused around the threat of "rolling up the buses," because, for my colleagues, losing their livelihood was a pressing, motivating concern. Teachers didn't lose their ability to form meaningful personal relationships with students, and the best, most creative teachers still found ways to teach lessons that spoke directly to students in spite of the education reform movement's emphasis on standardization, testing, and quantification. The rhetoric of reform in my school didn't involve teachers as agents in the process of changing a school that was labeled "In Need of Improvement"; it treated them as laborers who couldn't be trusted to do a good job in the classroom without adequate coercion to perform. Teachers and principals, though not all perfect, should not be treated with such suspicion. And the threat of closing down a school with no support offered to address the underlying issues should not be a regular tool wielded by policy makers. While the numbers may rise and tell a story of improvement, the day-to-day reality ultimately shows less effective teaching, decreasing motivation from both teachers and students, and lower authentic achievement.

Alex Diamond taught social studies for two years at Melrose High School in Memphis, Tennessee, before beginning a worldwide teaching tour that has taken him to South Korea, Perú, and now Colombia. He is currently teaching at the University of San Buenaventura in Medellín, Colombia, where he enjoys perfect weather, riding his bicycle, and speaking Spanish while riding his bicycle in perfect weather.

You're It!

On Being Targeted for Turnaround

MEGAN BEHRENT

Under the mayoral control of billionaire Michael Bloomberg, the closures of New York City public schools were decided by the Panel for Education Policy (PEP), a thirteen-person group that shuttered 160 schools from 2003 to 2013. A trip to the PEP was like a trip to Versailles, pre-French Revolution. As hundreds of eloquent and passionate speakers fought for their schools, members of the panel played games or texted friends on their Blackberries and mentally planned their next cocktail party. You could almost hear them muttering, "Let them eat cake," under their breath. The panel itself was made up of members mostly appointed by the mayor who went along with every decision he made. The one time mayoral PEP appointees stepped out of line to object to the use of standardized test scores as the basis for promotion of students to the next grade, they were fired.[70] That was in 2004. For the rest of Bloomberg's tenure, the PEP followed the mayor's policies without a hint of resistance.

In 2012, the threat of school closure landed at my school. That year, thirty-three schools were targeted for Bloomberg's "turnaround" model, in which the entire staff of a school is removed and forced to reapply for their jobs—with the proviso that a maximum of 50 percent can be rehired. Our school had first come into the Department of Education's sights two years earlier when state officials deemed it to be "persistently low-achieving" (PLA) because our four-year graduation rate was slightly below the city's average. This designation was a byproduct of New York's application for federal Race to the Top funds, which required states to identify such schools and impose one of four restructuring models as a condition of receiving federal School Improvement Grants. As a result, my school became a "transformation" school, arguably the least draconian of the four models. We were given three years to raise our graduation rate and were required to implement a variety of changes, including piloting parts of a new teacher evaluation system that, for the first time, required test scores and other measures of student learning to be used to determine 40 percent of a teacher's annual evaluation.

The evaluation system became law in 2010, but much about how it would be implemented was left up to negotiations between the New York City Department of Education and the United Federation of Teachers (UFT), the union that represents more than one hundred thousand educators and support staff in New York City's public schools. On December 31, 2011, the city's DOE officials walked out of negotiations with the UFT despite a deadline imposed on them by the state that threatened the loss of all Race to the Top funds should the parties fail to reach an agreement. The sticking point? The UFT wanted some semblance of fairness for appeals by teachers deemed "ineffective" two years in a row. Under the new system, the DOE wouldn't have to prove that a teacher was incompetent in order to take away his or her license. An accusation from the administration would suffice, and no appeals would be allowed.

With millions of dollars in funding at stake from Race to the Top, Bloomberg went on the offensive. Unable to reach an agreement through negotiations, he announced that thirty-three schools that had been classified "restart" or "transformation" were now to be subjected to the severe "turnaround" model (made famous in Central Falls, Rhode Island, in 2010),[71] complete with the provision that the entire staff would be fired and a maximum of 50 percent could return. Bloomberg used his State of the City address to announce this proposal. The next day, we were asked to distribute a letter to students for their parents from School Chancellor Dennis Walcott. Among other highlights, it stated:

> [U]nfortunately many of the conditions the UFT insisted on would have made it harder for us to replace a poor-performing teacher with someone who will better serve our students. As a result of our inability to get the UFT to agree to real accountability, the State Education Department suspended your school's grant funding.

It went on to persuade families of the benefits of the "turnaround" plan, which was described as an admittedly "aggressive" plan that would nonetheless allow the DOE to "screen existing staff using rigorous standards for student success, and to re-hire a significant portion of those staff," thus "enhanc[ing] the quality of teaching and learning in your school." This information was disseminated at the end of the day on a Friday before a long weekend and before the staff had been apprised of any of the details.

As a result, students were sent home in a fog of confusion amid finals and one week before Regents exams, the state tests that students are required to pass in order to graduate high school. The last thing they needed was to worry about the future of their school. So much for "children first," the name Bloomberg had given to his education reform agenda.

The idea that removing 50 percent of teachers in a school would be anything but devastating and disruptive fit in with the general logic of education reform, according to Bloomberg and Walcott. In this dystopia, eliminating schools improves them. So, too, does eliminating teachers apparently make them better teachers.

Or, at least some teachers and some schools. In 2011, Bloomberg had been "incredibly concerned" about the disruptions caused by layoffs from state budget cuts if seniority provisions weren't eliminated.[72] When it came to my school, however, firing half the staff was not destabilizing, but progress. We stood in the city as an anomaly to everything Bloomberg promoted. It is a large comprehensive neighborhood high school that accepts anyone who lives in our zone year-round. Many of our teachers live in or are from the neighborhood in which we teach. New schools with new teachers shouldn't have to handle the disorder of mass firings, but it was productive for a school with history and roots in its community.

Of course, the whole proposal was completely illegal, and was, in fact, later deemed to violate the UFT contract by the arbitrator and state judge who ruled on the UFT's lawsuit in response to the mayor's turnaround plan.[73] In anticipation of legal challenges, the DOE attempted to exploit an ingenious loophole. Because schools that had been closed were allowed to apply the turnaround model, the city could shut a school down and reopen it one day later, allowing them to displace staff at will.

As a consequence, my school and the thirty-two other PLA schools in the city were slated to close on June 30, 2012, and reopen the next day— in the same building, with the same students, but with a new name and new number. Teachers would not have any claim to a job in the school and would become ATRs (Absent Teacher Reserves, who maintain their current salary, but are shuttled around the city as substitute teachers). We would be allowed to reapply for our jobs with the understanding that, at most, 50 percent of us would be rehired.

It would be impossible to overstate the demoralization that permeated the building in the wake of this announcement. In effect, teachers were encouraged to see their coworkers as competitors for their jobs rather than collaborators. Students, no matter how successful they had been at our school, were suddenly deemed failures, their hard work unrecognized. Everyone at the school was concerned about how being called "persistently low achieving" would impact our school and our own individual futures. This struck us as all the more unfair because we had never received anything but complimentary reviews from anyone who had actually entered the building, observed classes, and had any significant contact with our school community. In the face of this demoralization, our staff and students rallied to defend our school in any way they could.

Despite this label, the reality was that we were not failing. My school was deemed PLA because our four-year graduation rate was below 60 percent. It was 59 percent. We had received an A on our report card in 2007[74] and Bs every year since. To justify this about-face, Walcott argued, "It's not just the letter grade—and the letter grade is extremely important, we take great pride in the letter grade . . . but you also have to take a look under the hood."[75] For once, we all seemed to say the same thing. These reports and evaluations of schools don't tell the whole story. In practice, though, an F was enough to close a school, yet an A or B would not guarantee that it stayed open.

What Walcott acknowledged for a moment is what we as teachers knew every day that we worked in our school: the "data" cherished by education reform demagogues says little about what really goes on. If you look at my school on paper, you will find a student body made up of more than three thousand students with a graduation rate that is only barely below the city average. Dig a little deeper, and you will see that up to 40 percent of our students are classified as English language learners by the DOE, though they should more accurately be referred to as "emergent bilinguals," since many already speak two languages. Many of these students are recent immigrants who, understandably, have difficulty graduating in four years. The reality is that all accepted research on language acquisition shows that it takes at least five to seven years to become academically proficient in a language.[76] Even that number assumes that students are already proficient in their own language, which is not always the case for those whose formal education has been interrupted. As one teacher at my school explained recently, the reason students don't learn faster is "because they're human, with human brains."

A school like mine has more than three thousand of them. Many of those stories begin in Albania, Uzbekistan, Bangladesh, the Fujian province of China, Pakistan, the Dominican Republic, Tibet, and Mexico. They are stories told in at least thirty-seven different languages, and no data can encapsulate the lessons one could learn from the student population in my building. There's no space on a school report card to measure the genuine multiculturalism that thrives when students share their ideas, cultures, and histories. They can't see the song and dance performances at our myriad school events, where Katy Perry mingles effortlessly with Indian dance, American rap, and a Chinese dragon dance. They aren't accounting for our flourishing theater program or our range of successful teams from football to cricket. That several of my former students are now colleagues says more about the success of our school than any measure of success they've created in the DOE. There's no algorithm that they've produced to tell the story of the student who arrived in the country in ninth grade and nonetheless graduated as the valedictorian with a full scholarship to a prestigious university. It doesn't let us show the student living in temporary housing who surmounted the odds to become the first in her family to graduate from high school. Some of our students were born in war-torn Kosovo, whose earliest memories are of escaping bombs and gunfire; others struggle with disabilities or work long hours to earn money for their poverty-stricken families in the United States or abroad. To reduce all of this to a school's graduation rate is to ignore everything that is fundamental in education. Far from increasing accountability, it puts pressure on schools to ignore what students need in favor of what looks good on paper.

In June 2012, an arbitrator ruled that Bloomberg's plan was in violation of the contract with the UFT,[77] a decision upheld in July 2012 by a New York State Supreme Court judge.[78] My own school was one of a handful of schools that had been removed from the turnaround list prior to the court decision. At less fortunate schools, the mass exodus of teachers who feared for their future was damaging, to say the least. Furthermore, the "failing" label made it difficult to recruit new classes of incoming freshmen. As a result, despite the legal win, many teachers were displaced and students harmed by the turnaround experiment, even if it was never fully implemented. And although they had won this turnaround effort, a modified version of the teacher evaluation system they had initially tried to force on schools like mine was unleashed across the city without union input on its implementation. It was steamrollered ahead through an arbitration decision made by the New York State Education Commissioner (and later, US Secretary of Education) John King still as flawed and untested as it had been in 2010. Using a combination of the Danielson Rubric and "value-added measures" from test scores,[79] these evaluations imposed more numbers onto realities that cannot be so easily defined. Art, music, and physical education teachers were rated based on assessments for subjects they didn't teach, bubble tests were given to kindergartners, and the first Common Core exams were so arduous that, around the city, educators reported huge increases in vomiting, nosebleeds, suicidal ideation, and even hospitalizations.

Students, parents, teachers, and administrators want to be more than just a score and want to operate without fearing what will happen if the numbers show that they are failures. New Yorkers have spent over a decade being defined in this way, and many want something else from their education system. There is hope for the future as communities refuse the logic of failure and the simplicity of bar graphs and instead look for alternatives that educate whole children, treat teachers as real people, and understand schools as sites of complex learning.

Megan Behrent is an educator, writer, and activist in Brooklyn. She is currently an assistant professor of English at NYC College of Technology, CUNY. Before teaching at City Tech, she taught English at Franklin D. Roosevelt High School in Brooklyn for fifteen years. She also taught writing courses at Touro College and SUNY Stony Brook. She is a contributor to Education and Capitalism *(Haymarket Books) and has been published in* Workplace: A Journal of Academic Labor, NYS TESOL Journal, *the* International Socialist Review, Labor Notes, New Politics, *and the* Harvard Educational Review.

After the Takeover

Critical Educators Need Not Apply

TIMOTHY BERNIER

After reading that the Academy of Urban School Leadership (AUSL) was taking over six of the ten public schools slotted to be turned around in Chicago during the 2012–2013 school year, I knew crucial information was not getting out about AUSL's role in fixing "failing" schools, their treatment of teachers who work under them, and their vision regarding the education of our children. For those unfamiliar with the nonprofit, AUSL is a powerful management group in Chicago that "turns around" schools declared failing and in need of closure. One key feature of AUSL's turnaround protocol includes firing and replacing the entire school staff—all of the teachers, clerks, lunchroom staff, and administrators—so they can start anew.

I spent four years teaching at Chicago's first official turnaround school. Without a doubt, the first three years presented their own challenges, but it was during my last year with AUSL that I witnessed the Chicago-based private contractor fervently push the deskilling of teachers while removing all extracurricular activities and arts programs in favor of excessive test preparation. It was after this raw exposure to the AUSL agenda that I came to understand that the AUSL board believes education reform is achieved through blind obedience and driving teachers to teach to the test in hopes of serving up data that "proves" their students are learning.

When I started at AUSL, I had already taught for five years in the inner-city of Chicago. I even had a couple years' teaching experience on my hiring principal, who was also new to the turnaround network. My hiring principal was young, Black, idealistic, and ready to change the way schools were run in low-income neighborhoods. For the first few years, our principal shielded our team from the AUSL standardized agenda, but as the network's demands became more persistent, the pressure to deliver took its toll. After four years as the school's principal, I believe he finally left our school out of this frustration.

AUSL's choice for our replacement principal was a white Harvard graduate who had a very difficult time adjusting to the neighborhood's South Side "urban" culture. Where our old principal had always been outside after the bell rang, oftentimes until the last student was picked up—talking with parents, discussing and handling discipline issues—it was not uncommon to see our new principal do a quick walk-around outside, then dip back into the building within a matter of minutes. When it came time for our new principal to address problems with parents or speak to community members about issues happening in the school or around the neighborhood, he would often be found in his office behind closed doors, leaving the heavy lifting to our assistant principal.

It became clear that our new principal did not value being informed about what was happening in the community. This was apparent, time and again, when violence would erupt after school or before school hours and we were not made aware of those situations until our students brought it to our attention during class. He had no excuses. Indeed, he had a plethora of resources, but lacked the wherewithal to tap into them. For example, in our building, we had a community activist and a security guard who lived in the neighborhood and were at our school daily, along with a few teachers who grew up in and around the area who knew the community intimately. Yet our principal seemed not to know how to utilize their knowledge and experience to build his understanding and create an authentic connection with the community.

To give you a snapshot, the neighborhood where I taught was a place where gunshots ended recess before its time and children came to school hungry and overwhelmed with personal trauma and inner turmoil. It was (and continues to be) an environment where drive-bys, drug use, gang violence, homelessness, and poverty are an everyday reality. Similar to all of the inner-city schools where I've taught, the real challenge was found in working to earn students' respect, build genuine relationships, and create an environment of trust, respect, and rapport.

As a light-skinned Colombian, I had learned early in my career that I had to work hard to show my students and their parents that I was not just another "poverty pimp"; I was there because I genuinely cared about their community and was authentic in my desire to be a part of a movement to create regular opportunities for my students to wrestle with and take action around topics and themes involving social justice and civic engagement. My goal was to create a classroom environment that resembled a think-tank or creative studio, where students felt supported in their efforts to invent and construct knowledge rather than uncover it. I was working to lead my students to be and become critically conscious, active in voicing their concerns, and relentless in working to create positive change in their school and community.

During my first three years, my hiring principal had supported me in my attempts to teach, learn, and create meaning and understanding with my students. He trusted me. He trusted our team. However, when he left, everything changed. Just as the new principal quietly failed to create connections with members of the community, the AUSL board openly disregarded the importance of creating a context where students had an opportunity to develop an awareness of themselves as agents of social change. It just wasn't part of their process. It didn't translate well into the test-driven environment they were working to establish, and this became a major point of contention between the management group and me. It was at this point that I found myself practicing what I taught and began directly challenging and questioning the methods our new administration chose to employ.

Directly after my hiring principal left, I began to speak out against the new administration's initiatives to push excessive test prep that took the place of afterschool extracurricular activities, half-day electives (classes that students had created and voted for), and regularly scheduled art and music classes. I also called the administration out on their secret curriculum meetings with select AUSL-trained teachers instead of with a group of both AUSL and regular Chicago Public School teachers. As violence from the neighborhood spilled onto our school grounds, I called for a heightened awareness from administrators in relaying important information about issues the community had been facing that directly affected students, staff, and teachers. And when my colleagues and I voted against additional professional development revolving around test-taking strategies for the upcoming state test, the AUSL board personally came to our school to intimidate teachers until they held an unprecedented second vote to pass it. I spoke out then, too.

During this second vote, I wondered aloud what had happened to schools as venues for independent thought, disagreement, dialogue, and debate. I asked those around me what had happened to schools as hubs for issues involving cultural democracy. We all knew the answer, even though no answers were shared. At this particular school, we all felt the pressure to teach to the test coming from our administration and the board, but we knew teachers and students needed more than what was expected and provided by AUSL (more opportunities to engage our students in social-emotional learning, to dialogue around issues affecting our school and community, to contextualize the curriculum, to deal with discipline using restorative practices . . .), but we were a school on academic probation, and no one from the administration seemed to care about anything beyond the numbers.

As the year went on, I continued to protest in small ways during meetings and discussions with teachers and administrators. I also wrote an open, schoolwide letter to my colleagues and school leaders after sitting through yet another infuriating data-driven team (shaming) meeting. The principal responded by publicly denying that my frustrations had merit, and wanted to follow up with a one-on-one discussion to go over my concerns, after suggesting (again publicly) that this school might not be the right fit for me. Though that never happened, what did follow were new rounds of daily classroom visits for the next three months. Each time the principal visited my classroom, he furiously scribbled away in his notebook, yet not once did he initiate a conversation about what he observed. Never did he impart advice, offer constructive criticism, or describe his motivations, even after I had asked him to engage in multiple debriefing sessions.

During one visit, the new principal was accompanied by AUSL's now famous *fake* "PhD," who had come down to observe me in action.[80] The principal did his normal rounds, walking and talking with students, and then began writing in his notebook in the corner of the room. The "Doctor"—who was also the director of curriculum and instruction—spoke with one student for less than a minute, and then pulled up a chair and turned his back to me and my class. He sat there for twenty minutes, staring plainly at one of my bookshelves. Arms folded and leaning back comfortably, the "Doctor" did not move from his seat. As I conferenced with students, I had him in the corner of my eye, hoping to see him turn around to witness the learning and the creating of meaning in which my students were engaged. He never turned around; he didn't waver.

The activity in which my students were engaged was that of constructing dialogue poems about the gentrification that was currently happening in Englewood (a South Side neighborhood in Chicago). They were following an outline using research they had compiled the previous week and were in the throes of inquiry and construction. This was my toughest fifth-grade class (academically and behaviorally). On this day, however, my students were fully engaged, excited, and working with a productive buzz. Critical dialogue, investigation, and writing were all well underway—and continued—as the uninterested director of curriculum and instruction sat in the corner with his back to my class. I had never been so disrespected in my short time as a teacher. The "Doctor's" message to me was loud and clear: he didn't care for me, my methodology, or the critical pedagogy I employed.

As I sat in the back of the room, facilitating one-on-one writing conferences, listening to my students' concerns, leading them to brainstorm ways to iron out the wrinkles in their drafted poems, I wondered, *how are my students interpreting the director's behavior?* After twenty minutes, the principal finished his notes and then tapped the director (who was still staring at the wall) on the shoulder. They both exited as quietly as they had come in. When the door closed behind them, I took a deep breath and continued on with the lesson, silently incensed.

The unannounced observations continued, and the principal's intimidation tactics were wearing down my psyche. It was around this time that I went to a Saturday workshop set up by CORE (Caucus of Rank and File Educators) and found out that I was not alone in my frustration. Just being among colleagues who believed in the kind of education I fought for daily was rejuvenating and reassuring. I can't tell you how many times I would be one of two people standing up at our weekly meetings expressing my opinions and concerns about certain issues and having little to no support from my colleagues. Afterward though, when our weekly meetings were adjourned, there would oftentimes be a small stream of teachers coming into my room agreeing with my points and commending me for having the courage to stand up and say something. My colleagues didn't want to risk their position at a time when teachers were being laid off and "pink-slipped" by the hundreds (thirteen hundred teachers and five hundred PSRPs [paraprofessionals and school-related personnel] were issued pink slips at CPS during the summer of 2010). I didn't blame them. It was a nerve-wracking time. However, for me, this was an issue worth fighting. We were nearing the end of the 2010–2011 school year, and dismissal slips were already rumored to have been sent to our home mailboxes. Surprise visits continued throughout the school, and the principal and his administrative staff had already made it clear (written and verbally) that if you didn't like the new test-driven environment that AUSL was creating, you needed to look elsewhere for a job.

At the Saturday workshop sponsored by CORE, we went around the room and introduced ourselves. As I listened to teachers share their names and the schools from where they came, the sheer number of teachers attending this workshop that were currently employed by AUSL took me aback. The title of the workshop: How to Deal with an Abusive Principal. Right then I knew that this issue, this fight, was bigger than me. After the workshop, I had a renewed sense of confidence that helped me to be proactive in combating my principal's intimidation tactics. Instead of dreading seeing my principal in the hallway, I began urging him to sit down with me and share his observations every chance I saw him. My persistence finally wore him down, and he agreed to have a conference with me. One conference—after what had to amount to over fifty unannounced visits (at least one visit per day, per week).

In the meeting that followed, my principal declared that he felt my classroom management seemed to be an issue. I asked him for suggestions as to how to manage the class better. He responded by saying that I should talk to one of my colleagues about it. I responded by saying that I would do that, but again I asked him if there was any advice he could give me *right now*. He offered the idea of stopping class to call home on my cell phone. He also directed me to go to the resource room and look up some behavior management resources. When I prodded him for more practical ideas, he became flustered and stated that he was not prepared to talk about this right now. I continued the conversation by asking him what other trends he noticed and what I could do to, in his opinion, improve my craft. He stated that many times when he observed my class he noticed that I did not have 100 percent of my students' attention 100 percent of the time. I asked him for some ideas about how to maintain 100 percent attention 100 percent of the time, to which he responded, "I'll get back to you with some ideas" (he never did). He also stated that the work the kids were doing did not meet his expectations, and that I needed to scaffold my lessons better. When I asked him for some suggestions as to how to do that, he said he would think about it and get back to me (he never did). I asked him if he would come into my classroom and model some of the things that he was asking me to do, and after an uncomfortable pause, he agreed. He said he would get back to me with a date (you guessed it, he never did). Coincidentally, he didn't observe me that last month unannounced. The last time he came into my classroom was in mid-April for my second—and final—official observation.

That last year with AUSL, I was conscientious in leading my students to build and refine their skills in critical thinking, close reading, narrative and expository writing, and speaking and listening. Some of the projects my students engaged in that year included running a full trial of Christopher Columbus and his Spanish soldiers, a Haymarket Riot role-playing, a poetry slam dealing with themes surrounding social justice, and the writing of epistle poems surrounding Martin Luther King Jr.'s march through Chicago. They explored and recreated the Wisconsin Uprising (mock protests) and created digital stories to support our attempts at engaging in participatory action research.

These were the projects that were on my mind when I went into my last evaluation of the year, hoping that some of the discussion would revolve around the important work my students had accomplished. When I walked into his office, the principal and assistant principal showed me the Danielson Performance Rubric and asked me to rate myself. I rated myself as proficient in most categories and distinguished in two. I supported the distinguished ratings with specific examples, activities, and situations throughout the year. After hearing me out, the principal and assistant principal then handed me a Danielson Teacher Profile sheet with four "grades" already on them. The grades totaled three B minuses (which translated to below basic) and one unsatisfactory. It felt like a sucker punch. They proceeded to tell me that I was rated—on the whole—as a below basic teacher.

When I asked how they came to this conclusion, they cited a number of low grades my students had earned during the first quarter of the year, the lack of "professional posters" on my wall, a disorganized classroom, and a chaotic setting. I argued with them about the fine line between absolute chaos versus the organized chaos stemming from the many creative environmental and social justice inquiry and project-based lessons I engaged my students in throughout the year. They responded by saying there were more levels to this rubric than what was shown in front of me, and that was how they ultimately came up with my rating. I asked them to explain this process further, wondering aloud that if there were more levels, details, and descriptions accompanying this particular rubric, then why were they fitting me into such a narrow box? They hurriedly stated this was the form they were using for all teachers, and pushed to move the conversation forward.

I couldn't move forward. I responded by telling them that this evaluation felt like a set-up. That their labeling me with a "below basic" rating—at the end of the year—had nothing to do with constructive criticism or any genuine attempt to lend assistance in helping me improve my craft. Even if the rating were true, not once during the year had they pulled me aside to discuss any of their concerns. Not once had they offered me support, mentoring, or even a chance to engage in a dialogue or give feedback on what the principal had been so diligently taking notes on for months. There had been no presented opportunities for me (or for my colleagues) to engage in critical, meaningful professional development sessions that didn't deal with

ISAT test prep or NWEA-test readiness. Instead, all that had been offered were scripted test-prep templates and endless staff meetings around the Danielson Framework and how to interpret the AUSL checklists concerning compliance, data accumulation, and the use of prepackaged lessons. There had been no opportunities to grow or improve in our style or craft, or to increase our knowledge and understanding of social-emotional learning or the content of the subjects we taught daily.

I continued to defend my position by stating that this particular school had become a place where educators couldn't grow. It almost seemed that they had purposely let problems and struggles continue within our ranks, especially with CPS teachers, by purposefully withholding notes, suggestions, and meetings so that we would "fail" according to their rubric. That way, I reasoned, they could recommend that we not return and could instead fill those spots with new, young, inexperienced AUSL-trained teachers.

It was at this point that I asked them both, as educators, *as professionals*—having seen me in action for the past four years (previously an AUSL executive, the principal had been around us for a couple of years as an advisor to the administration before entering the role of principal); having witnessed all my students' various accomplishments throughout my time at this school (including, but not limited to leading a teach-in around "living green," writing letters to the aldermen around obtaining an empty lot for a community garden, running a food/clothes/toy drive for the homeless, engaging in a critical literacy project around human rights, voicing concerns publicly about the relentless violence in the community . . .), my talking with students personally about what they were learning, with parents about what their kids were bringing home and discussing, *in addition to* my having raised my students' standardized test scores over the 2007–2010 school years in *all* the subjects I taught—"Can you honestly, professionally rate me as a below basic teacher?" They both said, almost robotically and in sync, "Yes. According to this, the Danielson Rubric, you are a below basic teacher."

I sat there dumbfounded. It was at this time that the principal waved his hand toward the door, not even meeting my gaze, indicating the meeting was over. I stood up slowly and stated that I didn't agree with their evaluation and their ratings, and that I would not sign this unfair and biased evaluation. As I write this and I think back to this day, in my fourteen years as an educator I had never felt so disrespected, disillusioned, and unappreciated.

Teaching is hard enough without being overtly disrespected, bullied, intimidated, and directed to teach scripted lessons on a regular basis. I've learned a lot from my experience with AUSL. I've learned that we need more teachers willing to share their love for learning, willing to infuse and create lessons dealing with civic engagement, willing to lead students to rethink and reevaluate history as well as our present place in society versus accepting and pushing rote teaching of fragmented skills. Teachers who adhere to, advocate for, and practice a critical pedagogy believe in leading their students to create knowledge and engage in creative processes, critical thought, and the understanding and challenge of power dynamics. To do all of this while fulfilling the multiple roles that teachers are tasked with every day, especially under the direction of an abusive administration who thinks that school improvement is solely tied to standardized test preparation, feels nearly impossible. And yet, there are teachers who are in schools like this across Chicago—across the country—who not only deal with, endure, and overcome abusive administrators, but create and experience significant small wins with their students regularly, despite the adversity they face daily from the leaders of their school.

It's time to rethink AUSL and all nonprofit and profit private contractors that emphasize rote learning, scripted lessons, and excessive test prep and that refuse to provide teachers with professional development that highlights the studying and implementation of research-based best practices, social-emotional learning, and restorative methods. I mean, really, when has positive and meaningful change ever been a result of abusive practices that highlight and encourage the deskilling and disempowering of critical educators?

Timothy Bernier is a veteran teacher of twelve years in Chicago, teaching at the middle and high school level. Timothy earned a master's degree in elementary education from Roosevelt University, he holds a Type 03 teaching certificate, and he is currently in his second year as an induction coach with New Teacher Center Chicago.

From Whittier to Greenleaf

A Community-Based Transformation Story

LIZ SULLIVAN

Before I became a teacher, I was an organizer with the United Farm Work-ers. Organizing and teaching seemed separate to me until Oakland's new small-school reform began. Then my knowledge of both worlds positioned me to participate in a unique way during a remarkable period of growth and creativity in Oakland schools. In 1999, I left the classroom and became an organizer with Oakland Community Organizations (OCO), an Alinsky-style grassroots group that connected families with reform-minded edu-cators. OCO partnered with the Bay Area Coalition of Equitable Schools (BayCES—now called the National Equity Project) and with the Oakland Unified School District (OUSD) to create forty-seven new public schools. During the same period, thirty-three charter schools opened in Oakland. The pressure from charter schools spurred the district to undertake serious reform by creating its own new schools.

Greenleaf Elementary School is one of Oakland's success stories, but the journey of transformation was long and hard.[81] In 1999, Greenleaf was Whittier Elementary, one of dozens of schools that languished in the poorest neighborhoods of Oakland. Reforms had come and gone. Con-troversies over curriculum had erupted and blown over. Whittier endured. The school was located just above International Boulevard, a scruffy, tree-less thoroughfare filled with car repair shops, nail salons, tattoo parlors, wash houses, liquor stores, and Mexican markets run by immigrants from Yemen. Pastel bungalows with bars on the windows dotted the avenues. Rose bushes peeked through chain-link fences, while pit bulls barked at passersby. Two blocks to the east sat the housing projects that had given birth to a notorious drug gang, the 69 Mob. One block to the west stood an old church building that once housed the Black Panther Party's community school and was now the home of the Acts Full Gospel Christian Academy. The building's history gave eloquent testimony to the community's desire for a school that would match its aspirations.

The backyard of a drug house abutted the Whittier playground, and St. Bernard's Catholic Church was located directly across the street. That was how OCO got involved with Whittier—through the St. Bernard's local organizing committee. Parents were concerned about crime and drug dealing near the school, and they came to the organizing committee to do something about it. The school was facing other problems, as well. At the time, California ranked its schools in two ways: the Academic Performance Index (API) compared each school to a standard measured by the state test, and a "similar schools" score compared each school to a set of one hundred schools serving children from similar socioeconomic backgrounds. The API ran from 200 to 1000, with 800 being the goal. In 1999, Whittier's score was 360, roughly what a school would get for students putting their names on the test. It had the lowest possible similar schools rank, a "1," and in fact Whittier was the lowest performing school among its cohort of one hundred similar schools. Whittier was, quite literally, one of the worst schools in the state.

Matt Hammer was an organizer at OCO who wanted to address the larger issues the school was facing head on. He tried to understand what was happening at Whittier by getting to know the people involved. He adhered to a community-organizing principle: those closest to the problem should be part of the solution. Matt got to know the new principal, a thoughtful woman who was building strong relationships with families. She wanted to change the school, and she saw Matt as a potential ally. Matt talked with parents, being careful to engage both Latinx and African American families. Whittier was located in a neighborhood that had once been overwhelmingly Black and now was becoming more and more Latinx. He used the state test score data as a tool for agitation, asking parents why they thought the scores were so low. No one had an answer.

When Matt showed me the data, I was disturbed, not by the low scores, but by the fact that Matt put such stock in standardized tests. I saw the test as a tool of oppression: it was designed to confer advantage on those who already enjoyed it. Since our country has a legacy of racism, this meant that middle-class white kids usually scored well on the test, and low-income children of color usually scored poorly. But Matt saw the test in exactly the opposite way: it was a tool for liberation. The test allowed parents to hold schools and districts accountable because it revealed the systemic inequities between education for the rich and education for the poor, between schools for middle-class white children and schools for low-income children of color.

One of the Whittier parents to whom Matt showed the standardized test scores was a retired navy man who had adopted a daughter late in life. He was an elder raising a young child. This situation was not uncommon in East Oakland. I met Jim at a meeting in the OCO office at the Eastmont Mall. He spoke with the gentle drawl of his native Alabama and told stories with a wry, self-deprecating sense of humor. Jim had dropped out of school in seventh grade during the Great Depression, and his unfinished education haunted him, despite a successful career in the navy. When he retired from the military, Jim took the extraordinary step of returning to school. He enrolled at Mission High in San Francisco and graduated thirty-three years after dropping out. Eventually he received a bachelor's degree in management from Cal State East Bay. Jim was an active and involved Whittier parent, as committed to his young daughter's education as he had been to his own. A premise that OCO adheres to is that parents must be treated as full partners in their children's education. There is a tendency for educators to dismiss families from low-income neighborhoods and to see people like Jim as exceptions to the rule, but I have found through my organizing experience that every family has something positive to contribute to their child's education.

Matt continued to talk with Whittier families, getting to know more and more people, but he struggled to find an analysis of what was going wrong, a lever that would allow parents to truly transform the school instead of reacting to symptoms like dirty bathrooms, fights on the playground, and unfilled teaching positions. Then a teacher from another school gave Matt a book by Deborah Meier called *The Power of Their Ideas*. Meier made a passionate argument for the school as a community of learners and for relationships as the building blocks of success. She critiqued America's factory model of education in which knowledge is stamped into children as they move from one grade to the next, like parts on an assembly line. For Meier, school size mattered because it impacted the quality of relationships. Big schools tended to be anonymous. Children could fall through the cracks, and ineffective teachers could hide. But small schools lent themselves to the creation of community: it was possible for the principal to know every child by name and for school staff to know children's families. It was possible for teachers to collaborate across grade levels and subject areas. In a small school, everyone's work was public.

OCO persuaded School Board President Robert Spencer to sponsor a trip to New York so that Oaklanders could see Deborah Meier's schools, and some other new schools, firsthand. More than a dozen people headed to the Big Apple, including Jim and the Whittier principal. I went as well, and the trip to New York changed my life—it helped me decide to leave the classroom and return to organizing. When I saw the vibrant, rigorous, safe schools in East Harlem and the South Bronx, I realized that we had settled for utter mediocrity in California. I also saw firsthand the power of creating a school that had internal unity around a clear vision. This meant an end to central office mandates for one-size-fits-all instruction, and it also meant an end to classrooms as personal fiefdoms in which teachers individually decided what instructional approach they preferred. Knowing that it was possible to create such high-caliber schools in low-income neighborhoods, I felt morally compelled to do so.

As OCO began to push for more small schools like we had seen in New York, Dennis Chaconas became superintendent in the spring of 2000. He had grown up in a working-class neighborhood not far from Whittier, and had gone all the way through Oakland public schools, graduating from Fremont High. He spent most of his career as an educator in Oakland schools. Dennis loved the idea of creating new schools, both as a way to fight the overcrowding that was rampant in East Oakland and as a way to create models of excellence. With his full support, the school board approved a new, small, autonomous schools policy that allowed for the creation of ten new schools over a three-year period. The idea caught fire in the Fruitvale district, which was ground zero for crowded schools. But during this period, the only reform to touch Whittier was a scripted phonics program called Open Court Reading. Chaconas saw Open Court as a temporary measure "to stabilize the patient" rather than a long-term answer for Oakland's literacy woes. With Open Court, Whittier's test scores inched upward. Now it ranked ninety-seventh among its cohort of one hundred similar schools.

The average tenure of an urban superintendent is about two and a half years, and the clock was ticking for Dennis Chaconas. A large deficit was discovered in the budget, and in June of 2003 the state took over the school district. Dr. Randolph Ward became Oakland's state administrator. The idea of small-school reform took on a different form under state administration: new school creation would be a remedy for low performance rather than a solution to overcrowding. One of the small-school principals, Hae Sin Thomas, became the director of New School Development and put together an in-district incubator to create new schools. She was careful to embed the value of family and community partnerships into the DNA of the incubator.

It would have been natural for Whittier to enter the incubator and be redesigned as a district school, given its dismal performance on the state test, but that was not to happen without a fight. I remember the afternoon I found out that the state administrator was trying to turn Whittier into a charter school. My boss, Ron Snyder, told me that he had just received a phone call from the special assistant to the state administrator. She was faxing over a document for us to look at. It was going to be publicly released in three days. My boss was a tall middle-aged man, a former Jesuit with salt and pepper hair and a mustache that he twisted when he got nervous. The fax came through and we pored over the document together. It said that thirteen Oakland elementary schools were being put out to bid in a "request for proposals" (RFP) process. Anyone who had a good idea for how to fix one or all of the schools could submit a proposal to take them over—a university, an educational entity, or a charter operator.

Ron called the special assistant, put her on speakerphone, and we began to ask questions. She seemed irritated, as if the merit of the idea was obvious and we were a little slow.

"Why are you putting these schools out to bid? Why not incubate them as new schools within the district?" I asked.

"The incubator is too full," she said. "The middle schools are there. If we add thirteen elementary schools, it will push the incubator beyond its capacity."

"What's the timeline for the RFP?" my boss asked.

"The proposals are due in three weeks." I shot a look of disbelief to Ron. Who could write a decent proposal to redesign a school in just three weeks? The district's own incubation process took two full years.

"How are families going to be involved in the RFP?" I asked.

"We are putting the RFP up on the website where everyone can read it," the special assistant responded.

"But most of the families don't have computers or Internet access," I objected.

"You can print the RFP and go over it with them," she said curtly.

The phone call ended on that sour note, and Ron and I sat for a few moments in stunned silence.

"What the f...?" I finally said. "Why are they doing this? They know that three weeks isn't enough time. This doesn't make any sense."

"Yeah," my boss agreed. "Something's going on. There's more to this." We started calling school board members to see what they knew, and the true story quickly emerged. The state administrator had convinced a Silicon Valley nonprofit called the New Schools Venture Fund to bankroll the creation of a charter management organization (CMO) run by a top district administrator. The CMO was called Education for Change, and it would break off from the district. The RFP was an act of political theater, to make it seem like there was an open process and that anyone could bid to take over the schools. When all the crappy proposals thrown together in just three weeks had been submitted and reviewed, Education for Change would emerge as the superior choice. But OCO believed that parent and community partnership was critical to successful reform, and there had been no public discussion of turning a chunk of the district into a charter network. The people closest to the problem, the families, had not been consulted at all.

"These are our schools," I told Ron. "These are the big overcrowded elementary schools that gave birth to the new small-schools movement—Jefferson, Hawthorne, and Whittier are on this list."

"Yep," he agreed, "and lots of the families belong to our member congregations."

"We can't let them do this, Ron. We have to fight."

Ron twisted his mustache and furrowed his brow. Thoughts flickered in his eyes like clouds crossing the sun. We hadn't challenged the state administrator because we didn't have enough power. Dr. Ward was accountable only to the state superintendent of public instruction, Jack O'Connell, who was accountable to the statewide electorate. We were a teeny tiny frog in an ocean-sized pond. Fighting would mean dropping the work we were doing in the new small schools we had just opened—schools like Ascend, International Community School, Life Academy, and Think College Now. Finally Ron said, "Liz, let's find out what the families think."

OCO had not been active in Whittier for a couple of years, and there was a new principal. But since many Whittier families attended St. Bernard's, it was not difficult to reconnect with parents. Peter Haberfeld, a former California Teachers Association organizer and a friend of mine from the United Farm Workers, now worked for OCO. Peter's organizing roots went back to voter registration in Mississippi during the Civil Rights Movement. He started talking to families, and found that Whittier parents wanted to have a say in the fate of their children's school. OCO took the position that the thirteen schools should have the option of staying within the district, and that families should decide whether their school would join Education for Change or be redesigned in the district incubator.

But the state administrator pushed ahead with his plan to charterize the schools. According to California charter law in 2005, only tenured teachers could convert a public school into a charter. The person tapped to run Education for Change was the supervisor of the thirteen principals whose schools were now being offered up in the bidding process. He persuaded the principals to support the charter, telling them that they would keep their jobs. The principals then set about recruiting teachers to sign the charter petition using the same pitch: everyone would keep their jobs. The implied threat was reconstitution, a consequence offered by No Child Left Behind in which all or most of a school's staff is replaced. OCO organizers spent as much time talking with teachers as with parents, helping them understand their rights.

Very few Whittier teachers signed the charter school petition, so the state administrator decided that he would reconstitute the school. His plan couldn't move forward, though, because the Whittier principal had not done observations and evaluations of any of the teachers. So the district sent in a tough veteran administrator to do the job. She formally observed all untenured teachers. Based on her observations and subsequent evaluations, many Whittier teachers were fired. One of the teachers was from the community. With great sacrifice, she had worked her way up from the position of teacher's aide. The district had conducted an early version of a value-added calculation, trying to figure out which teachers were really moving the kids in Oakland. This teacher came out as a strong performer. But for some reason, she didn't get a good evaluation from the woman doing Whittier's observations and evaluations. She was "non-re-elected," which is legalese for the dismissal of untenured teachers. Whittier parents were furious about her firing, but there was nothing that could be done to prevent it.

Of the thirteen schools put out to bid, two joined Education for Change, and three were admitted to the incubator. Before the school year ended, OCO held a large public meeting at St. Bernard's and the state administrator came. We asked that the incubator be an option for the remaining eight schools and that parents be allowed to decide if their school should become a charter or enter the incubator. The state administrator agreed, and he also accepted our invitation to meet personally with the parents in each of the remaining schools before the end of June. We hit a reset button, and this time flatlands families would be treated as partners in their children's education, just like parents in the hills.

A new principal was assigned to Whittier, Monica Thomas. She was a young woman originally from Ukiah who had been vetted through a community selection process run by Hae Sin Thomas and her New School Development team. At first Monica was leery that OCO would try to undermine her authority. Peter, with the help of a small organizing team, coaxed disillusioned parents to suspend disbelief long enough to make a strong impression on the new principal. Monica was delighted when she realized how perceptive and earnest the parent leaders were about improving the school. She listened to the parents' concerns and proposed a course of action: "I'm glad you're bringing up these problems, but, please, also bring solutions. I need your good ideas." She divided a sheet of chart paper down the middle. On one side she listed all the problems, and on the other side she asked parents to brainstorm solutions. Before the meeting ended, they agreed on two or three solutions to try in the coming week. When they met again, Monica checked to see if parents thought the solution had worked. If so, that problem was crossed off the list. If the solution had not worked, the parents brainstormed a better solution. This continued week after week, until all of the complaints had been crossed off the list and Monica had won the parents' trust.

Meanwhile, a district administrator met with families to discuss the fate of Whittier—should it become a charter or should it be incubated within the district? Peter took parents to visit Ascend, one of the new district schools in the Fruitvale neighborhood. The head of Education for Change was invited to make a presentation to parents, but he declined. The Whittier parents voted to enter the incubator, and the state administrator accepted their recommendation.

Monica put together a design team that included parents, key teacher leaders, and the community outreach coordinator, Rodolfo Perez. They began to meet weekly. Since parents had been so angered by arbitrary teacher firings the previous year, the team spent a lot of time talking about what good instruction looks like. They watched videotapes of master teachers; they went into classrooms to observe instruction; and they reflected on what they saw. Gradually the team constructed a vision of the kind of teaching they wanted: an inquiry-based approach with integrated thematic instruction. One of the design team leaders was a veteran Whittier teacher who had become an English language development coach. Because this respected veteran was part of the design team, their work was taken seriously by the whole staff. The proposal was submitted to the state administrator and to the board of education. The state administrator approved the proposal, and Greenleaf was born. Whittier teachers who wanted to teach at Greenleaf had to reapply for their jobs, and parents participated in the teacher interviews. Some Whittier teachers were hired for Greenleaf and some were not, but this time parents understood why.

Greenleaf opened in 2007 and grew gradually, starting with grades K–2 and then adding a grade each year until finally Whittier graduated its last class. Monica was principal of both the new school and the old school during the transition period, and test scores in both schools increased under her leadership. When Greenleaf came fully into its own, student achievement began to rise dramatically. The school was so successful that the district allowed it to add a middle school. In 2013, the last year for which state test results are available, Greenleaf scored 818 on the API and had a similar schools rank of 8. Parent volunteers proudly wear school t-shirts, photos of every student adorn the leaves of a tree painted in the entryway, and the quiet buzz of student conversation spills out into the hallways. Greenleaf is still a neighborhood school, serving the families who live on the avenues that cross International Boulevard. The student population has gotten poorer, and more Latinx over time. One of the things that I love about Greenleaf is that its name evokes a legacy as well as hope for the future. John Whittier was an abolitionist poet, and his middle name was Greenleaf. The school's website notes that John Greenleaf Whittier was dedicated to "social justice, creativity and scholasticism." I still work with families in Oakland public schools, and my focus is still school transformation. But now, instead of taking parents to New York or Los Angeles to see a really good school serving low-income children of color, I take them to Greenleaf.

Liz Sullivan is the director of Community Engagement for the Oakland Unified School District. She is a teacher and community organizer who has worked with district and charter schools in Oakland to support family leadership development since 1999. For twelve years, Liz directed education organizing for Oakland Community Organizations (OCO) and played a major role in Oakland's small-school reform. She has consulted with nonprofit organizations that work with parents, including the East Bay Asian Youth Center and Great Oakland Public Schools, and helped the Education for Change Charter Network develop a democratic governance model that involves families as full partners. She was the cofounder of a neighborhood Montessori preschool and then taught bilingual kindergarten for eleven years in the Hayward Unified School District prior to joining the OCO staff. Her first job was organizing farm workers for the United Farm Workers (UFW) in the late 1970s.

CHAPTER 5

EQUITY

From Here to Educational Justice

A better education system is often presented as the best hope our country has to create a more equitable society. This has been articulated by President Barack Obama and others, who extol "that most American of ideas, that with the right education, a child of any race, any station, can overcome whatever barriers stand in their way and fulfill their God-given potential."[1] And President George W. Bush used this message regularly in speeches about No Child Left Behind. "We must work as a society to extend the American Dream to *todos* – to everybody," he said in 2001.[2] Thus far, the public education system has not been up to the task, particularly for our country's most marginalized students.[3]

As we move into the next era of school reform under the Every Student Succeeds Act, the education of these students will become even more squarely the central concern of public schools, because they have literally become the majority of students we serve. Low-income students now make up 51 percent of the public school population,[4] and students of color outnumber white students in public school enrollment as well.[5] In 2014, immigrant children, those who either came from another country or have at least one immigrant parent, represented 25 percent of all children in the United States.[6] Looking ahead to 2023, the most recent projections show the number of kids who are Latinx, Asian, or have parents of two or more races will continue to grow.[7]

There's a lot of ground to make up before the United States can claim that we are justly educating these students. The differences in educational attainment between white students and students of color, rich and poor students, students with disabilities and general education students, and English language learners and native English speakers show up in a variety of school-related outcomes, including but not limited to test scores,[8] grade promotion,[9] placement in gifted and talented programs,[10] access to advanced coursework,[11] engagement with quality curriculum that demands higher-order thinking,[12] high school graduation and dropout rates,[13] college readiness,[14] college access,[15] and college graduation rates.[16]

In theory, the No Child Left Behind Act of 2001 (NCLB) was all about correcting these achievement gaps, in large part because it required states to track the performance of "subgroups" instead of looking at all students together. Armed with data from this law showing differences in achievement by race and class, members of the education reform movement have justified their policies through the rhetoric of the Civil Rights Movement and a stated goal of achieving "equity." They claim that measuring student learning, teacher effectiveness, and school success with test scores ensures a minimum level of quality, and if all children have access to a quality education that prepares them for a college or career of their choice, then the promise of public education will be fulfilled.

But setting and enforcing minimum standards will never produce the equal playing field presupposed by the American Dream. Working for true equity demands a long view, looking back to acknowledge and openly discuss an often unjust history and respond to its effects, particularly when it comes to resource distribution. It takes rooting out bias and discrimination from our policies and institutions or creating new ones based in real inclusion. It also means urgently working with schools in the system that exists now to remove barriers to access, opportunity, and achievement.

Parents and communities, organizers and activists, civil rights groups, educators, and researchers have tried to realign the equity conversation along these lines, pushing for a shift in language from the achievement gap to the opportunity gap. In the process, they have called out contexts, policies and practices that have been overlooked by the mainstream education reform movement, including many of the out-of-school and in-school factors detailed below. [17] By its very nature, the discussion of how to achieve educational equity is expansive. It won't be solved through any of the singular issues explained here; however, they provide a good starting place to move the United States towards educational justice.

OUT-OF-SCHOOL FACTORS

Poverty and Racism

Officially, a household is defined as being in poverty if its annual income is below $23,624 for a family of four. Even with that incredibly low bar, a full 20 percent of American children qualify as living in poverty, and almost 39 percent will experience poverty for at least one year before they turn eighteen.[18] Sixty-five percent of Black children, 62 percent of Native American children and 62 percent of Latinx children qualify as low-income or poor.[19] These are astounding numbers, particularly when we begin to understand the role that poverty plays in academic achievement, health, and life outcomes.

Parents who have more money can provide more enrichment and resources for their children, creating learning opportunities during out-of-school time. But often the effects of poverty hit on an even more basic level. Three-quarters of public school teachers see students come to school hungry on a regular basis, and 81 percent of teachers report that this happens at least once a week.[20] If there isn't affordable housing available, or if someone loses their job because low-income work is more likely to be temporary and families have to move, then students have to change schools. The resulting mobility brings down their achievement and contributes to steady rates of student turnover that negatively affect even those students who stay.[21] Families living in poverty also deal with more threats to their children's safety. In a Pew Research Center survey in 2015, 55 percent of lower-income parents reported worrying about their children being attacked, and 47 percent worried their children might be shot.[22]

Increasing numbers of studies also show the detrimental effects of poverty on health, from obvious environmental factors such as lead poisoning, air pollution, and less access to quality pediatric care or healthy food to more insidious factors like the crippling effects of stress on the body and brain.[23] Researchers have discovered a direct link between poverty and the development of brain structure, particularly in areas of the brain related to language, reading, executive function, and spatial skills.[24] In a review of much of the related research, the American Academy of Pediatrics concluded that toxic stress caused by poverty and discrimination can lead to long-term physical and mental health problems, impair the brain's ability to develop coping mechanisms or to learn new skills, and permanently modify a person's DNA.[25] And because of the link between race, income, and wealth, all of this disproportionately affects children of color.

For the most part, schools don't have the capacity to push students beyond these systemic obstacles in ways that fundamentally transform their life outcomes, but they are one of the few places remaining that even tries. In the past decade, poverty in the United States has increased,[26] while the availability of comprehensive public services to support struggling families has decreased. Large cuts to social services and programs were made after the 2008 recession at the state and local levels, many of which have not been restored.[27]

Drawing attention to these challenges for students and schools is often lambasted by education reformers. By bringing up the effects of racism and poverty, "too many educators have simply given in and given up," as former Education Trust Vice President Amy Wilkins wrote, "and in so doing they have surrendered their students to a dim future at the cold and lonely margins of our economic and cultural mainstream."[28] For this group of reformers, "education does not get fixed by beating one's chest over race and income," Jeanne Allen, founder of the Center for Education Reform, wrote in 2016. "Education advances for the downtrodden when we provide for the creation of great new schools—and from the competition that ensues as a result."[29]

While there is ample research suggesting that schools will never be able to completely solve these systemic problems on their own,[30] schools, districts, and states have developed programs that create additional opportunities for young people and their families. Doing this work within a school framework can include guaranteeing high-quality early childhood education,[31] expanding the community schools model, offering wraparound services,[32] and adding staff to support specific and labor-intensive problems like absenteeism.[33] Many of these options have been embraced by all kinds of schools, including some charter schools, and were included as strategies for school improvement under the Every Student Succeeds Act (ESSA), hopefully signaling that these resources will move into schools across districts in a comprehensive, rather than piecemeal, way.

Funding

What would it take to fund schools well enough so they could provide all students with what they need in order to achieve academically? Sadly, this is not considered a relevant question by most policy makers. State and federal legislatures do not look at the standards that they want students to achieve and compute the resources it would take to get kids to reach them. They do not wrestle with the true cost of what research shows is required to promote high achievement for special education and English language learners, nor do they quantify the additional services required for students living in poverty.[34] When the question has been presented about what states should be required to spend in order to provide, at the very least, an "adequate" education, states have responded by denying responsibility for anything beyond the most basic requirements for student learning. During a school funding case brought against the state of New York, then Governor George Pataki and the state's lawyers claimed that an adequate education only meant the opportunity to learn through the eighth grade.[35] More recently, lawyers for the state of Pennsylvania argued that their obligation under the state constitution was only to keep public schools open.[36]

Instead of figuring out what's actually needed by schools, state governments rely on funding formulas that begin with a percentage of the budget that feels amenable to legislators to devote to education for the year. Based on that number, they assign a dollar amount for each student. Some states use a weighted formula that gives additional funding for special education students, English language learners, or students living in poverty, though many don't. Fourteen states actually provide *less* funding to districts with higher concentrations of low-income students, and eighteen states provide little to no additional money to districts serving low-income students.[37] Add to that inadequate foundation the vastly different amounts of money raised through local taxes, including property taxes where higher-value homes clearly produce higher revenues for schools, and the gap grows further. Even within districts, because salaries are usually linked to how many years teachers have been teaching, the schools with the most experienced, best-qualified teachers—who are disproportionately in higher-income, whiter schools—receive more funding.

In 2014, 91.4 percent of all school money came from state and local governments.[38] The remaining 8.6 percent of federal funding does not close these funding gaps and occasionally widens them further. A report by *U.S. News & World Report* found that 20 percent of all Title I money—the federal funds targeted for low-income students—goes to districts that actually have a high proportion of wealthy families because of an outdated formula that doesn't account for concentration of poverty, particularly in rural areas and smaller cities. In practice, this means that a place like Nottoway County, Virginia, where more than 30 percent of students live in poverty, receives $775,000 each year from Title I funding, but Fairfax County, Virginia, a well-known wealthy suburb near Washington, DC, with an 8 percent poverty rate, receives $20 million in Title I funds.[39] Additionally, a higher percentage of Title I funding is given to states that invest more in education, meaning that wealthier states get more money because they can spend more, and poorer states get less money because they don't have money to spend.[40]

This structure of school funding across all levels of government results in a drastically unequal system. When comparing districts at the top and bottom income quintiles across the United States, districts at the bottom of that scale receive an average of $1,200 less per student. When we consider race, the schools in the quintile serving the most students of color receive an average of $2,000 less than the quintile of schools serving mostly white students.[41] The outliers on the extremes of these scales are often much worse. In Pennsylvania, for example (the state where all they feel they are obligated to do is keep the school doors open), no state funding formula exists to equalize spending between rich and poor districts, creating a range of spending of from $9,800 per student in the poorest districts to almost three times as much—$28,400 per student—in the richest districts.[42]

The city of Detroit provides a startling example of what inadequate funding means inside schools. Public education there went into a fiscal crisis after years of mismanagement by the state alongside declining student enrollment, resulting in repeated budget cuts. In 2016, teachers took to Twitter to document the crumbling of their schools' basic infrastructure and followed this with a series of "sick-outs" to draw attention to conditions that literally made them and their students sick. City inspections confirmed the presence of rodents, mold, water damage, and more —an average of fourteen violations per school visited.[43] The lack of funding has produced both teacher layoffs and teacher shortages, along with larger class sizes and a lack of basic materials like textbooks.[44] All of this has happened along the most economically segregated school district boundary in the country: Detroit's child poverty rate sits at 49 percent, while in the next district over, Grosse Pointe, just 6.5 percent of children live in poverty.[45] Grosse Pointe is also over 95 percent White and 2 percent Black, while Detroit is about 11 percent White and 83 percent Black.[46]

The national mismatch between funding and need defies common sense, not to mention a large body of research proving why schools serving disadvantaged students should get more money and how these resources can lead to improved academic achievement.[47] Comparisons between the test scores of American students and students in other countries are reported regularly as an indicator of the sorry state of our public education system. Apparently less noticeable is that the majority of the countries that we so desperately want to beat in achievement spend more per student in lower-income school districts than in higher-income ones, while the opposite remains stubbornly true in the United States.[48]

Segregation

One policy stands out as the most effective school funding redistribution plan we've ever tried: the desegregation of public schools.[49] With its near-complete erosion, it's not incredibly surprising that major inequities in how schools are funded across this country persist.

In the 1960s and 70s, years after the Supreme Court's *Brown v. Board of Education* decision has been handed down, school desegregation made progress through busing, district mergers, urban-suburban partnerships, race-based student assignments, school district rezoning, and federal litigation and sanctions, among other means. But beginning with the 1974 Supreme Court decision to end busing (*Milliken v. Bradley*), the United States essentially gave up on integration as a fundamental goal of education reform. Stripped down by decades of federal and state policies and court decisions reversing integration orders and in the absence of any coherent housing policy, desegregation policy as it exists today mostly includes voluntary city-to-suburbs transfer options and magnet schools that are supposed to attract suburban white students while holding slots for urban students of color.[50]

As a result, schools are more racially segregated now than they have been since the 1980s, and are increasingly moving in that direction.[51] From 1993 to 2011, the number of Black students attending schools whose student population was 90 percent or more Black and Latinx grew from 2.3 million to 2.9 million.[52] The Latinx student population has grown tremendously over the past four decades, while also growing increasingly segregated, particularly in the West. In 2011, 45 percent of all students enrolled in Western public schools attended schools with 90 to 100 percent students of color. White students are the most racially isolated group in the country, removed from different cultures and perspectives at a time when our country is becoming increasingly diverse.[53] These patterns have coincided with a growth in income segregation in schools over the past twenty years, miroring the widening gulf between the rich and the poor in the United States.[54]

Increased race and class segregation has resulted in an uptick in schools that are defined by both. Sixteen percent of all schools in the United States now have student populations where 75 to 100 percent of students are Black or Latinx *and* 75 to 100 percent of students are eligible for free or reduced-price lunch. There are twice as many schools with these extreme levels of "double segregation" than there were in 2001, the year NCLB was passed.[55]

The reform policies of NCLB and the Obama era have largely ignored these segregation patterns. The preferred strategy has been to try to create better schools, whether they are segregated or not, an outgrowth of reformers' belief that the power of in-school factors can overcome larger societal problems.[56] So while Race to the Top offered states additional money for creating a new teacher evaluation system or lifting the cap on charter schools, absolutely no weight was given to districts looking to create plans for integration. Meanwhile, policies such as school choice and test-based accountability actually exacerbate the problems of race- and income-based segregation, directly contributing to the growth of hypersegregated schools.[57]

Keeping schools segregated not only goes against the purported American values of diversity and inclusion, it also runs counter to established research. Segregation has been clearly tied to lower test scores and worse life outcomes for students of color, whose schools tend to have fewer resources, higher teacher turnover, less experienced and less qualified teachers, less access to creative and challenging curriculum, more exposure to narrow test-based lessons, and lower-quality learning materials and facilities.[58] Segregated schools also hurt white students, though it's not as obvious when we narrow our view of educational quality only to test scores. Plenty of research has demonstrated that the isolation of white students contributes to the development of implicit biases that disrupt learning processes, leads to oversimplified approaches to problem solving, limits exposure to multiple perspectives, and stunts the ability to work with people from diverse backgrounds.[59] Overwhelmingly, the research shows that integrated classrooms produce higher academic achievement and social and emotional benefits for *all* students.[60]

As Dr. Gloria Ladson-Billings notes, both school desegregation and funding equity are two interventions that show incredible results for students and yet have never received full implementation and testing.[61] Under ESSA, much of this remains true. The basic funding structures remain in place, and there are no additional federal funds for creating greater equity between states, districts, or schools.[62] As for integration, parts of the law offer priority in grant competitions for charter schools that have "racially and socioeconomically diverse student bodies" and there is increased funding for magnet schools, one of the more popular tools for voluntary school integration. School diversity or changes in funding formulas *could* be included as part of school and district improvement plans, but, as with much of ESSA, it will largely be up to states to decide whether to address systemic issues of educational injustice in their plans.[63]

IN-SCHOOL FACTORS

Out-of-school factors create the context for students, families, teachers, and communities and shape the conditions for learning; however, there are a number of things happening inside schools that also have drastic implications for educational equity.

Punish and Reward

Within a broader movement calling for changes in policing and the criminal justice system, discipline has emerged as a critical issue in how schools shape students' chances for academic success. Since the implementation of zero-tolerance policies in schools in the 1990s, the number of school suspensions, expulsions, and arrests has dramatically increased, spurred further upward during the years of NCLB.[64] Under this form of school discipline, students of color, students with disabilities, and LGBTQ students have been disproportionately targeted.[65] The disparities in discipline between white students and students of color have been shown to persist even when they are part of the same socioeconomic class and they do not account for significantly different rates of misbehavior.[66]

In Meridian, Mississippi, the Department of Justice filed a lawsuit against the public school system for its routine use of exclusionary discipline for even the smallest infractions. The school system had outsourced all of its discipline to the local police, so when there was a problem, an officer would automatically arrest the child in question, including students as young as ten years old. One child went to jail over thirty times directly for school-based infractions such as wearing the wrong colored socks or being a few minutes late, sometimes staying in the detention facilities for weeks on end. Although Meridian's population is a little over 60 percent Black, for years it was exclusively Black students who were arrested for small, nonviolent offenses.[67]

Meridian provides an extreme—although sadly not entirely unique— example of what has come to be known as the school-to-prison pipeline. A report by the Center for Civil Rights Remedies at the University of California, Los Angeles, estimated that in just one school year, U.S. public school children lost almost 18 million days of instruction because of suspensions.[68] One study analyzed the long-term academic impact of student suspension rates on reading and math outcomes and found that school suspensions account for about one-fifth of the achievement gap between Black and white students.[69] Students who have a history of suspension are also more likely to drop out and become involved with the juvenile or criminal justice systems.[70] The American Academy of Pediatrics and the American Psychological Association both came out with policy statements detailing the academic, social, and emotional harm that is done to students under zero-tolerance policies.[71] Given what we know about how poverty, trauma, and stress affect the brain, it's easy to see why these kinds of punishments often don't improve students' misbehavior.[72] Research has also shown that these policies make schools less safe overall and depress the academic outcomes of even nonsuspended students, too.[73]

Intensive community organizing, research, and activism around this issue has led to widespread calls to end the school-to-prison pipeline, and more states, cities, and districts are responding with initial reforms.[74] This has resulted in a drop in suspensions—a 20 percent decrease in two years—yet the racial disparity in discipline during that same time grew. Black K–12 students are now almost four times as likely to be suspended as white students, up from three times as likely.[75] Researchers have also found that some schools are simply using other forms of exclusionary discipline, including a doubling of the in-school suspension rates among African American high school students in Chicago.[76] ESSA requires that states report on school discipline and work with districts to reduce the use of exclusionary discipline. What's clear from some of the most recent numbers, though, is that more is needed to shift how educators respond to student behavior, including additional training and support for teachers on classroom management, implicit bias, empathy, and alternative approaches like restorative justice to fundamentally change this problem.[77]

Within schools, opportunities are also restricted for students based on the classes that students are placed in. Even in schools that are not outwardly segregated, students are often put into different, racialized tracks. Some students, generally white and East Asian, are placed in honors, Advanced Placement (AP), or International Baccalaureate (IB) classes where they continue to gain on achievement scores. Meanwhile, other students, more often Black, Latinx, and Southeast Asian, are placed in general or remedial education classes and receive less of everything: less experienced teachers, less engaging curriculum, less exposure to content, and, as a result, less learning and annual losses on measures of achievement.[78] Some scholars have referred to tracking as "silent segregation," because it removes many of the benefits of integrated schools and has clear negative impacts on students.[79] A meta-analysis of four decades of research on detracking schools, on the other hand, showed significant positive effects on the academic achievement of students who would have been placed in the general or remedial classes and no effects on academic outcomes for students who would have been in advanced classes.[80]

Perceptions and Expectations of Students

At the root of decisions about how to discipline students and who gets classified as gifted are educators' conscious and unconscious perceptions and judgments of young people. These can play out in smaller ways, too, down to the daily interaction between teachers and students, and they can powerfully shape young people's experiences with school.[81] In the classroom, when teachers hold negative views or low expectations of students, they might call on them less, reject their ideas more, praise them less and criticize them more, offer less time for them to answer questions, and provide less support and guidance to find the right answer.[82]

Even when not intentional, these expectations are often linked to race. In a 2016 study of teachers' expectations, researchers at Johns Hopkins University found that, when assessing the same Black student, white teachers were more likely than Black teachers to predict that the student would not graduate from high school. Black and white teachers' expectations for their white students' futures, however, were generally the same.[83] Research has also shown that the expectations of teachers affect historically marginalized students more, meaning that teachers' behaviors have an outsized effect on those students; and for students who belong to more than one vulnerable group, the impact is even greater.[84] Dr. Claude Steele has spent a lifetime documenting the effects of "stereotype threat"—when people internalize the perceptions of what their group is or isn't supposed to be like, succeed at, or do—on students in all levels of education.[85]

Many education reformers might claim that this is exactly what they've been saying when they make impassioned arguments about challenging what President George W. Bush loved to call "the soft bigotry of low expectations."[86] At base, it seems as if we're all fighting for the same thing: education as a path to a more just country. In praxis, the ideas are different. The high-expectations, no-excuses mantra focuses on education as a path for future economic success: the college students can attend, the career that can take them out of their neighborhood. A more holistic and empowering approach values who students are when they enter the classroom, acknowledges their socioemotional needs, engages with the families and communities they are a part of, and adapts to their styles of learning.

Before the recent hyperfocus on accountability, there was a movement for multicultural education that is largely absent in current debates around education reform. Within the breadth of research around multicultural education and culturally responsive pedagogy, researchers have documented the ways in which some students' cultures have been more valued within schools, with devastating effects for the achievement of Black, Latinx, Native American, and other nondominant groups of students. They argue that by ignoring and sometimes even erasing students' cultures from their education, including youth, hip-hop, and pop culture, we are failing to meet students' needs and exacerbating the opportunity gap.[87]

In their 2011 book *Creating the Opportunity to Learn,* Dr. Wade Boykin and Dr. Pedro Noguera write about culture as one of a series of "asset focused factors" that educators should incorporate into schools if they want to successfully reach all students.[88] If teachers are pushed to recognize students' strengths, create supportive and engaging learning environments, and use research-based practices alongside care and love, schools can create appreciable differences in students' outcomes. This is a model of education that centers on students, in all of their complexities and humanity. And while it doesn't ignore the context that creates inequity, it also accepts the responsibility that education is powerful in the ways it can shape young people's lives.

Ultimately, the fight for educational equity is about how we value people's lives. If our goal in the next era of education reform is to take the American Dream from rhetoric to reality, our investments at systemic, school, and individual levels will speak for themselves. As James Baldwin said in his speech "A Talk to Teachers," "Any citizen of this country who figures himself as responsible—and particularly those of you who deal with the minds and hearts of young people—must be prepared to 'go for broke.'"[89]

TEACHERS' STORIES

The stories in this chapter describe examples of educational equity in practice. The first two stories offer differing perspectives on a similar concern: an early childhood teacher, Michelle Gunderson, and a college educator, Ellen Baxt, show how the focus on accountability has ignored the acknowledgment and development of students as whole people over the course of their K–12 education. Anthony Bromberg then takes us into a school using restorative justice, allowing readers to see an alternative to excessive discipline in action and hear how it's shaped this teacher, his students, and his school. Lynne Gardner-Allers discusses a district process for textbook selection and how teachers fought for the adoption of culturally relevant resources in their schools. The last story in the collection is co-written by John Lockhart and Greta McHaney-Trice. The two taught a sociology unit to fourth graders that helped students explore the conditions, history, and context that affected their schools and develop the type of critical-thinking and literacy skills that make for real education.

Holding on to Child-Driven Teaching in a Data-Driven World

MICHELLE GUNDERSON

As you enter the first-grade classroom there are children spread out on the floor making puppets to accompany a song they will perform that afternoon. Other children are playing with blocks on a carpet, making train stations and signs for their newly constructed world. You see some children sitting in a tight circle helping each other learn to cross-stitch—threading needles, solving their sewing problems, and waiting patiently for help. There is a certain productive hum in the classroom. When you teach in the early grades, you know this sound when it happens. It is the sound of happy children learning through satisfying and dynamic play.

During my twenty-nine years of teaching I have witnessed children's determination to learn when provided the appropriate tools and opportunity. Given a pegboard with colored pegs, a child will create patterns and designs over and over again while learning number concepts to one hundred. It is through this work that a true internal understanding of numbers happens, not through worksheets or drills. When you witness children working with puzzles, you see natural problem solving when they turn, slide, and flip a puzzle piece into place. This is a very sophisticated geometric progression of rotation, transformation, and reflection. This is the type of experiential learning that builds the groundwork for later abstract thought. Maria Montessori once said that play is the work of childhood. I believe play is the essence of childhood—the way that children make sense of their world.

This is the true rigor of early childhood.

Rigor is one of the words co-opted by education reformers who believe that the problems in our education system would be solved if only we raised the bar higher for children. We just need to make teachers and children work harder, and like a magic wand has been waved, children will miraculously start learning. There are two problems with this argument in terms of child-driven instruction. First, it views the purpose of childhood as preparation for adult life without honoring the intrinsic worth of childhood itself. Second, it views learning as having a linear trajectory—as if children learn increasingly difficult tasks at a steady and consistent rate. We know from brain research that children do not always learn at the same pace, and that plateaus in learning have definite benefits. Think of a child learning to play the piano. Playing the same song over and over again and staying at the same level actually has its benefits in solidifying skills. The same is true with many other aspects of learning. Another choice word that enters into this narrative is *grit*. What if we could find out why some children are more resilient than others? If we could measure and enculturate this resilience—this grit—more children would learn. Yet, this ideology that making the world tougher for kids and teachers is the tonic for what ails our schools is usually reserved for poor children in urban schools. It is inequitable, it is unjust, and it does not take into account how children develop and learn.

If we reclaim *rigor* and *grit* and decide to take a stance that treats children as fully human, we would turn this narrative on its head and use the words *accomplishment* and *determination* in their place. The famous child psychologist Erik Erikson identified the primary grades as a time when children experience a conflict in personality development that he labels "industry versus inferiority." During this stage, ages six to ten, children strive to complete more and more complex tasks. When a child experiences encouragement from caring adults during this process, strong feelings of competence develop. On the other hand, school experiences and curriculum based on a false sense of rigor have the potential for the opposite effect. If children are given tasks that are too difficult or developmentally inappropriate, they often develop feelings of doubt and inferiority, which impede their ability to persevere through the inevitable struggles that come with learning.

I teach first grade in the Chicago Public Schools. Our school is located in Lakeview and is in a neighborhood where most children walk to school, something that is becoming a rarity in Chicago, where children crisscross our town in buses to go to specialized schools or charters. Our students come from many different places, many different family constellations, and various socioeconomic conditions. Forty percent of our students receive free and reduced-price lunch, and then some of our students live on Lake Shore Drive and wake up each morning with a luxury high-rise view of Lake Michigan. The classroom scenario in the opening paragraph is what a typical afternoon looks like in our classrooms in the early grades at our school. It is beautiful. It is child centered. But in a world of Common Core State Standards, teacher accountability based on tests, and rigor, it comes at a price.

I have always been fortunate in finding mentors over the last twenty-nine years while forging my way as a teacher. My training as an early childhood educator comes from the National College of Education (now National-Louis) in Evanston, Illinois. National College was an institution started by Elizabeth Harrison and was supported and influenced by Jane Addams, two women at the forefront of the kindergarten movement. The school's beginnings were rooted in Froebel's teachings of experiential learning and play. Froebel, who created kindergarten, was one of the first educators to realize that young children have distinct needs and that they are not just miniature adults. My mentor during those years was Betty Weeks, a nationally renowned early childhood educator. I literally learned at her feet as I sat on the rug in her classroom learning the magic of storytelling and the wonder and importance of play in children's lives. I experienced a teaching world that took into consideration the needs of the whole child—social, emotional, academic, and physical. Once you have experienced so much beauty, a place where people are honored and enriched, there is no way you could want anything else for the children in your life.

I have made it my life's work to pass this knowledge on to others. The Chicago Public School system, however, is a difficult place to sustain progressive education inside our classrooms. In the last four years since the Common Core State Standards were created, we have seen an increasing amount of testing, with top-down management and control over classroom activity based on these tests. There has been a push toward data-driven instruction, using the information from these assessments to guide classroom practice. It might, on the surface, make sense to follow that logic: test children, evaluate the information, and adapt what you are doing to meet needs. The problem is the underlying assumption that the tests being used actually measure something, and that a set of standards can actually guide the complexity of what happens in a classroom.

Let me give you an example from my classroom practice. Our school system insisted that early childhood teachers use a test called DIBELS (Dynamic Indicators of Basic Early Learning Skills). You could not invent a worse test. DIBELS measures discreet skills in reading acquisition such as letter fluency (how fast you name letters), phonemic awareness (breaking down sounds), decoding (reading nonsense words), and reading text passages. These tasks are all important subsets of learning to read, but they do not constitute the act of reading. There is very little information that DIBELS provides that helps diagnose and approach the complexity of teaching reading. A teacher already knows these isolated factors about their children by listening to them read text from real books. The assessment takes an inordinate amount of time to administer, so that the very children that reformers label as "urban" and "challenged" in my classroom lose four and a half weeks of reading instruction out of a forty-week school year just for one test. This is wrong, this is not happening in wealthier school systems, and this is what inequity looks like.

With the time limits from administering the test and the narrowing of our curriculum to meet only these standards, what and how educators teach has increasingly been taken away from our professional judgment. At the heart of the Common Core Standards is the premise that the purpose of education is the production of students who are "college and career ready." This is the antithesis of everything I believe in as a progressive educator. I believe that the purpose of education is to educate a populace of critical thinkers who are capable of shaping a just and equitable society in order to lead good and purpose-filled lives. I also believe that the purpose of my students' education is not just to become productive members of the workforce. I view my students as fully human and expect that my job is to develop their interests, ideals, and character as well.

This is highly complex and moral work that cannot be done according to a timeline of standards, and it cannot be tested. One afternoon last year a student asked if he could choreograph the life cycle of monarch butterflies. Five of his friends volunteered for the ballet, and they set off to work without adult instruction. After two sessions of rehearsals, they were ready to perform, complete with narration and accompanied by a Beethoven sonatina. At the end of the ballet, the narrator said, "And sadly many of the monarchs didn't make it on their migration to Mexico." There were tears streaming down my face as I watched the children whither to the floor—this undertaking was filled with so much beauty, learning, and ability. The ballet was better and more creative than I ever could have planned or directly instructed. Child-centered, art-infused learning is only possible when we honor the time and space for this work to take place. In a world where teachers are held to a script and every minute of the day must be spent on standards-directed learning, this does not happen.

The influence of Common Core and teaching to the test is felt everywhere in the Chicago schools—in professional development sessions provided by my school district, in the materials being purchased, and in the discussions regarding student achievement. Earlier this year I was called in to a professional development touting the virtues of the Common Core–aligned EngageNY curriculum for first-grade math. The lessons that we analyzed at our professional development were very abstract and were based on pencil and paper activities. This is not how young children make sense of their mathematical world. They need hands-on interaction with materials and work that they care about—not information or problems on a worksheet.

Common Core influences are also prevalent in the teaching materials purchased by the district. This year I was so excited to receive Lucy Calkins's new units of study in writing. I admire Calkins's work very much—it is always well researched and thoroughly piloted in urban classrooms very similar to mine. The teacher talking points and management in the earlier version guided my students through a writing process that was child friendly. The lessons were short and concise, and were more about what the children produced than the teacher presenting as if she were the "sage on the stage." I was crestfallen when I opened these new Common Core–aligned materials. The lessons are much too long for my students, and there is much more teacher talk before children are released to work on their own. A primary premise in early childhood is that children need time to experiment and explore in order to learn. Sitting for too long and listening to an adult has very minimal effect with younger students. Children at this age learn by doing, and the teacher's role is as a guide and consultant.

It is what I am seeing in all of the materials I have reviewed that claim to be aligned to the Common Core. In the name of rigor, the lessons are very adult centered, with too much teacher input and not enough direct activity centered on the children. This type of direct instruction is promoted as necessary for children in Chicago schools to catch up; yet, it is the very opposite of the type of instruction children receive in our progressive private schools. A narrow, teacher-directed curriculum is acceptable for poor kids, but not for children whose parents can afford a nonregimented, child-friendly education. Can you imagine Education Secretary Duncan saying to his children's teachers at Sidwell Friends, "Please read a script to my children today. That's how I think they should learn."?

So how is it possible to create a classroom where students are immersed in play-based learning in this climate? I do none of this work alone. I work with a strong team of teachers. We are all experts in early childhood education, grounded in developmental practice, and committed to child-centered learning. It is not a coincidence that we happen to be teaching together. Our principal believes in shared leadership, and teachers are always part of the hiring team. Unlike many administrators in our system, our school leader is not intimidated by independent professionals. One of our goals in hiring is to identify educators with a strong progressive education background and a passion for this work. We are a faculty of professional educators, not a staff of deskilled workers controlled by top-down management.

When they looked into the testing practices in our building, the early childhood teachers approached our principal about our concerns with DIBELS. We made a case for why it was not working in our building and asked to use another tool. In the end, we decided to use Fountas and Pinnell's diagnostic. I am not promoting the use of this particular assessment in this essay. What I am saying is that we decided which tool works best for our context, approached our school leader with our professional concerns, and were able to make the change that benefited our students. In many other schools, this type of activity would be regarded as insubordination, and a teacher's position would be on the line. We all still have our jobs.

Another way we preserve progressive education in our classrooms is through strong union ties and activism. The team of teachers I work with align themselves with a social-justice framework and use the structures provided by our union contract to protect our classroom practice. We are a school that had a 100 percent vote to strike in 2012, and there are several teacher-activists on our faculty who have leadership roles in the Chicago Teachers Union. Through our union-negotiated contract, each school must have a Professional Personnel Learning Committee, and we follow this structure to the letter. This committee is in charge of school-based professional development, the recommendations for curriculum changes and purchases, and any other activity that affects teaching and learning in our building. Through this committee work we are able to make our voices heard and challenge the multitude of reforms that want control of our teaching and classrooms.

The work to preserve progressive educational practice and equity in our schools takes place on a much larger scale than just my schoolhouse. I am part of a growing group of social-justice unionists around the country who work for workplace justice as well as equitable education for our students. Along with national groups such as United Opt Out and the Network for Public Education, we are working together to decrease the overuse and abuse of tests. Several activists in the Chicago Teachers Union are advocating a complete rejection of the Common Core State Standards as a framework for teaching and learning. This is never-ending work, and occupies a large part of my time.

A few years ago a student teacher noticed my advocacy work. She said to me, "I didn't go into teaching to be political." I did not answer her statement at the time, but let her watch my work. She became increasingly aware of the outside influences over our classroom practice and grew into one of the strongest unionists I know. Teaching is political work. It is probably the most political action inside the human experience—helping students learn how to make decisions themselves.

I realize that my situation is not shared by everyone. I consider myself part of the "old guard." My children are raised, my family income is stable, and I work in a city with a strong teacher union whose philosophy and political framework closely align to my own. I am afforded a situation where I can speak out loudly and the repercussions are minimal.

And I say—all children deserve an education that honors who they are, promotes justice, and helps them lead good and fulfilled lives.

Michelle Gunderson is a twenty-nine-year teaching veteran. She currently teaches first grade in a neighborhood school for the Chicago Public Schools. Ms. Gunderson is vice president for elementary schools for the Chicago Teachers Union and is a nationally known teacher-activist. She is a leader in the social-justice unionism movement and currently serves on the steering committee for the United Caucuses of Rank and File Educators (UCORE). Ms. Gunderson is a doctoral student at Loyola University Chicago, where her studies focus on teacher activism and classroom practice.

Preparing the Whole Student for College

ELLEN BAXT

As graduation rates rise in New York and other cities across the country, one might imagine more students enrolling in and graduating from college. Yet, as more students gain entry to institutions of higher education, few bring with them the skills required to successfully complete college-level work. This is particularly acute at the community college level. In New York City, only 22.2 percent of the students in the class of 2012 graduated with college ready scores, despite record-high graduation numbers. Of those, the top 10 percent of schools in the city, generally gifted and screened schools, accounted for half of those students.[90] The overall number of college ready students arriving to campus is low, and their lack of college preparedness jeopardizes their chances for success from the start.

I work at an intensive remedial program in a large community college system, recently developed as an alternative to the traditional remedial courses the college has offered for decades. The program has been very successful, and most students finish relatively quickly, in contrast to the college's typical remedial courses, which have not been as successful in helping students progress into credit-bearing courses and through to graduation.

Fundamental to this program is the recognition of the real skill levels of the students. Some remedial courses start their curriculum at too high a level and move too quickly, attempting to cover a wide swath of topics in little detail. This ignores the depth of the academic and social gaps typical of students who earn diplomas but who have not yet mastered high school— and in many cases middle school—material. Despite the fact that students entering community colleges now have been subject to tests designed to end "social promotion" starting in the third grade and continuing through middle school, many still are not able to read, write, compute, and analyze at the college level. Many students are surprised to learn that they require remedial instruction and are unaware of their own academic strengths and weaknesses. To truly address the needs of today's incoming students, community college remedial courses must begin with the most basic building blocks of reading, writing, math, and social-emotional development, placing an emphasis on communication and critical thinking as opposed to more surface-level skill drills.

So we start where students need us to, and over the semester, students practice academic and nonacademic skills from simple to complex, preparing them for credit-bearing college courses. In reading and writing courses, we begin with the most basic elements of gleaning meaning from text, eventually building to writing a ten-paragraph literary analysis. The sense of relief is palpable when students learn that they do not have to hide their confusion or questions, and are instead encouraged to express their uncertainties. Recognizing the importance of their social skills, we also work on patience, scholarly respect, collaboration, mental stamina, and self-advocacy. It is this acknowledgment of their skills that allows students to move beyond shame into accomplishment. This is achieved through deep-level work, with a focus on discussion, the expression of ideas, and the articulation of reasoning as opposed to a focus on procedures, formulas, and memorization. As those college-level skills have been pushed out of K–12 schools to make room for test prep, we have to reintroduce them into college remedial courses.

Apart from the basics of reading, writing, and math, one of the major skills that we see missing from students' repertoires is how to have scholarly discussions. When classes are discussion based, students learn vocabulary as well as the ability to express complex concepts through verbal and written language. Even math classes can be discussion based, with students explaining their thinking process and the steps they took to solve problems. But intellectual dialogue is a new arena for many new community college students. Many of their previous learning experiences were dominated by short, superficial questions and answers and test preparation. While some may have worked on group projects or engaged in debates, these experiences were likely few and far between. Consequently, most students are unaccustomed to expressing their thought process and thinking aloud, and may be uncomfortable speaking in front of a large group. While most college classes expect that students will share their ideas with the whole class, few prepare them to do so. We help them develop this muscle of dialogue.

Nationwide, the six-year graduation rate is 39 percent.[91] Many students enter college with academic deficits, hampering their ability to accumulate credits in a timely manner, but social-emotional underdevelopment is responsible as well. Many have difficulty working productively in groups, persevering when faced with difficult tasks, taking risks to share new ideas, or disagreeing with others respectfully. Many were overlooked, pushed out, or ignored in high school due to behavioral challenges, disabilities, or growing frustration with their education and, despite the rhetoric on standards, were not held to high expectations. Just as we recognize students' true academic levels and use that as a starting point for instruction, the same must be done for social-emotional skills, which can be taught and learned just as academic skills are.

I see on a daily basis how social-emotional skill deficits have a significant impact on students' ability to learn through scholarly exchange. Shaheem and Lori didn't like each other. Although we tried to maintain a positive classroom environment, they often antagonized each other. One day, after being goaded by Lori, Shaheem called her a bitch. Later I asked Shaheem what other words he could have used to express his disagreement respectfully. He was completely stumped. He didn't even really understand the question. "That's how we speak where I'm from," he said. What followed was a vocabulary lesson, including definitions, standard usage, and opportunities for practice. College is a different environment from the one that most community college students are accustomed to. It is a middle-class environment, while most of my students come from poor and working-class communities. Many of my students exhibit behaviors used successfully in their neighborhoods and are unaware of the academic and social expectations that will make them successful in college. As emphasis on standards and testing reign, there is less time for more nuanced conversations about setting and code switching that would help students beyond steering them to choose the correct multiple-choice answer.

Instead, students feel a disconnect with their new college environment and conclude that they don't belong. They often feel like outsiders and isolate themselves from their peers, many of whom are going through the same thing. Students may think that their college-going is an accident, or more accurately, a mistake. Many begin college ineligible for credit-bearing classes, after all, so they must not be smart enough for college. When they do well, they may think it is due to luck, but doing poorly confirms that they should not be in college at all.[92] Their ability to persist relies on the knowledge that college *is* for them, participation is their right, and no one has made a mistake. As with acquiring other skills, gaining the knowledge of belonging is one that requires practice. For educators, this demands repetition of the message that college exists for them. Teaching the language, customs, and geography of college will make students feel like new residents, not tourists. Just as we acknowledge their academic gaps, we must also address their college-culture gaps.

Teaching students about college culture and expectations is much like teaching any skill. Instructors and advisors teach college-going vocabulary much the same way they teach any vocabulary, through providing definitions and opportunities for practice. Colleges can't assume that students are familiar with terms such as *bursar, office hours,* and *syllabus,* because most of them have not been taught these terms in earlier educational settings. Many community college students are the first in their family to attend college, and they often have to learn by trial and error how to navigate this complex, confusing, and often labyrinthine system. Many students are unfamiliar with how colleges are structured—for example, what a major is, how majors are grouped into departments, and different types and levels of degrees. All of this is information that can be taught and learned. When colleges ignore these gaps in knowledge, students receive the message that they should know it already. And that assumption often leads to "impostor phenomenon," making students feel that they have landed, as if by magic, in a place never intended for them.

Many students also enter college with a profound lack of self-esteem and deep feelings of self-doubt. These feelings have often been built over years of low test scores, lack of thoughtful adult attention and respect from the school systems in which they were raised, and a lowering of expectations. One of the comments I've heard most frequently as students exit the program is, "I'm more confident now." The confidence students develop makes an enormous impact on their ability to persist when faced with difficult tasks. As with vocabulary acquisition, students will need modeling, practice, and feedback. Rather than telling students what they did right, we apply the academic rigor used in the classroom to the teaching of confidence building. We ask students to identify their achievements and the strategies they used to improve their performance. This increases students' self-awareness and builds their analytic and communication skills. When students hear about their achievements in their own voices, they develop their muscles of confidence building. Like building the stamina for reading longer and longer texts or performing more and more complex computations, students improve persistence through the awareness of their own progress, even when it is small. In addition, when I notice students struggling with confidence, I pull them aside and privately tell them, "I'm proud of you." This can be an emotional moment, particularly if it is a new experience for them. Some students may never have heard those words applied to them before. They may be shocked and even nervous to have someone pay such close attention to them. Based on past experiences in education, many students think that a meeting with the teacher is necessarily punitive, and they often see staff in a policing role. Taking time to have positive interactions with students on an individual basis helps them to reshape those ideas.

Another conversation that seems to be absent in college is about the many fears that students bring with them to college that have real impacts on their ability to persist. Underlying some students' refusal to take a guess, work in groups, or speak up is fear. Discussing fear is taboo in American culture. As adults we are supposed to be strong, independent, decisive, and brave. Harboring fear is a big burden on students, and helping them release some of that burden makes space for all the new information they are trying to acquire. It also builds their muscle of courage. Like confidence, courage is something that can be practiced and developed. Being courageous does not indicate the absence of fear. Rather, it indicates the ability to say "yes" despite the strong pull of fear screaming "no!"

I address students' fears in a couple of ways: First, acknowledge it. Because it is taboo to discuss fear, students, like other adults, are often ashamed to admit they have it. Acknowledging it normalizes their feelings and lets them know they are not alone. Second, use dialogue to dispel it. Often students self-sabotage due to fear. Discussing their fears in detail can ultimately deflate them. Once students understand that making mistakes is a fundamental part of the learning process, they are often more willing to take risks.

Beyond their general academic and social-skill needs, young people sometimes enter college with untreated, undiagnosed, or ignored mental health issues. Darla was a quiet student, though she performed well on written assignments. She often looked disheveled and seemed unfocused at times. She did well on independent classwork, but when assigned group work, she opened her binder, turned it upside down like a tent, and hid under it, quietly refusing to interact with her peers. For the first two weeks, she arrived on time in the mornings but didn't return from the lunch break. One day it was the dentist. Another, she had to take care of younger siblings. There were vague mentions of other appointments. Darla's stepmother called frequently to discuss her progress. During one of these calls, I learned that she did not have appointments or responsibilities at home, and that Darla regularly called her stepmother during the midday break, telling her she had gotten in trouble at school and needed to be driven home.

Eventually, we recognized that Darla had so much trouble socially that she couldn't interact with her peers. We guessed she didn't quite know what to do with herself when other students were chatting and forming personal bonds over lunch. I suggested to the staff that for the next two weeks, we take turns eating lunch with Darla, hoping that she might stay for the afternoon class if we could get her there. And it worked. After two weeks, we no longer had to eat lunch with her, and she maintained good attendance. She dismantled the binder tent and slowly began interacting with her peers. Later, we learned the full story. Darla was a survivor of incest, victimized over the course of many years. The assailant was her mother's boyfriend. Despite Darla telling her mother about her victimization, her mother planned to marry him. That semester, Darla decided to press charges and was embroiled in long and terrible court proceedings.

Before attending our program, Darla had enrolled in several remedial classes at various colleges but didn't pass any of them. Certainly Darla was one student who needed a creative response to her social-emotional challenges that she likely would not receive in most typical remedial classes. Underlying this intervention is the assumption that all students can be successful, and that the responsibility is on educational staff to assess students' needs and devise solutions, even unorthodox ones. Administrators must share this view, allowing educators the space to develop creative solutions to complex problems.

Another unorthodox concept in education is love. It has been replaced by zero-tolerance policies that more closely resemble penal systems than they do models for the development of humans. Great teachers love their students, but love is a little bit shameful these days. It is unscholarly, unquantifiable, and its impact on students is certainly underestimated. Teachers show love for students through insistence on the excellence of their work, acknowledgment of achievements even when they're tiny, encouragement of individuality, acknowledgment of risk taking, an insistence on respect for all, and an unwavering belief in the ability of individuals to achieve their goals. We also show love by subverting our authority in the classroom and inviting students to take the reins. However, in our capitalist society, we're discouraged from loving people who experience difficulty. When I was a college student, I heard a lecture that had a profound impact on me. Miep Gies, the woman who protected Anne Frank and her family, said,

When we're children, we're taught by our parents that if we behave, everything will work out fine. So, people who have a problem must have made a serious mistake. Why should we then help them? . . . If you ever decide to help people who are in trouble, you need the courage to face the opposition of many of your friends and family members.[93]

Many community college students are those people in trouble. They have been homeless, abused, addicted, and jailed. And the systems in which we live do not necessarily support our helping them. Our school systems pressure us to treat all students the same, under the guise that equal means fair. Struggling in a new environment, these students can come across as nervous, rude, untrusting, and ungrateful, but they also recognize love. And one way we show love is by seeing our students as individuals, with unique strengths, challenges, and needs.

Students recognize loving commitment from the way a teacher looks them squarely in the eye, delivers bad news honestly and good news joyfully. They experience love and belonging when a teacher insists on respectful behavior from all and when she takes a personal interest in students, asking about their bands, jobs, children, and goals. They even experience it when she raises an eyebrow to chatting in the corner or earbuds in ears, because they know it means she values everyone's time and commitment to their education. She treats them as scholars-in-training. Love does not come from gooey, fake sentiment; it comes from an insistence on excellence. These are the kinds of standards we can support—not standards of data and procedures, but standards of attentive caring.

The achievement gulf is wide and dangerous. Ninety percent of my students are students of color. Applied here, attentive caring is antiracist action. It presumes that all students are intelligent beings worthy of care, likely to meet challenges, and able to make lasting contributions to the intellectual life of the institution. Developing the whole student—academically, socially, and emotionally—is a way to honor the histories and talents of all students.

Ellen Baxt is a professional developer with the City University of New York (CUNY) Language and Literacy Programs. She has taught ESL in the CUNY system, the Brooklyn Public Libraries, various community organizations, and in Recife, Brazil. She developed the advisement program for CUNY Start, an intensive alternative to standard remedial courses in CUNY. She lives in Brooklyn, New York, with her daughter.

This Is What Restorative Justice Looks Like

ANTHONY BROMBERG

"All over the world I see them wearing my hat, and they know where I'm at . . ." sings Javion, "Jay," at the center of a semicircle of admiring young men. He stands tall, his acolytes crouching and standing around him, his arms carving through the air to the rhythm he creates deftly with his words. Jay is a tenth-grade student who receives special education services. This is his favorite moment of the school day. "I'm bringing the moment of truth . . ." Nearby, in part of an orbit of a group overlapping slightly with Jay's, Cameron, "Cam," a charismatic ninth grader who also receives special education services, jokes to his friends, "Oh-ho, man, you hear that. It's ridiculous!" He is a successful basketball player with an outgoing personality.

"Man, you need to shut your mouth," Jay says directly to Cam.

"Chill, bro," Cam laughs.

"Man, I don't have time for this. F– you!"

"What?" Cam responds, dropping his backpack. The students take a step toward each other. The atmosphere changes instantly. The crowd merges, growing into a haphazard circle around them. They cuss at each other, slowly circling. The crowd vibrates, nervous, expectant.

Two assistant principals feel the palpable energy change and hear the noise. Hearts fluttering, they run over to interrupt the growing mob. They get there and are able to step between Jay and Cam before a punch is thrown, though the potential combatants continue to talk.

What happens now? A year ago, both students would have been sent home for three days.

Before school the following morning, I arrive early, in the role of newly appointed social and emotional learning lead teacher and a campus restorative justice advocate hoping to help transform our discipline paradigm, having been asked to lead a harm-repair circle. I greet Jay and his aunt, Ms. Hart, along with one of the assistant principals, Mr. Mayo, an experienced administrator, in the front office. We shake hands with Ms. Hart, who immediately wants us to know her primary concern is that Jay not be the only one who gets in trouble, but that the other child be held responsible as well. Everyone has agreed to be here voluntarily, but this is new, and who knows what to expect.

"I've seen it happen before," she says.

Mr. Mayo leads us to a conference room across the entry hall, where we meet Cam and his mother, Ms. Walker, who immediately goes up to Ms. Hart and shakes her hand.

"I'm so excited to meet you," she says. "I was in Mr. Mayo's office yesterday when he called you, and I heard how much you cared about Jay and wanted him to be responsible."

"Oh, well, it's nice to meet you, too," Ms. Hart replies, surprised.

After everyone settles down, Jay looking alert, Cam resigned, I introduce the circle and our intentions for being there: to openly hear everyone's perspective and reach consensus about what harms need to be healed and how we can all be accountable for their healing.

Beginning with a discussion of what happened, Jay shares. "I was singing, and I was in my zone. I get real caught up, and I take it seriously. Maybe Cam didn't mean what I thought he did, but I don't really know him, so I kind of jumped to that. I'm working on that, but it's hard."

"Thank you, Jay," Ms. Walker says. "That means a lot to hear you show that kind of self-awareness. Cam and I have been talking about it, and I think we can relate. He takes acting real seriously too. Do you study singers?" Jay bobs his head affirmatively. "Cam will watch a movie over and over. He studies too. Sounds like y'all had a miscommunication." Ms. Hart nods too.

As the circle moves forward to focus on who was harmed, I mention all of the other students who saw these two scholars treating each other with disrespect. Were they harmed?

"It's true," Mr. Mayo chimes in. "I think you two know it, a lot of the kids look up to you. They'll follow your lead. You're charismatic and smart. You've got to use that positively."

Then Ms. Walker and Ms. Hart share similar perspectives, "It's the same at home, your cousins and siblings are hurt if you set this kind of example. And we had to take off work to be here. And if you'd gotten suspended, then who'd have been really hurt?"

The women talk at length, building off of each other's wisdom and sharing the experiences and values they believe should shape Jay and Cam's futures. The young men are listening. The atmosphere in the room is warm and supportive and full of high expectations.

Eventually, we transition to talking about what each of us can do to repair the harm. First, it's suggested that Jay and Cam talk to each other, and not make assumptions in general if they ever think they're being disrespected. That'll be hard, but worth it they say. Cam has opened up now and shares, "Most people don't know this about me, but I'm actually shy. I don't always like to talk to people I don't know." They also agree to talk to the younger children at home about making positive communication choices and finally to shaking hands out in front of everybody at lunch to show they're cool. Ms. Hart and Ms. Walker say they'll continue to talk to their students at home while I make an agreement to check in each week and visit them during lunch. The scholars also agree that they'll come to Mr. Mayo if any tensions arise during their school days. Consensus on these agreements is reached with one go-round of the talking piece.

As we wrap the circle up, Ms. Hart and Ms. Walker begin planning to collaborate in their neighborhood. Ms. Walker shares that she loves taking Cam with her to visit elder-care facilities, and Cam lights up. "They have such great stories to tell," he says. And Jay smiles when Ms. Hart shares about how he uses producing music as a creative outlet to deal with stress.

At this point, the principal pops her head in because it's time for the students and me to get to class. "How'd it go?" she asks. "Very well. Thank you. Can we stay in here and keep planning for a little while?" Ms. Hart asks the principal, who nods. "We've got some things to talk about."

Jay and Cam have, with some growth moments along the way, continued successfully through eleventh and tenth grade, respectively. Jay has gotten up on stage at multiple school events and shared his music, while Cam continues to play sports and has costarred in a student-made film.

Restorative justice provides an alternative framework to traditional, exclusionary discipline practices. Knowing that relationships are at the core of human learning, schools are increasingly turning to restorative approaches. The idea is that when someone or something is harmed, a community should embrace both the responsible and the harmed parties and, together, plan for restitution rather than isolating those involved and using punishment to attempt to coerce future behaviors.[94]

The restorative symbol is the circle. We literally sit in circles. And listen. And talk as the talking piece goes around the circle. If you've got it, you talk. If you don't, you listen, deeply. While facilitators help structure the circle, every voice carries equal importance. There are infinite variations of how circles can be used, but they're mostly variations on two themes. In community-building circles, the goal is to give each member access to express their truth and connect while shared meaning on a topic is created. In harm repair, we work to build consensus around accountability and the supportive path to restitution, repairing whatever harms have occurred.

Our campus is one of the two largest high schools in a national top-twenty urban-population city. We are similar to many schools nationwide with approximately two-thirds of our students receiving free and reduced-price lunch and 77 percent of our students self-identified as Hispanic/Latinx. When our current lead learner stepped in, she made lowering the suspension rate and promoting social and emotional learning (SEL) priorities, so we started with a class to help all ninth graders and made restorative practices a bedrock of our curriculum. We are also the first high school in the district to have a full-time restorative coordinator. Through training in circling and restorative responses from the coordinator, our local restorative advocacy group, and devoted teachers like myself, we began to put the practices into use across the campus. Still, implementing restorative practices has not been without challenges. Working with the well over 2,500 students and 150 adults on campus on any given day, plenty of communication and logistical (as well as mindset) challenges ensued. The key to restorative growth has been leveraging student voice.

Over the course of our first year of implementation, students became progressively bigger advocates for and leaders of restorative practices. First, they began leading the circles in our ninth-grade SEL classes and then in other areas of the school, some even reporting circling with their friends and family outside of school hours. We've had circles with administrative, counseling, custodial, and office staff, with school resource officers and educational leaders from the district offices. Students have participated in almost all of them. Using academic circles to spur literary discussions about symbolism in our Advanced Placement English IV classes helped us to go from five to thirty-two students who passed that AP test in one year.[95]

One scholar, a twelfth grader named Luisa, went from being in a harm repair circle at the beginning of the year to becoming one of the biggest circle advocates on campus, eventually leading the first two circles at our feeder middle school. Luisa's circles went so well that the school plans to use circles in their advisory classes in the upcoming year. Another scholar, a twelfth grader nicknamed "G," became a similarly strong voice in restorative leadership. One day I was asked to coguide a tour of district leaders around the campus. The tour was during my sixth-period class, where G was the student coteacher. The note I left for the sub simply said to let G lead a circle. As I shared our campus with the district leaders, they expressed interest in seeing the classroom being led by a student. I was cautiously optimistic the spirited class wouldn't be too rowdy, so I led the group in that direction. There had, of course, been no reason to feel cautious! We entered the room to find all thirty students fully engaged in G's circle, sharing deeply how they saw the world. Everyone was rapt.

In our SEL classes, we held community-building circles weekly, chairs arranged in a circle so all could easily make unobstructed eye contact. Another twelfth grader, Gem, facilitated one such circle about dreams. Her opening was a poem she wrote on dreams. "I want to talk about dreams, those lifelong schemes . . ."

The first response round begins with an icebreaker: 1 to 10, how is your day/what animal do you feel like?

Gabriel (a twelfth grader and class mentor): I didn't know if I was going to share this today, but, honestly, I'm a 2. We're having some trouble at home. There's arguments. It's hard.

Gaia (a ninth grader): I'm like an 8.7 today. Got an 87 on my algebra test, so that was pretty good, but I'm sorry to hear that, Gabriel. We know you care about your family a lot.

Julio (a ninth grader): Well, today I'm a polar bear, because you know I stay frosty. I hear you, it's hard right now, Gabriel, but you're a frosty dude. I've seen it. You will bounce back.

Then we check in about our values: Who inspires you to reach your dreams?

Half the circle (ninth graders): My mom. She works so hard. She does so much for us . . .

Luna (a ninth grader): My older brother. He screwed up some, but he's really come back from that, and I'm proud of him. And he's always there for me. He listens.

Elizabeth (a twelfth grader): My best friend inspires me. She's so creative, and she makes me laugh.

The core of the circle is the body rounds. There are usually three to five questions/opportunities to tell stories. Gem asked students to share about one dream they dream for themselves.

Gaia: I'm not going to lose sight of my dream to go to graduate school and become a doctor. I know I've got to keep that algebra grade up.

Maggie (a ninth grader): Honestly, I can't see that far ahead right now. My dream is just to graduate. I've got to stop being absent so much, right, Mr. B? (*she grins at the teacher*).

Gem (pointing to Elizabeth and Gabriel as well): Hey, we're almost there, and graduation's an important dream to focus on. There are plenty of moments when it's not easy, and you're right. You don't want to be absent and lose credits in ninth grade, because it makes so much extra work. I had to make up a couple of credits at the beginning of the year, and it was such a pain. My dream now is to actually move away, go to college, and make sure I choose the right major for me.

Maria (a ninth grader): That does seem like a long way off, but I know it's not. Right now I'm focused on making the top band and getting my engineering grade up to an A. I will figure out how to work with that teacher yet. And to avoid drama the rest of the year!

Gem closes the circle with a brief activity to help everyone take the values and thoughts they've shared into the rest of the day with them. In this case, she invites everyone to tell the people around them, or even to get up and walk around the circle, sharing with all that they can make their dreams a reality. High-fiving, hugging, and "you can do it!" happen all over the room.

As the year progressed, both our district and the restorative nonprofit we work with began bringing observers to campus regularly. Interested educators from the district, other cities around Texas, and across the country from as far away as California and Georgia have come and participated in our circles. The most common question they brought up after circling was: do students really share like that and *support* each other like that every day? The answer is yes. But it also gets messy and scary. And implicitly: yes, this is absolutely possible on every campus.

Restorative practices are always rooted in our shared humanity and in acknowledging that every member of the learning community is valuable and deserves the best possible education. Embracing restorative practices takes us on a relational, communication-based journey of ever-increasing authentic equity that, like a circle, never ends.

Anthony Bromberg is an assistant principal in Austin, Texas. Previously, he taught English language arts and social-emotional learning for ten years. He is a restorative practices and social and emotional learning advocate currently completing his master's in principalship as part of the University of Texas at Austin's antiracist leadership program.

Rethinking Educational Equity

When "Equal" Isn't Enough

LYNNE GARDNER-ALLERS

In our national efforts to close the achievement gap, "educational equity" can carry many different meanings. In K–12 school and district policies, equity as an underlying value is often used to represent a desire for everyone to be the "same" and "equal." As a high school social studies and language arts teacher for over thirteen years in the largest school district in Oregon, I witnessed this belief shape the adoption of curriculum materials and resources that failed to support the unique and multidimensional perspectives of our schools. When faced with a diverse student population and communities that have been historically neglected, is "equal" enough?

In 2006, Portland Public Schools (PPS), enacted a districtwide plan to curtail the disparities between students and schools across the city. The scope and shape of such a plan was guided by the vision of our new superintendent, who had recently moved to Portland from an East Coast school district in 2004, an outsider to our local community. Under her short but tumultuous time as superintendent, six of the district's ninety schools were closed, several elementary and middle schools were forced to merge into a K–8 model, and a districtwide scope and sequence alignment model around a "common core" was set in motion. In many ways, her reign was a reaction to the combined effects of a disappointing lack of leadership from the former superintendent and a series of devastating voter-approved ballot measures that slashed our schools' budgets. Realizing the effects that these cuts had wreaked on our schools, voters approved a local-option levy to help restore funding lost from the previous measures; this allotted approximately $4 million for our district to use on purchasing new textbooks and classroom materials.

One of the first actions this plan included was a curricular initiative to establish a "common core" curriculum program for all of the nine comprehensive high schools in the district. This term is not to be confused with the Common Core State Standards that have become embedded in education discourse today, though it exemplifies a shift in the language that educators and politicians use to codify a defined body of knowledge necessary for all students. For PPS, the common core curriculum involved establishing a framework to recognize and define equity as everything being the same in each school. In order to create this sameness, the logic followed, all schools should offer the same courses, same school schedules, same state standards, and same curriculum.

Prior to the common core curriculum, many neighborhood high schools had developed unique course offerings, depending on student interest and teacher expertise. For example, at one high school, all freshmen took an introduction to law course; at other schools with International Baccalaureate programs, anthropology or philosophy were offered. District officials argued that a common core curriculum ultimately served students who requested in-district transfers. Approximately 20 percent of the student population was estimated to leave their neighborhood school and transfer to another school in the district. To ensure the success of those students at their new school, one of the initiative's first policies involved purchasing identical curricular resources, such as textbooks, for every grade level. To accomplish this task, the district organized curriculum adoption committees in stages for high school core courses. Language arts, or English, and social studies were selected for adoptions first; world languages, math, and science would convene the following year.

Teachers were invited by principals to participate in the adoptions. The twelve high schools in PPS were represented by at least one social studies teacher each, a volunteer position that required us to listen to textbook representatives (think car salespeople but with books), assess the materials, talk to each other about our individual school's needs, and take curriculum samples back to our schools to discuss them during department meetings to be sure we were being inclusive in our voting process. We were to represent the voices of our fellow social studies teachers and students of our diverse school communities to find what was best for everyone. At least, that was what many of us believed.

My pedagogy is highly influenced by critical theory and the education liberation philosophies of Paulo Freire, Michael Apple, bell hooks, and Peter McLaren, among others. Equally important in my professional development, I am fortunate to live in one of the epicenters of Rethinking Schools, a nonprofit education group committed to social justice in education action in schools and teacher practice. These perspectives provide me with a critical lens through which to view both content and curriculum used in my classes. As one of many PPS teachers who self-identify as a social-justice educator, I believed the curriculum adoption process was an opportunity to have conversations around providing equitable curriculum for our students based on our individual site needs and unique neighborhoods. However, many of us who were selected or volunteered for the adoption committee were equally concerned about losing the individual integrity of our unique courses at our schools through the common schedule process. Many of us considered the student transfer rate a minor problem, and it did not seem as concerning in comparison to the inequitable support of materials and curriculum supplies that some schools desperately needed. Furthermore, many of us designed our own curriculum, meaning we created a "unit" or "path" based on the interests of our students that included academic and nonacademic content and skills. For many of us, our participation on this committee was an opportunity to select materials we could use based on our knowledge as classroom teachers.

When educators talk about making curriculum and materials choices, it's not about deciding on a single kit or defined set of lesson plans that everyone will use. It's about what resources, texts, films, documents, artifacts, and the like we will have access to plan our year of study around. These choices determine the themes, definitions, perspective, and content that are the foundation for what we can do in the classroom. As a language arts teacher, I enjoyed the freedom to select a variety of district-purchased literary texts to develop my curricular path or choices with my students. The choice of texts offered me the luxury to not teach from a standard language arts textbook, which failed to appeal to my students' interests in reading for many reasons. When I switched to teaching global studies, the district supplied me with a traditional, Western-perspective textbook. Social studies textbooks, distinctively heavy with short chunks of information, timelines, and questions at the end of the chapter, did not suit my approach to teaching social studies; nor did they ever provide a curriculum that matched my pedagogical style of critical historical inquiry. Even more important, my students hated them.

Although the population of our students of color at my high school was relatively small compared to other PPS high schools, several of my students self-identified as Native Alaskan, Native American, African, Chinese American, Korean American, Croatian, Mexican American, Mexican, and African American. They wanted to learn about their histories, and resisted teachers who used these textbooks by skipping or failing class.

Many social studies teachers in my district saw this pattern and shared the goal of designing and teaching a curriculum that did not represent a dominant white or middle-class perspective. These teachers believed that such an adoption of resources would benefit our students and help build a more representative curriculum. Those of us who agreed to participate with the adoption had very high hopes that we would be able to represent these concerns and address the limitations of our current resources.

Once the adoption process began, it became clear that equity in the common core meant something different for teachers, community members, and district officials. The adoption of curricular resources was undisputedly needed for many of our schools, but the common core did not recognize the needs of our individual high schools and students. Portland high schools are located in fairly segregated neighborhoods, not only by socioeconomic standards, but also by race and ethnicity. By insisting that equity meant the same, Portland Public Schools developed systemwide changes that failed to understand the academic, cultural, linguistic, and economic needs of our students and their school communities. A few teachers from schools often labeled by district and state officials as "underperforming" expressed concern about the lack of cultural identities and perspectives represented in the economics textbooks we reviewed. "Mainstream America" or "white, middle-class America" was overrepresented in the texts' photographs, graphs, and images in the same ways as before. Similarly, many of us voiced serious concerns that some of the American history textbooks the district considered adopting portrayed the complex histories of indigenous people in the margins, as a side story to the main stories of pilgrims, pioneers, and presidents. Overall, many teachers were concerned that we were adopting another whitewashed curriculum for our social studies classes.

Several community members who were also part of the adoption process had similar concerns. The combined positions of some of the parents on the parent adoption committee and our teacher committee formed a unified front on many of these issues because we were concerned about the impact it would have on our students. It was also apparent that the committees lacked representation from a more needed group: the students themselves. Several teachers brought up their absence in the adoption process. At the very least, we encouraged the school district to distribute textbooks that made the "final cut"—books that were highly recommended in our voting process—to all of the high schools for their input. The curriculum director thought it would be too expensive to send the books around to each school and that it would fail to meet the district's procurement deadline. The compromise was to send the selected books to four school locations, where community members were invited to look at the materials and voice their opinions about the committee's choices. In a school district with more than seventy different languages spoken by our students and parents, an invitation to view curriculum materials was extended only to those families who spoke the more dominant language groups within the district; unfortunately, this community outreach was not met with much success.

Teachers from our more marginalized school neighborhoods attempted to offer their perspectives on what their students needed to compensate for parents who were unable to attend the textbook adoption sessions, and passionately argued for more flexibility. Their arguments were met with a colorblind rhetoric that argued that students who were "not achieving" would rise to the challenge if given the *same* textbooks, or similar curricular materials, as "high-achieving" schools. The common core "must" be common, they argued, and officials went ahead with adopting the textbooks that we were fighting against. And yet our committee was also charged with a different adoption plan for schools with more advanced programs, such as Advanced Placement and International Baccalaureate (IB). Common core textbooks did not meet the needs of these coveted programs, and a different set of texts was required to support students in college-preparatory courses. Ultimately, certain types of students influenced the decision to diversify the textbook choices, but not the types of students that many of us had advocated for.

In the end, after months of negotiations and compromises, district officials, some parents, and teachers solidified the choices for the adoption. Many teachers adamantly called for the adoption to also include ancillary materials to critique the limited or misrepresented information in the textbooks. One text, in particular, was highly contentious: Howard Zinn's *A People's History of the United States*. This was a text many of us wanted to use in regular and advanced classes. We argued that we could use the essays as a way to show our students how to be critical thinkers and write persuasive arguments with historical data. We talked to parents on the other adoption committee and had their approval of the text. And we had asked several students who were already familiar with the text if it was a good choice for students. Overwhelmingly, they agreed it was. Finally, teachers who had voted in support of the district decisions for most of the textbooks did not offer any opposition to purchasing *A People's History of the United*

States. In the end, however, district officials, who were not as enthused as our colleagues, parents, and students, did not agree with our choice. Even though we had a majority vote on our committee, they overruled the process of the adoption. We learned that even the adoption process was not as equitable as we had imagined it was.

As the district finalized its approved adoption, the creation of a "common core" via curricular materials did nothing to address decades of inequities between our neighborhood schools. Schools located in higher socioeconomic neighborhoods that wanted certain books but did not get them simply acquired funding for the resources they wanted through individual school fund-raisers. Schools without these means were left with only the textbooks purchased and approved by the district. The idea of equity, it seemed, meant schools would receive nothing more and nothing less from the district. Status quo was symbolically represented by the adoption of approved district textbooks with nothing to account for schools with limited fund-raising capabilities.

Today, I am teaching global studies after taking a two-year leave of absence to pursue a doctoral degree in education from the University of Oregon. My decision to leave my school for another degree in education was undeniably associated with the experiences I had in this adoption process and with the district policies around equity and curriculum. The loss of autonomy and lack of appreciation for professional expertise continues to affect my students and my classroom's lack of resources on a daily basis. The extremities of our district's curriculum process can be summed up by a closer examination of my school's use of the textbooks we were forced to adopt: four of five teachers teaching freshmen social studies do not use the new textbook (although the global studies class has been conveniently retitled "Modern World History" after the new textbook), compared to all four IB teachers using the textbooks approved just for their classes. This small sample is quite significant, given the numbers of students in these classes: maybe 5 to 10 percent of our students in each freshmen social studies class will take an IB history class in which the district financially supported the purchase of historically equitable texts. While our school strives to include more students of color in our IB program, there are disproportionately small numbers of underrepresented youth in IB classes. In our tracked system, district approved testbooks persistently remain in "regular" social studies classes, which serve more of our students of color. In these classes, the available texts continue to reflect traditional and whitewashed versions of American history, government, and economics.

A teacher friend of mine once told me that to achieve equity, some groups will have to give up what they already have access to and other groups will need more due to a long history of disparity reflected in our current institutional systems. The differences between the types of textbooks some schools were able to purchase on their own versus other schools that had no choice reflects a basic inequity: we can't get resources that are best suited for our students. Our schools are unique, and our students are, too. This must be a consideration in determining how we educate in an inequitable society. "Equity" must mean more than "same" if we are to create a truly equitable system that benefits all students in every school.

Lynne Gardner-Allers has been teaching high school social studies and language arts in Portland Public Schools for over seventeen years. In addition to teaching a variety of social studies courses at all grade levels, she continues to be an active participant in local school- and district-level curriculum development and adoption processes. She is also a doctoral student at the University of Oregon. Her research interests include theoretical conceptions of knowledge production in social studies as a discipline, teacher education, and social-justice curriculum.

What Got Left Behind

Fourth Graders Uncover Inequity and Find Their Voice

JOHN LOCKHART AND GRETA MCHANEY-TRICE

We met at an annual progressive educators' conference, the North Dakota Study Group, as two concerned, justice-oriented educators who felt that the testing and accountability mindset increasingly constrained meaningful learning in schools. Stark differences exist between our backgrounds. John, barely thirty and biracial, grew up in California. His laid-back demeanor and incessant questioning of systems often contrasted with Greta's Southern upbringing. A Black woman in her midfifties, she was keenly aware that despite sweeping social change, Blacks still couldn't take for granted what whites could.

We challenged each other's ideas about racism, teaching, fulfilling state mandates, and how we as teachers could best work with marginalized families. Rather than succumbing to increasing pressure, becoming disempowered, and just teaching to the test, we began teaching together to prove to ourselves that we could do something to offset bleak and demoralizing school conditions while engaging students in quality learning. We asked ourselves (1) how could we resist the mandates of testing, teach progressively, and include social justice, and (2) can we help students understand social inequity and how it affects them?

We engaged Greta's thirty-two fourth-grade students in conducting sociological inquiry and personal identity work, work that is not normally a part of school curriculum. A standard school approach would have students read some basic sociology texts, answer some questions on worksheets, and perhaps watch a film. We challenged our students to be "sociologists" who attempt to "explain human behavior" through questioning, observing, and analysis to generate knowledge. Framing their work, we continuously asked our students to examine the questions: where have we come from, where are we at, where are we going? The key to this unit was to constantly engage students in conversation, have them work with their own and each other's stories, question statements and situations to uncover underlying causes, and assemble a narrative of their own.

GRETA

Touted by Black preachers, teachers, and parents alike as I grew up in the segregated South, education was seen as the beacon of hope and opportunity for the Negro, the equalizer, if you will. Gaining access to it was heralded and depicted by the courageous efforts of the Little Rock Nine and many others before and during the modern Civil Rights Movement. The words of Frederick Douglass, "To educate a man is to unfit him to be a slave," had inspired many out of slavery, through the era of Jim Crow, and into the fight for desegregation. I saw the disparity we faced in schools, materials, and the like. I don't recall being in despair, understanding that hard work and study would make the difference one day.

Though I knew injustice and segregation presented daunting challenges, the greater, more permanent damage imposed on my psyche and identity was less apparent, but manifested itself in my choice to withdraw from college the first time I attended. With the end to legal segregation and with few teacher-mentors like those I had had in my early school years, who had understood, acknowledged, and could address racism's damage, I floundered, disillusioned as I observed many less adept students flourish. Upon returning a few years later, Jay MacLeod's *Ain't No Makin' It* powerfully helped me to realize that lowered teacher expectations of minority students often resulted in their low aspirations and achievement.[96] Consequently, providing equitable learning opportunities in a society where racism and class oppression continue to thrive requires a *different* kind of teaching, similar to those of my early teachers, who worked to impart to me the same awareness Frederick Douglass discovered: success does not always depend on intellect and efforts alone, and mental enslavement is as potent as physical enslavement.

Returning to college, I embraced MacLeod's work and social-justice theories that articulated systemic educational abuse. Such ideas were absolutely critical to the teacher I was becoming, forever motivated to counter the prevailing narratives of "deserved" defeat and inherent inadequacy, historical messages of inferiority still prevalent in many more places than just our schools. My past experiences and emerging epiphany shaped a teaching philosophy to elevate students' consciousness, exposing the contradictions and constraints of a society that espouses egalitarianism while perpetuating conditions that privilege those in political and economic power; had I known better, I would not have lived in self-defeat for leaving college.

When I started teaching, I made the space in my classroom and curriculum to meld academic skills students needed with recognizing many of the social realities that certain students faced because of race and class. One time, before the legislation reshaped schools, a student shared in class that he and his mom were followed in the mall "just because we were Black," suspected of stealing. I asked the class, "Does that really happen?" Most, but not all, of the Black students—about 50 percent of the class—fervently nodded yes, while the other students either shrugged their shoulders uncertainly or voiced a definite no.

In a spontaneous act, we walked three blocks to the neighborhood gas station mart to test this idea. DeMarcus, a Black male student, went into the store. About three minutes later he rejoined us after being watched and asked by "a man" if he wanted to buy something. Then Aaron, a white student, volunteered to go inside. Returning much later, he confessed he'd only returned because he himself felt weird about the time he'd been gone. The clerk only asked him as he left, "Hey, isn't there school today?" The look on his face as he shook his head in disbelief: priceless! Before, he had vehemently denied that Blacks were treated differently in stores. This experience transformed Aaron's ideas, as well as his classmates'. Transforming minds—a purpose to teach.

Back then I had the latitude to let the curriculum fit students' needs, interests, and lives, a function fundamental to student-centered teaching, creating opportunities to educate and expose students to injustice and inequities. When the state made test scores the way to measure student achievement, teacher quality, and school worthiness, my district, like others, reacted to satisfy the demands. The imposed pacing guides, quarterly assessments, and grade-level expectations restricted space to teach beyond the prescribed curriculum. Staff meetings and professional development sessions became trainings centered on scores—viewing students in terms of aggregated percentiles and adequate yearly progress—a dehumanizing paradigm shift. This led to systematized actions that further marginalized students who did not perform well by subjecting them to more pull-out tutoring, test-prep programs, rote memorization, and drills for recall. Teacher and student enthusiasm waned.

Michigan's Department of Education reported in 2003 that 85 percent of those on the "high priority" list of failing schools were in urban centers, with 50 percent in Detroit. Nine out of ten students in schools deemed failing were students of color, while only one out of four students in schools that made adequate yearly progress were students of color. A decade later, little has changed. Government mandates still have not fixed problems of disparity, exacerbating them in many places while constraining schools and teachers from teaching in ways that actually educate those most likely to stay or end up in poverty. Moreover, these mandates have all but eliminated pedagogical opportunities to address situations in ways that would be effective for my students' needs. In dismay and with some despair, I often discussed this dilemma with other professional colleagues like John.

JOHN

Growing up in the 1980s and '90s on the suburban peninsula of San Francisco, I found classroom life in my Catholic elementary school, where half of my classmates were of color, pretty dull. School was a place where I had to show that I knew certain things to get good marks but wanted and thought there should be something more. My working-class parents scraped by, but always managed to feed us and pay the very reduced rate tuition, teaching us lessons to live right, to do well at school because that would help, and that we'd be out of the house at eighteen and have to make our own way in the world. Though they were an interracial couple, they didn't talk about race much with us, and it wasn't until I went to high school in San Francisco that I began to understand the importance of institutional structures, opportunity, and life chances. I was teaching science in a Portland, Oregon, high school with a large number of poor and working-class students when the federal government enacted its legislation, and I saw my administrators immediately narrow their focus to student test scores. By the time I left there in June 2003, the school leaders were pressing us to do more test preparation, an important curricular move toward teaching to the test.

I moved on to get my doctorate at Michigan State, choosing to teach the urban section of a course to student teachers who were completing their internships in Lansing high schools. Most of the student teachers were middle-class white women, and like many entering teaching in urban schools, they were filled with good intentions as they started their careers. They, too, reported feeling a lot of pressure to teach in traditional ways and do things at a basic level, with eyes firmly placed on the test scores. Most troubling for me was to hear some of the interns blame students for their social problems while paying little attention to or considering their own inability to teach them effectively. They used middle-class frames of reference from their own schooling history to make sense of their students' lives, and subtly blamed their students for not learning, absolving themselves from their responsibility to engage their students. I wanted to find classrooms in the area that were really working for students of color and that presented a different kind of education than test preparation.

JOINING FORCES IN THE CLASSROOM

The two of us—Greta, an award-winning teacher, and John, an aspiring professor finishing graduate work—decided to teach a unit together to reinvigorate our beliefs in the purpose of education and push ourselves to provide a really meaningful experience for Greta's thirty-two students. For twelve weeks, we had students use project-based learning to conduct a sociological investigation where they attempted to explain human behavior in relation to education. Our main goals were that through literature, history, media, inquiry, observation, and writing, the students would (1) confront inequity in systems, especially schools; (2) have opportunities to study themselves within their social and political environments; and (3) have out-of-classroom experiences within, and focused on, the Lansing community and daily life. At the end of the project, students would write their own narratives combining their research, inquiry, and experiences.

Our first day started with John's personal narrative that focused on his journey through school systems. As we talked about why some people failed to make it through "successfully," students' perceptions about where and how they saw themselves quickly emerged. In most of their minds, success or failure was pretty much up to the individual student, mainly one's study habits and hard work. Although a few asserted that some teachers care and others do not, students had little consciousness of how other factors impact one's life chances. The rest of their statements about school focused on getting to college and getting a job, standard reasons given for the purpose of school. By fourth grade, most students who struggled at all with school already blamed themselves, without considering teachers, parents, and other family members, resources, curriculum, and the myriad policy makers who help decide what gets taught and why. John queried the students as to why they thought so much of schooling was filling in bubbles and doing worksheets, and if this was what they enjoyed doing. One student paused and replied, "Because they want to tell you *what* to think and not teach you *how* to think?" There was a brief moment of silence in the classroom.

To give them perspective beyond elementary school, we invited six former students from the school to speak as a panel about life after sixth grade, including preparing for the future. Greta's elementary school feeds into Olds High School, whose population had consistently and drastically declined, partly because some families took advantage of the state's school-choice policy, opting out of the district to the so-called better schools, which were predominantly white, middle-class, and suburban. The elementary school had experienced its own demographic changes, being one of the district's last schools to become a Title I school. It was losing its long-held reputation as a "good school."

Five of the panelists attended Olds, though Chantelle had recently transferred there from Suburban High, where Sandra attended. Chantelle passionately spoke about having felt culturally and socially isolated at Suburban: "Everybody thinks that Suburban High is all that and Olds ain't, but I'm doing better at Olds, and Suburban is not what everybody thinks. There are problems there and kids fight, too. I went because my parents wanted me to go, but I didn't feel right, it's just different." Sandra nodded in agreement and went on to explain that she didn't really mind, and could deal with the "differences." Dominic shared: "Olds is perceived to be a bad school, but they got some good teachers and some bad teachers. I didn't let it stress me out . . . It's mostly the bad kids that don't go to class and get into trouble. It's like a business, the manager may be good, but the employees are the ones that make it a bad business."

Like the fourth graders, the high school panelists blamed student behavior for any academic problems rather than examine systemic factors. Near the end, though, the discussion shifted from the usual cliché advice of listen to your teachers, do your homework, and hang around good kids to other factors: teachers, parenting roles, gender, class, and race, and their effects on school success. Ronald and Ashley commented on how Black boys got in trouble, even suspended, for doing the same actions that girls did, such as entering and exiting school through improper doors. Ashley, the only white panelist, shared how school security would let her go through the prohibited doors while Black boys got suspended for doing so. We noted many heads nod in affirmation as others shook theirs in obvious disbelief, yet the panelists garnered students' respect and credibility, impressing them, since they once had been where the students now sat. The exchanges were rapid. With excitement high, the panel session ran over into the coveted computer class time as students asked many questions and shared some similar stories. But nothing we had planned prepared us for what happened next.

The panel members were about to leave but wanted to see some of their former teachers. After escorting students to computer class, Greta returned to thank the panelists. She heard a very loud ruckus and noticed Ronald visibly upset, shaking, nearly in tears. The others began to explain that they had convinced him to visit a particular teacher. Once they had shared why they had come to the school that day, the teacher remarked, "Oh, Ronald, I did not think you would have made it past middle school!" The teacher had a reputation for being insensitive to African American males, and some parents had requested their child not be placed in this class. This prompted Greta to explicitly bring it up with the students when they came back from computer class, asking, "Why would this upset Ronald? Was his hurt and anger justified?" We continued to use these opportunities to address our recurrent theme of having students analyze events such as this. Without assessing intent, we let the students speak to the impact and consequences of what had occurred. They debated among themselves the plausible explanations, for example, "maybe he did not like the teacher" or "the teacher wasn't thinking," and began to use evidence to support their notions. They responded with such things as, "Ronald had left smiling after doing a good thing by taking his time to come and talk to us, and the teacher was wrong for upsetting him like that!" "That teacher is a racist, because my mom says so!" These are nine- and ten-year-olds grappling with things they don't normally talk about in a classroom—or perhaps in their lives at all—in real time as issues arise, including those involving the students they had just met and now viewed as new role models.

Like good sociologists, we also wanted to look to the past for perspective, so we read much of *Narrative of the Life of Frederick Douglass*. They'd studied Douglass's epiphany as he realized that his pathway to freedom depended on his learning to read, and that the masters *knew* the slave would "become unmanageable and of no value" once educated. He wrote: "It was a new and special revelation . . . I set out with high hope, and a fixed purpose, at whatever cost of trouble, to learn how to read . . . I owe almost as much to the bitter opposition my master held as to my mistress." We read and reread this passage, until Rynnelle spoke out loudly, "I get it, I get it! It's like there are two kinds of slavery!" We went on to talk about both physical chains and the mental chains that lock the mind, which are much harder to break—the *slave mentality*.

Students were beginning to accept the idea that, while the physical captivity of slaves was often horrific, Douglass realized that the psychological damage of ignorance and self-debasement worked to keep slaves in bondage. Greta explicitly asked, "Are poor kids or Black kids all bad or not as smart? Was it the slave's fault for being a slave?" We pointed out that, clearly, Douglass was capable of learning but was denied opportunity and resources, an inequity that made all the difference. We pointed out to students how different opportunities and resources—like differential access to computers and field trips as well as curricular options for college-bound courses and electives in the so-called good schools—play a major part.

As we continued studying historical circumstances, students began to understand power in more complex ways. While watching selections from the documentary *Slavery and the Making of America*, students questioned why the slaves didn't do more about their condition, with James saying amidst a chorus of agreement, "Shoot, I would have just killed the master or something." The film emphasized how the institution of slavery was tied to international markets to make money through the production and trading of goods, including slaves, a concept broader than just lazy masters, as the students initially had conceived. This prompted Briana to say, "You mean it's like how the slaves picked cotton for the masters, and Kanye West sings *Money, Money*, and it makes money for the producers and labels, but not the rappers? And that is like a kind of modern-day slavery?" Her profound statement to her peers indicated a heightened awareness that we'd hoped to see about who's in control and why. Examining the social, more complex context of power and oppression as a structure and not merely the plight of individuals helped the students begin to understand how systemic inequity can remain in society and impact everyone.

We asked students to think about the effects of race and class in their daily lives and about events that interfere with educational attainment. John told the class about being stopped on his bicycle and detained by the Lansing police for no reason other than "you fit the description" of someone they claimed to be looking for. A class discussion ensued on the role of the police, the meaning of "protect and serve," and why so many more Latinos and Blacks, especially males, drop out of school and end up in jail. The class was animated as many of the Black students argued that the police are racist, with a couple sharing how the police have interacted with their own family members. Echoing Greta's earlier class that had visited the gas station mart, many of the white students began to argue that the police only stop people that are bad, but when pressed by our asking "in what ways was John bad for riding his bike home at night?," these students stumbled on their words. The cognitive dissonance and disbelief was palpable.

This discussion greatly affected Casey, a disengaged biracial student who often misbehaved, and whose father had recently been incarcerated. With our help, Casey researched and learned about the connection between dropping out of high school and the statistical likelihood of ending up in prison. Later, in his own narrative entitled "Being Bi-racial," Casey wrote about the different methods of discipline used by his custodial white mother and his black father, who is "all about discipline." He confronted aspects of his social world and some inconsistencies in it, such as the differences in how his parents allowed him to behave. By his *choosing* to write about it, we assert he was challenging the ways he conceived of these parts of his life and his outlook on school, his behavior, and his future. This met our goal of providing him and other students with a space to study themselves within their own social and political environments.

We purposefully designed tasks where students gathered artifacts and data to construct and reflect on their work and not just recite facts. These tasks helped structure information so they could write narratives of their own lives. We emphasized that the narrative was not just the important act of them telling their stories, but was also connected to larger social, cultural, and historical ideas, another key objective. We also helped students to engage in the affirming and informative experience of presenting part of their narrative near the end of the school year to a gathering of parents, loved ones, and other school personnel. Despite the fact that these topics would not show up on a test, this project easily met key state standards for skill building. Michigan's social studies benchmarks explicitly "require active, social studies inquiry" and state, "students should engage in disciplined inquiry, analysis, and argumentation . . . It entails learning how to read, write, and use the social studies to understand and participate in the world around us" so students can frame important problems and questions. Our project met this benchmark better than any textbook or pacing guide could have through the students' stories, multimedia presentations, and parent interviews.

One student drafted a written piece that focused on her mother's tragic murder and her current living situation. Diamond was too young to remember the events herself, but used knowledge from media and family accounts.

In her narrative, she explained why her older sister acted out at home and in school. She asserted, "When you don't have a mother, you don't get the same attention as you would from your real biological mother." Diamond, the sociologist, evaluated why her sister did poorly in school (a system) and examined the social issues that affected her, whereas before she had thought of her sister as just "being bad." Having learned new information about her life through this process, Diamond presented her work with an even demeanor and with pride and satisfaction, even though she was extremely shy. Her adoptive parent, her mother's sister, praised our efforts to help Diamond understand how the events of her mother's death impacted her yet today in school. She was amazed at Diamond's power, poise, and clarity in both her narrative and oral presentation. She assured us that both she and Diamond had learned a great deal. Could a raw test score or letter grade reveal as much about student growth?

Greta had spoken to some concerned parents early in the unit so they would understand what we were doing in the classroom, but our full engagement with families came when students interviewed their parents and invited them in for the presentations. Many of the parents shared how much they enjoyed the presentations, and moreover, how much they learned about the different experiences of their child's classmates, some of whom they thought they knew much better. At the same time they marveled at what the students were able to demonstrate. During the presentation, we seized the opportunity to explicitly compare this type of learning to what had become the norm of schooling—merely to pass tests. We encouraged parents to share their observations with school leaders, because their voices made a difference.

Greta's principal was extremely concerned about the school's Adequate Yearly Progress numbers, to say the least. However, when asked about the project two years later, she excitedly recalled the work, the presentations, the parents' pleasure, and her overall belief in the merit of the work. She especially focused on the power of the student presentations she had witnessed, especially Diamond's. She eloquently spoke on how the project marked "a great example of differentiated teaching," adding that students sometimes act out in schools because of some unmet emotional needs. She added that meeting some of these emotional needs would result in a better student. Originally, her main concern had been how the project would help scores. She has since changed her focus to a more humanizing look at students.

Through this project, we directly engaged in equitable teaching practices in several ways. First, as teachers, we developed a structure for the project: students would be sociologists doing personal identity work and studying themselves in relationship to each other, their families, and their city. Within this framework, all of our students engaged in the project because their own interests led them to choose what they wished to study and write about. The writing, speaking, and thinking involved pushed each student beyond his or her current level as students talked and wrote with each other and their teachers, and practiced academic skills like writing, editing, and giving a presentation of their learning. We helped raise student awareness about the social inequities that exist in school and society while undertaking serious, rigorous study and further developing academic and social skills in a humanized experience—more than satisfying the normal demands of public schooling. For the teachers, students, and families involved, it was an empowering experience—and one that will never show up on a test.

John Lockhart is currently working as an assistant principal in Portland, Oregon. Previously, he had been a mentor for first-year teachers, an associate professor of education preparing new teachers, and a public high school science teacher. John earned his PhD from Michigan State University and has also planned and implemented professional development and presentations in a variety of locations. He has actively worked with teachers and district leaders to increase racial awareness and engage in equitable classroom instruction.

Greta McHaney-Trice is a retired educator who spent fifteen years in elementary education and received the Michigan State University Outstanding Alumni K–12 Teacher Award in 2010. Post retirement, she is the executive director of Resolution Services Center, a nonprofit organization that helps schools implement restorative justice to reduce violence, suspensions, and disciplinary actions. She continues her commitment to progressive education, equity, inclusion, and social justice for students.

Notes

Introduction

1. Allie Bidwell, "Florida School District Opts Out of Opting Out," *US News & World Report*, September 2, 2014, http://www.usnews.com/news/articles/2014/09/02/florida-school-district-retracts-historic-testing-opt-out-decision.
2. Andrew Ujifusa, "A 'Common-Core Math' Problem: How Many States Have Adopted the Standards?" *Education Week*, June 30, 2015, http://blogs.edweek.org/edweek/state_edwatch/2015/06/a_common_core_math_problem_how_many_states_have_adopted_the_standards.html.
3. Kathy Christie and Jennifer Dounay Zinth, *Teacher Tenure or Continuing Contract Laws* (Denver, CO: Education Commission of the States, August 2011); Jennifer Thomsen, "50-State Comparison: Teacher Tenure / Continuing Contract Policies," Education Commission of the States, May 1, 2014, http://www.ecs.org/teacher-tenure-continuing-contract-policies/; Motoko Rich, "Teacher Tenure Is Challenged Again in a Minnesota Lawsuit," *New York Times*, April 13, 2016, http://www.nytimes.com/2016/04/14/us/teacher-tenure-is-challenged-again-in-a-minnesota-lawsuit.html.
4. Kathryn M. Doherty and Sandi Jacobs, "2015 State of the States: Evaluating Teaching, Leading and Learning" (Washington, D.C.: National Council on Teacher Quality, November 2015).
5. Diana Oxley and Julia Kassissieh, "From Comprehensive High Schools to Small Learning Communities: Accomplishments and Challenges," *Forum: For Promoting 3–19 Comprehensive Education* 50, no. 2 (2008): 199, http://www.schoolturnaroundsupport.org/sites/default/files/resources/forum_from_comprehensive_to_slc.pdf.
6. "Out of Control: The Systemic Disenfranchisement of African American and Latino Communities Through School Takeovers," The Alliance to Reclaim Our Schools, August 2015. http://www.reclaimourschools.org/sites/default/files/out-of-control-takeover-report.pdf
7. "Charter School Data Dashboard—National/Schools," National Alliance for Public Charter Schools, 2016, http://dashboard2.publiccharters.org/National/.
8. Alan Greenblatt, "New Orleans District Moves to an All-Charter System," nprED, May 30, 2014, http://www.npr.org/sections/ed/2014/05/30/317374739/new-orleans-district-moves-to-an-all-charter-system.
9. Daniel J. Losen and Russell J. Skiba, "Suspended Education: Urban Middle Schools in Crisis," eScholarship, September 13, 2010, https://escholarship.org/uc/item/8fh0s5dv.pdf.
10. Gary Orfield et al., *Brown at 60: Great Progress, a Long Retreat and an Uncertain Future* (Los Angeles: The Civil Rights Project/Proyecto Derechos Civiles at the University of California, Los Angeles, May 15, 2014). https://civilrightsproject.ucla.edu/research/k-12-education/integration-and-diversity/brown-at-60-great-progress-a-long-retreat-and-an-uncertain-future_
11. Andre M. Perry, "The Education-Reform Movement Is Too White to Do Any Good," *Washington Post*, June 2, 2014, https://www.washingtonpost.com/posteverything/wp/2014/06/02/the-education-reform-movement-is-too-white-to-do-any-good/.

Chapter 1

1. Rhema Thompson, "Too Much Test Stress? Parents, Experts Discuss High-Stakes Standardized Test Anxiety," *WJCT*, April 23, 2014, http://news.wjct.org/post/too-much-test-stress-parents-experts-discuss-high-stakes-standardized-test-anxiety.

2. John Annese, "Fears, Tears and Prozac Par for 3rd-Grade Course," Staten Island Advance, April 21, 2004, http://www.freerepublic.com/focus/f-news/1121963/posts.

3. Marion Brady, "One Mother's Story: How Overemphasis on Standardized Tests Caused Her 9-Year-Old to Try to Hang Himself," AlterNet, August 1, 2016, http://www.alternet.org/education/perils-standardized-tests.

4. Nanette Asimov, "Disabled Students Call Test Unfair / State High School Exit Exam Forcing Them Out of Classroom, Some Say," SFGate, March 2, 2003, http://www.sfgate.com/education/article/Disabled-students-call-test-unfair-State-high-2630208.php.

5. Natasha K. Segool et al., "Heightened Test Anxiety Among Young Children: Elementary School Students' Anxious Responses to High-Stakes Testing: Test Anxiety Among School Children," *Psychology in the Schools* 50, no. 5 (May 2013): 489–99, doi:10.1002/pits.21689; Joseph J. Pedulla et al., "Perceived Effects of State-Mandated Testing Programs on Teaching and Learning: Findings from a National Survey of Teachers," March 2003, http://eric.ed.gov/?id=ED481836.

6. Janet Y. Thomas and Kevin P. Brady, "Chapter 3: The Elementary and Secondary Education Act at 40: Equity, Accountability, and the Evolving Federal Role in Public Education," *Review of Research in Education* 29, no. 1 (January 1, 2005): 51–67, doi:10.3102/0091732X029001051.

7. Jay P. Heubert and Robert M. Hauser, *High Stakes: Testing for Tracking, Promotion, and Graduation* (Washington, DC: National Academy Press, 1999), https://www.nap.edu/read/6336/chapter/1, http://eric.ed.gov/?id=ED439151.

8. Allie Bidwell, "Florida School District Opts Out of Opting Out," *US News & World Report*, September 2, 2014, http://www.usnews.com/news/articles/2014/09/02/florida-school-district-retracts-historic-testing-opt-out-decision.

9. Jennifer McMurrer, "Choices, Changes, and Challenges: Curriculum and Instruction in the NCLB Era" (Washington, DC: Center on Education Policy, 2007); Farkas Duffet Research Group, "Learning Less: Public School Teachers Describe a Narrowing Curriculum" (Washington, DC: Common Core, March 2012); Sam Dillon, "Schools Cut Back Subjects to Push Reading and Math," *New York Times*, March 26, 2006, http://www.nytimes.com/2006/03/26/education/26child.html.

10. Wayne Au, "High-Stakes Testing and Curricular Control: A Qualitative Metasynthesis," *Educational Researcher* 36, no. 5 (July 2007): 258; see also: Heinrich Mintrop, "The Limits of Sanctions in Low-Performing Schools," *Education Policy Analysis Archives* 11, no. 0 (January 15, 2003): 3, doi:10.14507/epaa.v11n3.2003; Laura S. Hamilton, ed., *Standards-Based Accountability Under No Child Left Behind: Experiences of Teachers and Administrators in Three States* (Santa Monica, CA: Rand Corporation, 2007).

11. Derek Neal and Diane Whitmore Schanzenbach, "Left Behind By Design: Proficiency Counts and Test-Based Accountability" (working paper, National Bureau of Economic Research, Cambridge, MA, August 2007), http://www.nber.org/papers/w13293; Jennifer Booher-Jennings, "Below the Bubble: 'Educational Triage' and the Texas Accountability System," *American Educational Research Journal* 42, no. 2 (June 20, 2005): 231–68, doi:10.3102/00028312042002231.

12. Advancement Project, "Test, Punish, and Push Out: How Zero Tolerance and High-Stakes Testing Funnel Youth into the School-to-Prison Pipeline" (Washington, DC: Advancement Project, March 2010); Linda Darling-Hammond, *The Flat World and Education: How America's Commitment to Equity Will Determine Our Future*, 9644th ed. (New York:

Teachers College Press, 2010), 74–98; "5 Educators Arrested in El Paso Schools Fraud Scheme," Associated Press, April 27, 2016, http://bigstory.ap.org/article/49d0f7baf26a4c 5894e32aa8b302e7de/5-educators-arrested-el-paso-schools-fraud-scheme.

13. L. Valli and D. Buese, "The Changing Roles of Teachers in an Era of High-Stakes Account-ability," *American Educational Research Journal* 44, no. 3 (September 1, 2007): 519–58, doi:10.3102/0002831207306859; David Hursh, "Exacerbating Inequality: The Failed Promise of the No Child Left Behind Act," *Race Ethnicity and Education* 10, no. 3 (Sep-tember 2007): 295–308, doi:10.1080/13613320701503264; John B. Diamond and James P. Spillane, "High-Stakes Accountability in Urban Elementary Schools: Challenging or Reproducing Inequality?" *Teachers College Record* 106, no. 6 (June 2004): 1145–76, doi:10.1111/j.1467-9620.2004.00375.x.

14. Melissa Lazarín, "Testing Overload in America's Schools," Center for American Prog-ress, October 16, 2014, https://www.americanprogress.org/issues/education/report/ 2014/10/16/99073/testing-overload-in-americas-schools/.

15. Frederick M. Hess, "No More Mr. Rogers: Michelle Rhee Is Getting Tough with Teach-ers-Union Obstructionism," Frederick M. Hess, October 9, 2008, http://www.frederick-hess.org/5036/no-more-mr-rogers; Alyson Klein, David J. Hoff, and Catherine Gewertz, "Obama: Duncan 'Doesn't Blink' on Tough Decisions—Education Week," *Education Week*, December 16, 2008, http://www.edweek.org/ew/articles/2008/12/16/16duncan_ ep.h28.html; Andrew J. Rotherham and Richard Whitmire, "Time for Policy Leaders to Make the Tough Decisions in Education," *RealClearEducation*, September 20, 2014, http://www.realcleareducation.com/articles/2014/11/20/education_policy_decisions_1134 .html.

16. Philissa Cramer, "Following Bloomberg, Walcott Shifts on Teacher Ratings Release," Chalkbeat New York, March 2, 2012, http://www.chalkbeat.org/posts/ny/2012/03/02/ following-bloomberg-walcott-shifts-on-teacher-ratings-release/.

17. Aaron Pallas, "The Emperor's New 'Close,'" *A Sociological Eye on Education*, March 8, 2012, http://nepc.colorado.edu/blog/emperors-new-close.

18. Jennifer Medina, "The Rise and Fall of New York Student Achievement," *New York Times*, October 10, 2010, sec. Education, http://www.nytimes.com/2010/10/11/ education/11scores.html.

19. Victor Bandeira de Mello, "Mapping State Proficiency Standards onto the NAEP Scales: Variation and Change in State Standards for Reading and Mathematics, 2005–2009" (Washington, DC: National Center for Education Statistics, Institute of Education Sci-ences, U.S. Department of Education, 2011); Brian A. Jacob, "Test-Based Accountabil-ity and Student Achievement: An Investigation of Differential Performance on NAEP and State Assessments" (working paper, National Bureau of Economic Research, Janu-ary 2007), http://www.nber.org/papers/w12817; Jaekyung Lee, "Tracking Achievement Gaps and Assessing the Impact of NCLB on the Gaps," eScholarship, June 1, 2006, http:// escholarship.org/uc/item/4db9154t.pdf.

20. Rachel Aviv, "Wrong Answer: A Middle-School Cheating Scandal," *New Yorker*, July 21, 2014, http://www.newyorker.com/magazine/2014/07/21/wrong-answer; Alan Blinder, "Atlanta Educators Convicted in School Cheating Scandal," *New York Times*, April 1, 2015, http://www.nytimes.com/2015/04/02/us/verdict-reached-in-atlanta-school-testing-trial.html.

21. Jack Gillum and Marisol Bello, "When Standardized Test Scores Soared in D.C., Were the Gains Real?" *USA TODAY*, March 30, 2011, http://www.usatoday.com/news/ education/2011-03-28-1Aschooltesting28_CV_N.htm; Greg Toppo, "Memo Warns of Rampant Cheating in D.C. Public Schools," *USA TODAY*, April 12, 2013, http:// www.usatoday.com/story/news/nation/2013/04/11/memo-washington-dc-schools-cheat-

ing/2074473/; John Merrow, "Michelle Rhee's Reign of Error," Taking Note: Thoughts on Education from John Merrow, April 11, 2013, http://takingnote.learningmatters. tv/?p=6232.

22. Linda M. Calbom, "K–12 Education: States' Test Security Policies and Procedures Varied," Washington, DC: Government Accountability Office, May 16, 2013, http://www.gao.gov/ assets/660/654721.pdf.

23. Daniel Koretz, *Measuring Up: What Educational Testing Really Tells Us* (Cambridge, MA: Harvard University Press, 2008), 179–215; Richard Rothstein, Rebecca Jacobsen, and Tamara Wilder, *Grading Education: Getting Accountability Right* (Virginia Beach, VA: Economic Policy Institute, 2008), 58–70.

24. Council of Chief State School Officers (CCSSO) and the National Governors Association Center for Best Practices (NGA Center), "About the Standards," Common Core State Standards Initiative, accessed August 28, 2016, http://www.corestandards.org/ about-the-standards/.

25. Arne Duncan, "Beyond the Bubble Tests: The Next Generation of Assessments" (Achieve's American Diploma Project Leadership Team Meeting, Alexandria, VA, September 2, 2010), http://www.ed.gov/news/speeches/beyond-bubble-tests-next-generation-assessments-secretary-arne-duncans-remarks-state-l.

26. Lyndsey Layton, "How Bill Gates Pulled Off the Swift Common Core Revolution," *Washington Post*, June 7, 2014, http://www.washingtonpost.com/wp-srv/special/national/gates-foundation/.

27. William J. Mathis, "The 'Common Core' Standards Initiative: An Effective Reform Tool?" (Boulder and Tempe: Education and the Public Interest Center & Education Policy Research Unit, 2010), http://www.stopccssinnys.com/uploads/NAEP_The_Common_Core_Standard_Initiative_An_Effective_Reform_Tool___William_J._Mathis__Ph.D._University_of_Color.pdf.

28. Catherine Gewertz, "Common-Standards Watch: Montana Makes 47," *Education Week - Curriculum Matters*, November 4, 2011, http://blogs.edweek.org/edweek/curriculum/2011/ 11/common-standards_watch_montana.html?cmp=SOC-SHR-FB.

29. Stan Karp, "The Problems with the Common Core," *Rethinking Schools* 28, no. 2, Winter 2013/2014, http://www.rethinkingschools.org/archive/28_02/28_02_karp.shtml.

30. "U.S. Secretary of Education Duncan Announces Winners of Competition to Improve Student Assessments | U.S. Department of Education" (U.S. Department of Education, September 2, 2010), http://www.ed.gov/news/press-releases/us-secretary-education-duncan-announces-winners-competition-improve-student-asse. *"First time"*: Anya Kamenetz, *The Test: Why Our Schools Are Obsessed with Standardized Testing—But You Don't Have to Be* (New York: PublicAffairs, 2015), 92.

31. Duncan, "Beyond the Bubble Tests."

32. Elizabeth Phillips, "We Need to Talk About the Test: A Problem with the Common Core," *New York Times*, April 9, 2014, http://www.nytimes.com/2014/04/10/opinion/the-problem-with-the-common-core.html.

33. Carol Burris, "Educators Alarmed by Some Questions on N.Y. Common Core Tests," *Washington Post*, April 19, 2015, http://www.washingtonpost.com/blogs/answer-sheet/ wp/2015/04/19/educators-alarmed-by-some-questions-on-n-y-common-core-tests/.

34. *Example of 2015 state test roll-out:* Andrew Ujifusa, "Smarter Balanced Delays Spur Headaches in Wisconsin, Montana, and Elsewhere," *Education Week*, March 27, 2015, http:// blogs.edweek.org/edweek/state_edwatch/2015/03/smarter_balanced_delay_wisconsin_ montana_nevada_north_dakota.html. *Continuing problems in 2016, including score nullification:* Ty Tagami, "Georgia Computer Problems Disrupt Standardized Testing," *Atlanta Journal-Constitution*, June 5, 2016, http://www.myajc.com/news/news/local-education/

computer-disruptions-at-schools-nullify-results-of/nrHxY/; FairTest keeps a (long!) running list of these problems at http://fairtest.org/computerized-testing-problems-chronology.

35. Motoko Rich, "Test Scores Under Common Core Show That 'Proficient' Varies by State," *New York Times*, October 6, 2015, http://www.nytimes.com/2015/10/07/us/test-scores-under-common-core-show-that-proficient-varies-by-state.html.

36. Ray Hart et al., *Student Testing in America's Great City Schools: An Inventory and Preliminary Analysis* (Washington, DC: Council of the Great City Schools, October 2015); Liana Heitin, "State and District Leaders Vow to Reduce Testing, Stick with Yearly Assessments," *Education Week*, October 15, 2014, http://blogs.edweek.org/edweek/curriculum/2014/10/state_and_district_leaders_vow.html.

37. Sean Cavanagh, "Common-Core Testing Contracts Favor Big Vendors," *Education Week*, October 1, 2014, http://www.edweek.org/ew/articles/2014/10/01/06contract.h34.html.

38. John Richards and Leslie Stebbins, *Behind the Data: Testing and Assessment*, 2014 PreK–12 U.S. Education Technology Market Report (Washington, DC: Education Division of the Software & Information Industry Association [SIIA], 2014).

39. MDR, "Increases in School Instructional Spending Are Largest in Six Years," SchoolData.com, July 2015, http://schooldata.com/increases-in-school-instructional-spending-are-largest-in-six-years/.

40. Stephanie Simon, "No Profit Left Behind," POLITICO, February 10, 2015, http://www.politico.com/story/2015/02/pearson-education-115026.html.

41. Jesse Hagopian, "Our Destination Is Not on the MAP," in *More Than a Score: The New Uprising Against High-Stakes Testing*, ed. Jesse Hagopian (Chicago: Haymarket Books, 2014); Rachel Monahan, "Forget Teaching to the Test—at This Washington Heights Elementary School, Parents Canceled It!" *NY Daily News*, October 21, 2013, http://www.nydailynews.com/new-york/uptown/parents-opt-city-test-article-1.1492127; Owen Davis and StudentNation, "Turn On, Tune In, Opt Out," *The Nation*, November 5, 2013, https://www.thenation.com/article/turn-tune-opt-out/.

42. Juan Gonzalez, "Fed-up Parents Revolt Against State's Standardized Tests," *NY Daily News*, April 14, 2015, http://www.nydailynews.com/new-york/education/fed-up-parents-revolt-state-standardized-tests-article-1.2185433; Swapna Venugopal Ramaswamy, "Schools Seeing High Opt-out Rates," *Lower Hudson Journal News*, April 17, 2015, http://data.lohud.com/maps/examoptout/.

43. Katherine Reynolds Lewis, "Standardized Testing Hits a Nerve," *USA TODAY*, August 8, 2016, http://www.usatoday.com/story/news/2016/08/08/standardized-testing-hits-nerve/88301982/; Christina A. Cassidy, "Opt-out Movement Accelerates amid Common Core Testing," Associated Press, April 17, 2015, http://www.salon.com/2015/04/17/opt_out_movement_accelerates_amid_common_core_testing/.

44. Andrew Ujifusa, "A 'Common-Core Math' Problem: How Many States Have Adopted the Standards?" *Education Week*, June 30, 2015, http://blogs.edweek.org/edweek/state_edwatch/2015/06/a_common_core_math_problem_how_many_states_have_adopted_the_standards.html; Andrew Ujifusa, "Traction Limited in Rolling Back Common Core," *Education Week*, April 22, 2015, http://www.edweek.org/ew/articles/2015/04/22/traction-limited-in-rolling-back-common-core.html.

45. Catherine Gewertz, "State Solidarity Erodes on Common-Core Tests," *Education Week*, March 23, 2016, http://www.edweek.org/ew/articles/2016/03/23/state-solidarity-erodes-on-common-core-tests.html; Catherine Gewertz, "Reach of PARCC, Smarter Balanced Drops Sharply in 2015–16," Curriculum Matters, *Education Week*, March 28, 2016, http://blogs.edweek.org/edweek/curriculum/2016/03/Reach_of_PARCC_Smarter_Balanced_drops_sharply_in_2015-16.html.

46. Kate Zernike, "Testing for Joy and Grit? Schools Nationwide Push to Measure Stu-

dents' Emotional Skills," *New York Times*, February 29, 2016, http://www.nytimes.com/2016/03/01/us/testing-for-joy-and-grit-schools-nationwide-push-to-measure-students-emotional-skills.html.

47. Angela L. Duckworth and David Scott Yeager, "Measurement Matters: Assessing Personal Qualities Other Than Cognitive Ability for Educational Purposes," *Educational Researcher* 44, no. 4 (May 1, 2015): 237–51, doi:10.3102/0013189X15584327.

48. Peter Hill and Michael Barber, *Preparing for a Renaissance in Assessment* (London: Pearson, 2014), http://www.pageturn.co.uk/pearson/Preparing_for_a_Renaissance_in_Assessment.pdf.

49. Rothstein, Jacobsen, and Wilder, *Grading Education.*, 35-74, 99-118, 141-159

50. Darling-Hammond, *The Flat World and Education*, 305.

51. Rothstein, Jacobsen, and Wilder, *Grading Education.*, 152-156

52. The names of students, faculty, and the school have been changed throughout the collection. Dialogue is a composite and approximate. The poetry is from student writing.

53. In this story, the names of the people and school have not been changed.

54. Aviv, "Wrong Answer."

55. In this story, the names of people and the school have not been changed. All teachers, administrators, and school staff go by first names with students.

56. I hesitated somewhat to tell Reyna's story because I don't want others to glorify her story or view her from a deficit perspective. Reyna and I have talked at length; she has read and approved this paper and has encouraged me to share this story.

57. Title I schools are those with a certain percentage of students who qualify for free or reduced-price lunch, typically 40 percent or more of students must qualify for a school to be eligible for Title I funds. At New York Performance Standards Consortium schools, students must pass the New York State Regents Examination in English language arts, but the other Regents exam requirements are fulfilled by passing the performance-based assessments in social studies, literature, math, science, literature (and autobiography at Vanguard), www.performanceassessment.org.

58. Vanguard is modeled after Ted Sizer and Deborah Meier's small-school model and is a member of the Coalition of Essential Schools.

59. As in many urban high schools in underfunded districts, our students have attended elementary and middle schools lacking the resources our students deserve for strong educational experiences. Therefore, many enter Vanguard with gaps in their mathematics understanding. Approximately 80% of students qualify for free or reduced-price lunch, and roughly 95% are students of color. Around 70% of students enter testing below grade level in mathematics, and a third receive special education services. The school serves approximately 400 students. Statistics are approximate, as the student population changes each year, and this article discusses the school during the years 2001–2011.

60. Complex Instruction is a result of the research work of Elizabeth Cohen and Rachel Lotan at Stanford University.

61. Stanford professor Jo Boaler researched the Railside School math team's use of complex instruction with academically heterogeneous untracked courses and found that it resulted in greater achievement gains than the tracked and traditionally taught math classes. See J. Boaler and M. Staples, "Creating Mathematical Futures Through an Equitable Teaching Approach: The Case of Railside School," *Teachers College Record* 110, no. 3 (2008): 608–645.

62. Our weekly teaching load was distributed unevenly to allow for math team meetings almost all day on Wednesdays. We taught longer on Mondays, Tuesdays, Thursdays, and Fridays in order to have math team collaborative planning time on Wednesdays, when we taught only Advisory. This time allowed for math team meetings as well as partner meet-

ings with our planning partner, for example, the two ninth-grade math teachers could also meet to plan.

63. Not only did we focus on complex instruction and PBAs, we engaged in teacher-led professional development about lesson study, differentiated instruction, collaborative team teaching, and a host of other pedagogical strategies in order to meet the needs of our diverse student body.

Chapter 2

1. Barack Obama, "Remarks Honoring the 2014 National and State Teachers of the Year," May 1, 2014. Online by Gerhard Peters and John T. Woolley, The American Presidency Project, http://www.presidency.ucsb.edu/ws/?pid=105154.

2. StudentsFirst, "Thanking Our Teachers," StudentsFirst.org, October 5, 2011, https://www.studentsfirst.org/blogs/entry/thanking-our-teachers.

3. William J. Bushaw and Shane J. Lopez, "A Nation Divided: Results of the 44th Annual PDK/Gallup Poll of the Public's Attitudes Toward the Public Schools," *Phi Delta Kappan* 94, no. 1 (2012): 8–25.

4. Linda Darling-Hammond et al., eds., *Preparing Teachers for a Changing World: What Teachers Should Learn and Be Able to Do*, 1st ed. (San Francisco: Jossey-Bass, 2007); Linda Darling-Hammond et al., "Getting Teacher Evaluation Right: A Background Paper for Policy Makers," *National Academy of Education (NJ1)*, 2011, http://eric.ed.gov/?id=ED533702.

5. No Child Left Behind Act of 2001, Pub. L. No. 107–110, 115 Stat. 1425 (2002), http://www2.ed.gov/policy/elsec/leg/esea02/107-110.pdf.

6. Rod Paige, "Meeting the Highly Qualified Teachers Challenge: The Secretary's Annual Report on Teacher Quality," U.S. Department of Education, 2002, http://eric.ed.gov/?id=ED513876.

7. Jennifer McMurrer, *Implementing the No Child Left Behind Teacher Requirements* (Washington, DC: Center on Education Policy, 2007).

8. Bill Gates, "American Federation of Teachers," July 10, 2010, Bill & Melinda Gates Foundation, http://www.gatesfoundation.org/media-center/speeches/2010/07/american-federation-of-teachers.

9. "Carrots and Sticks for School Systems," *New York Times*, August 5, 2012, http://www.nytimes.com/2012/08/06/opinion/carrots-and-sticks-for-school-systems.html.

10. Stanford economist Eric Hanushek's figures total 5–10%. See: Eric A. Hanushek, "Lifting Student Achievement by Weeding Out Harmful Teachers," *Eduwonk*, October 31, 2011, http://www.eduwonk.com/2011/10/lifting-student-achievement-by-weeding-out-harmful-teachers.html; Eric A. Hanushek, "Valuing Teachers: How Much Is a Good Teacher Worth?," *Education Next*, Summer 2011, http://educationnext.org/valuing-teachers/. In the Vergara case, education researcher David Berliner estimated that maybe 1–3% of teachers were ineffective, and explained that he was offering a guess only. See Jordan Weissmann, "Fuzzy Math: The Guesstimate That Struck Down California's Teacher Tenure Laws," Slate, June 12, 2014, http://www.slate.com/articles/business/moneybox/2014/06/judge_strikes_down_california_s_teacher_tenure_laws_a_made_up_statistic.html.

11. "But the transformative changes needed to truly prepare our kids for the 21st-century global economy simply will not happen unless we first shed some of the entrenched practices that have held back our education system, practices that have long favored adults, not children." From: Joel Klein et al., "How to Fix Our Schools: A Manifesto by Joel Klein, Michelle Rhee and Other Education Leaders," *Washington Post*, October 10, 2010, sec. Opinions, http://www.washingtonpost.com/wp-dyn/content/article/2010/10/07/AR2010100705078.html; "The trademark of this new system is not just that the teachers'

unions are pre-eminently powerful. It is also that they use their power to promote their own special interests—and to make the organization of schooling a reflection of those interests. They say, of course, that what is good for teachers is good for kids. But the simple fact is that they are not in the business of representing kids. They are unions. They represent the job-related interests of their members, and these interests are not the same as the interests of children." From: Joel I. Klein and Al Sharpton, "Charter Schools Can Close the Education Gap," *Wall Street Journal*, January 12, 2009, sec. Opinion, http://www.wsj.com/articles/SB123172121959472377; Jeb Bush said, "They don't represent children so much as they represented adults—teachers, janitors and cafeteria workers." Bush during the summit called the public education system "government-run, unionized monopolies." From: Marc Caputo, "Jeb's Education Talk Omits the Words 'Common Core,'" *POLITICO*, February 10, 2015, http://www.politico.com/story/2015/02/jeb-bush-education-common-core-115087.html. See also Terry M. Moe, "The Staggering Power of the Teachers' Unions," Text, *Hoover Institution* (July 13, 2011), http://www.hoover.org/research/staggering-power-teachers-unions.

12. Dana Goldstein, *The Teacher Wars: A History of America's Most Embattled Profession* (New York: Doubleday, 2014); Educator and blogger Mark Weber goes through a list of teachers fired for political reasons, retaliation from a principal, or after false accusations at: Mark Weber, October 25, 2014, "@TIME Gets Tenure Wrong, Part I: It Is NOT Hard To Fire a Teacher," *Jersey Jazzman Blog*, http://jerseyjazzman.blogspot.com/2014/10/time-gets-tenure-wrong-part-i-it-is-not.html.

13. Richard D. Kahlenberg, "Bipartisan, but Unfounded: The Assault on Teachers' Unions," *American Educator* 35, no. 4 (2012): 14–18.

14. Robert M. Carini, "Teacher Unions and Student Achievement," in *School Reform Proposals: The Research Evidence*, ed. Alex Molnar (Greenwich, CT: Information Age Publishing, 2002), 197–215.

15. Randi Weingarten, President, American Federation of Teachers: "They—and the AFT—want a fair, transparent and expedient process to identify and deal with ineffective teachers. But they know we won't have that if we don't have an evaluation system that is comprehensive and robust, and really tells us who is or is not an effective teacher. That is essential for a fair and efficient due process system." From: Randi Weingarten, "A New Path Forward: Four Approaches to Quality Teaching and Better Schools," Washington, DC, January 12, 2010, http://www.aft.org/sites/default/files/wysiwyg/sp_weingarten011210.pdf.

16. Arne Duncan: "We also have to fix our method of evaluating teachers, which is basically broken. A recent report by the New Teacher Project shows that 99 percent of teachers are all rated the same, and most teacher rating systems don't factor in student achievement." From: "States Will Lead the Way to Reform," Secretary Arne Duncan's remarks at the 2009 Governors Education Symposium, June 14, 2009, U.S. Department of Education, http://www2.ed.gov/news/speeches/2009/06/06142009.html.

17. "The Department also believes that student growth should be one of those measures and should be weighted as a significant factor. For this reason, criterion (D)(2) (Improving Teacher and Principal Effectiveness Based on Performance) asks LEAs and/or States to develop evaluation systems that take into account student growth as a significant factor." From: U.S. Department of Education, *Race to the Top Program Guidance and Frequently Asked Questions* (Washington, DC, 2010), p. 21.

18. U.S. Department of Education, "ESEA Flexibility," Washington, DC. Updated June 7, 2012, https://www2.ed.gov/policy/eseaflex/approved-requests/flexrequest.doc, 3; Stephen Sawchuk, "Teacher Evaluations Key to State Chances for NCLB Waivers—Education Week," *Education Week*, December 12, 2011, http://www.edweek.org/ew/articles/2011/12/14/14waive-bargain_ep.h31.html. *State specific: Washington, Illinois:*

A. Klein, "How Much Political Juice Does the Ed. Dept Have in NCLB Waiver Renewals?" *Education Week,* January 26, 2015, http://blogs.edweek.org/edweek/campaign-k-12/2015/01/arne_duncan_entering_nclb_rene.html?r=920778480. *Maine:* Jay Field, "Maine at Risk of Losing 'No Child Left Behind' Waiver," *Maine Things Considered,* Maine Public, January 16, 2015, http://news.mpbn.net/post/maine-risk-losing-no-child-left-behind-waiver. *Kansas, Oregon, Washington:* M. McNeil, "NCLB Waivers in Kansas, Oregon, Washington at 'High Risk,'" August 15, 2013, http://blogs.edweek.org/edweek/campaign-k-12/2013/08/nclb_waivers_in_kansas_washing.html?cmp=SOC-SHR-FB. *California:* M. McNeil and A. Klein, "California's Hopes Dashed for NCLB Waiver," *Education Week,* January 9, 2013. *Texas:* M. Smith, "Williams: 'Conflict of Visions' on Educator Evaluations," *Texas Tribune,* February 11, 2015, https://www.texastribune.org/plus/edu/vol-2/no-4/texas-feds-still-locking-horns-no-child-left-behin/.

19. Derek Briggs and Ben Domingue, *Due Diligence and the Evaluation of Teachers: A Review of the Value-Added Analysis Underlying the Effectiveness Rankings of Los Angeles Unified School District Teachers by the "Los Angeles Times"* (Boulder, CO: National Education Policy Center, 2011), http://eric.ed.gov/?id=ED516008.

20. Barack Obama, "Remarks by the President on No Child Left Behind Flexibility," The White House, February 9, 2012, https://www.whitehouse.gov/node/120463.

21. *44 states:* E. Porter, "Grading Teachers by the Test," *New York Times,* March 24, 2015, http://www.nytimes.com/2015/03/25/business/economy/grading-teachers-by-the-test.html. *Compared to four states:* Kathryn M. Doherty and Sandy Jacobs, *State of the States 2013: Connect the Dots: Using Evaluations of Teacher Effectiveness to Inform Policy and Practice* (Washington, DC: National Council on Teacher Quality, 2013), http://www.nctq.org/dmsView/State_of_the_States_2013_Using_Teacher_Evaluations_NCTQ_Report.

22. Board on Testing and Assessment (BOTA), *Letter Report to the U.S. Department of Education on the Race to the Top Fund* (Washington, DC: National Research Council, October 5, 2009).

23. Amy Zimmer, "50,000 Teachers Could Be Rated Based on Students That Aren't Theirs: Union," *DNAinfo New York,* March 12, 2015, http://www.dnainfo.com/new-york/20150312/carroll-gardens/50000-teachers-could-be-rated-based-on-students-that-arent-theirs-union/; J. Jacobs, "How Is This Fair? Art Teacher Is Evaluated by Students' Math Standardized Test Scores," *Washington Post,* March 25, 2015; Elaine Weiss, *Mismatches in Race to the Top Limit Educational Improvement: Lack of Time, Resources, and Tools to Address Opportunity Gaps Puts Lofty State Goals Out of Reach* (Washington, DC: Economic Policy Institute, September 12, 2013), http://www.epi.org/publication/race-to-the-top-goals/. Another example of a teacher graded by someone else's exam here: J. Hiltz, "Teacher: What It Feels Like to Be Evaluated on Test Scores of Students I Don't Have," *Washington Post,* March 15, 2014, http://www.washingtonpost.com/blogs/answer-sheet/wp/2014/03/15/teacher-i-was-evaluated-with-test-scores-of-students-i-dont-have/.

24. Elaine Weiss, *Mismatches in Race to the Top;* Sean Cavanagh, "Race to Top Winners Feel Heat on Teacher Evaluations—Education Week," *Education Week,* September 14, 2011, http://www.edweek.org/ew/articles/2011/09/14/03evaluation_ep.h31.html; Stephen Sawchuk, "States' ESEA Waiver Bids Murky on Teacher Evaluations—Teacher Beat—Education Week," *Education Week,* November 23, 2011, http://blogs.edweek.org/edweek/teacherbeat/2011/11/states_esea_waiver_bids.html.

25. R. Rothstein, *How to Fix Our Schools,* Issue Brief #286 (Washington, DC: Economic Policy Institute, October 14, 2010), http://xa.yimg.com/kq/groups/10285308/416256905/name/Reading++how+to+fix+our+schools.pdf. *Teacher shortages:* M. Rich, "Teacher Shortages Spur a Nationwide Hiring Scramble (Credentials Optional)," *New York Times,* August 9, 2015, http://www.nytimes.com/2015/08/10/us/teacher-shortages-spur-a-nationwide-hiring-scramble-credentials-optional.html; Ross Brenneman, "Districts Facing

Teacher Shortages Look for Lifelines," *Education Week*, August 5, 2015, http://www.edweek. org/ew/articles/2015/08/05/districts-facing-teacher-shortages-look-for-lifelines.html?utm_ source=fb&utm_medium=rss&utm_campaign=mrss&cmp=RSS-FEED; Eric Westervelt, "Where Have All The Teachers Gone?" *All Things Considered*, National Public Radio, March 3, 2015, http://www.npr.org/blogs/ed/2015/03/03/389282733/where-have-all-the-teachers-gone; Shaina Cavazos, "Educators: Low Pay, Negative Perceptions Behind Struggles to Recruit Teachers," Chalkbeat Indiana, September 24, 2015, http://in.chalkbeat.org/2015/09/24/ educators-low-pay-negative-perceptions-behind-struggles-to-recruit-teachers/.

26. Dana Markow, Lara Macia, and Helen Lee, *The MetLife Survey of the American Teacher: Challenges for School Leadership* (New York: MetLife, 2013). https://www.metlife.com/ assets/cao/foundation/MetLife-Teacher-Survey-2012.pdf.

27. ACT, Inc., *The Condition of Future Educators 2014* (Iowa City: ACT, Inc., 2015). http:// www.act.org/content/dam/act/unsecured/documents/CCCR-2014-FutureEducators.pdf.

28. Richard Ingersoll, Lisa Merrill, and Daniel Stuckey, "Seven Trends: The Transformation of the Teaching Force," *Consortium for Policy Research in Education*, April 2014, http:// repository.upenn.edu/gse_pubs/241.

29. Mark Simon, "Is Teacher Churn Undermining Real Education Reform in D.C.?" *Washington Post*, June 15, 2012, http://www.washingtonpost.com/opinions/is-teacher-churn-undermining-real-education-reform-in-dc/2012/06/15/gJQAigWcfV_story.html.

30. Ingersoll, Merrill, and Stuckey, "Seven Trends."

31. *Though some charter schools:* M. Rich, "At Charter Schools, Short Careers by Choice," *New York Times*, August 26, 2013, http://www.nytimes.com/2013/08/27/education/at-charter-schools-short-careers-by-choice.html. *Substantial evidence about the positive role of experience:* G. T. Henry, C. K. Fortner, and K. C. Bastian, "The Effects of Experience and Attrition for Novice High-School Science and Mathematics Teachers," *Science* 335, no. 6072 (2012): 1118–1121, http://doi.org/10.1126/science.1215343; J. E. Rockoff, "The Impact of Individual Teachers on Student Achievement: Evidence from Panel Data," *The American Economic Review* 94, no. 2 (2004): 247–252; T. G. Carroll and E. Foster, *Who Will Teach? Experience Matters* (Washington, DC: National Commission on Teaching and America's Future, 2010), http://eric.ed.gov/?id=ED511985. *And the negative role that teacher turnover plays:* M. Ronfeldt, S. Loeb, and J. Wyckoff, "How Teacher Turnover Harms Student Achievement," *American Educational Research Journal* 50, no. 1 (2013): 4–36.

32. Linda Darling-Hammond, *The Flat World and Education: How America's Commitment to Equity Will Determine Our Future*, 9644th ed. (New York: Teachers College Press, 2010).

33. Elaine Allensworth, Stephen Ponisciak, and Christopher Mazzeo, *The Schools Teachers Leave: Teacher Mobility in Chicago Public Schools* (Chicago: Consortium on Chicago School Research, 2009), http://eric.ed.gov/?id=ED505882.

34. Daniel H. Pink, *Drive: The Surprising Truth About What Motivates Us* (New York: Riverhead Books, 2011); Matthew G. Springer, et al., *Teacher Pay for Performance: Experimental Evidence from the Project on Incentives in Teaching* (Nashville, TN: National Center on Performance Incentives at Vanderbilt University, 2010); Julie A. Marsh, ed., *A Big Apple for Educators: New York City's Experiment with Schoolwide Performance Bonuses: Final Evaluation Report* (Santa Monica, CA: Rand, 2011).

35. R. M. Ingersoll and M. Strong, "The Impact of Induction and Mentoring Programs for Beginning Teachers: A Critical Review of the Research," *Review of Educational Research* 81, no. 2 (June 1, 2011): 201–33, doi:10.3102/0034654311403323.

36. Kwang Suk Yoon et al., "Reviewing the Evidence on How Teacher Professional Development Affects Student Achievement. Issues & Answers," REL 2007-No. 033, *Regional Educational Laboratory Southwest (NJ1)*, 2007, http://eric.ed.gov/?id=ED498548.

37. Carrie R. Leana, "The Missing Link in School Reform (SSIR)," *Stanford Social Innovation Review*, Fall 2011, http://www.ssireview.org/articles/entry/the_missing_link_in_school_reform; C. Kirabo Jackson and Elias Bruegmann, "Teaching Students and Teaching Each Other: The Importance of Peer Learning for Teachers" (working paper, National Bureau of Economic Research, Cambridge, Massachusetts, 2009), http://www.nber.org/papers/w15202; Yvonne Goddard, Roger Goddard, and Megan Tschannen-Moran, "A Theoretical and Empirical Investigation of Teacher Collaboration for School Improvement and Student Achievement in Public Elementary Schools," *The Teachers College Record* 109, no. 4 (2007): 877–96.

38. Sylvia A. Allegretto and Lawrence Mishel, "The Teacher Pay Gap Is Wider than Ever: Teachers' Pay Continues to Fall Further Behind Pay of Comparable Workers" (Washington, DC: Economic Policy Institute, August 9, 2016); Cavazos, "Educators: Low Pay, Negative Perceptions"; Ilana Boivie, "The Three Rs of Teacher Pension Plans: Recruitment, Retention, and Retirement" (Washington, DC: National Institute on Retirement Security, October 2011).

39. Danielson 2014-15 Rubric, http://www.cfn107.org/uploads/6/1/9/2/6192492/danielson_2014-2015_rubric.pdf.

40. Bill & Melinda Gates Foundation, *Asking Students About Teaching: Student Perception Surveys and Their Implementation* (Seattle, WA: Bill & Melinda Gates Foundation, 2012), http://k12education.gatesfoundation.org/wp-content/uploads/2015/12/Asking_Students_Practitioner_Brief.pdf.

41. Massachusetts Department of Elementary and Secondary Education, "Implementation Brief: Using Student Growth Percentiles," Educator Effectiveness (Boston, MA, 2014), http://www.doe.mass.edu/edeval/ddm/GrowthPercentiles.pdf. When Riana asked for a citation from DESE, here was their response: "I think the best I can do is to suggest you cite the implementation brief and pointing out that it only applies to 4–8th grade Math and ELA teachers with more than 20 students in a given topic area. We don't have a published reference to the statistic. It is especially challenging because we at the state don't have a full way of knowing which teacher is actually teaching which students—so we only have our estimate, which may not be the same year to year even or content area to content area. The percent of educators that can be matched with SGP ranges from 16–18%."

Chapter 3

1. Charles L. Glenn, "The History and Future of Private Education in the United States," *Journal of Catholic Education* 1, no. 4 (1998): 7.

2. Ansley T. Erickson, "The Rhetoric of Choice: Segregation, Desegregation, and Charter Schools," *Dissent* 58, no. 4 (2011): 41–46.

3. *Progressive small-school educators:* Deborah Meier, *The Power of Their Ideas: Lessons for America from a Small School in Harlem* (Boston: Beacon Press, 2002). *Private school vouchers:* Jim Carl, *Freedom of Choice: Vouchers in American Education* (Santa Barbara, CA: Praeger, 2011).

4. "What Are Public Charter Schools?" National Alliance for Public Charter Schools, 2014, http://www.publiccharters.org/get-the-facts/public-charter-schools/.

5. In 2009–2010, 12% of charter schools nationwide were unionized. National Alliance for Public Charter Schools, "Unionized Schools, 2009–2010," The Public Charter Schools Dashboard, 2014, http://dashboard.publiccharters.org/dashboard/schools/page/union/year/2014.

6. "What Are Public Charter Schools?"

7. *6,700 charters serving 2.9 million students:* Grace Kena et al., *The Condition of Education 2015* (Washington, DC: U.S. Department of Education, National Center for Educa-

tion Statistics, May 2015). *Serving about 6% of the total:* "Fast Facts: Back to School Statistics," U.S. Department of Education, Institute of Education Sciences, and National Center for Education Statistics, 2015, http://nces.ed.gov/fastfacts/display.asp?id=372.

8. *Grown over 300 percent:* Kena et al., "The Condition of Education 2015." *Almost 2,000 new charter schools opened:* Leigh Dingerson, *Public Accountability for Charter Schools: Standards and Policy Recommendations for Effective Oversight* (Providence, RI: Annenberg Institute for School Reform at Brown University, 2014).

9. White House Office of the Press Secretary, "Fact Sheet: The Race to the Top," The White House, November 4, 2009, https://www.whitehouse.gov/the-press-office/fact-sheet-race-top; John White, "States Open to Charter Start Fast in 'Race to the Top': Education Secretary Seeking Autonomy with Real Accountability for School Innovators," U.S. Department of Education, June 8, 2009, http://www2.ed.gov/news/pressreleases/2009/06/06082009a.html.

10. Nick Anderson, "Report Says Performance of Arizona's Charter Schools Is Mixed," *Washington Post*, November 16, 2009, sec. Education, http://www.washingtonpost.com/wp-dyn/content/article/2009/11/15/AR2009111502585.html.

11. "Number and Percentage Distribution of Public Elementary and Secondary Students and Schools, by Traditional or Charter School Status and Selected Characteristics: Selected Years, 1999–2000 through 2012–13," National Center for Education Statistics, Institute of Education Sciences, November 2014, https://nces.ed.gov/programs/digest/d14/tables/dt14_216.30.asp.

12. *Low-income students:* Center for Research on Education Outcomes, *National Charter School Study 2013* (Palo Alto, CA: Center for Research on Education Outcomes (CREDO), Stanford University, June 2013). *Qualify as a high-poverty school and more likely to serve black students:* "NCES Fast Facts: Charter Schools," National Center for Education Statistics, Institute of Education Sciences, 2015, http://nces.ed.gov/fastfacts/display.asp?id=30.

13. CREDO, *National Charter School Study 2013*; Joshua Furgeson et al., "Charter-School Management Organizations: Diverse Strategies and Diverse Student Impacts," *Mathematica Policy Research, Inc.*, 2012, http://eric.ed.gov/?id=ED528536; George A. Scott, "Charter Schools: Additional Federal Attention Needed to Help Protect Access for Students with Disabilities," Report to Congressional Requesters. GAO-12-543, U.S. Government Accountability Office, 2012, http://eric.ed.gov/?id=ED533002.

14. Furgeson et al., "Charter-School Management Organizations"; Gary Miron et al., *Schools without Diversity: Education Management Organizations, Charter Schools, and the Demographic Stratification of the American School System* (Boulder and Tempe: Education and the Public Interest Center & Education Policy Research Center, 2010), http://eric.ed.gov/?id=ED509329.

15. "Death by a Thousand Cuts: Racism, School Closures, and Public School Sabotage" (Journey for Justice Alliance, May 2014), 3.

16. Title IV, Part C: "Expanding Opportunity Through Quality Charter Schools," Every Student Succeeds Act of 2015, Pub. L. No. 114-95, S.1177, https://www.gpo.gov/fdsys/pkg/BILLS-114s1177enr/pdf/BILLS-114s1177enr.pdf.

17. *Larger funding increase:* Frederick M. Hess, "The Every Student Succeeds Act and What Lies Ahead," *AEI*, February 16, 2016, https://www.aei.org/publication/the-every-student-succeeds-act-what-lies-ahead/. *Biggest funder of their expansion:* Lyndsey Layton, "Charter Love: Feds Give $157 Million to Expand Charter Schools," *Washington Post*, September 28, 2015, https://www.washingtonpost.com/local/education/charter-love-feds-give-157-million-to-expand-charter-schools/2015/09/28/006ad118-6613-11e5-8325-a42b5a459b1e_story.html. This is on top of the $157 million that the U.S. Department of Education gave to charter school expansion in September 2015; Center for Media and

Democracy, *Charter School Black Hole: CMD Special Investigation Reveals Huge Info Gap on Charter Spending* (Madison, WI: Center for Media and Democracy, 2015). Before the implementation of ESSA, the DOE had awarded more than $3.7 billion to charter schools since 1995.

18. Lauren Camera, "Donald Trump Goes All In on School Choice," *US News & World Report*, September 8, 2016, http://www.usnews.com/news/articles/2016-09-08/donald-trump-goes-all-in-on-school-choice.

19. *"Mercifully free"*: Evan Thomas, "Why We Must Fire Bad Teachers," *Newsweek*, March 5, 2010, http://www.newsweek.com/why-we-must-fire-bad-teachers-69467. *Laboratories of research and development*: Robin J. Lake, "In the Eye of the Beholder: Charter Schools and Innovation," *Journal of School Choice* 2, no. 2 (April 2008): 115–27; Christopher Lubienski, "Innovation in Education Markets: Theory and Evidence on the Impact of Competition and Choice in Charter Schools," *American Educational Research Journal* 40, no. 2 (July 1, 2003): 395–443.

20. *Spur improvement*: Arne Duncan, "Turning Around the Bottom Five Percent" (Speeches and Testimony, April 15, 2011), http://www2.ed.gov/news/speeches/2009/06/06222009.html. *System as a whole would improve*: "Charter Schools in Perspective: A Guide to Research," Public Agenda and the Spencer Foundation, In Perspective Series, June 2015. http://www.in-perspective.org/pages/a-guide-to-research.

21. "Five Pillars - KIPP Public Charter Schools | Knowledge Is Power Program," accessed March 28, 2016, http://www.kipp.org/our-approach/five-pillars.

22. *One of the most profound changes*: Duncan, "Turning Around the Bottom Five Percent." *Lessons about what works*: David Leonhardt, "Inequality Has Been Going on Forever . . . But That Doesn't Mean It's Inevitable," *New York Times*, May 2, 2014, http://www.nytimes.com/2014/05/04/magazine/inequality-has-been-going-on-forever-but-that-doesnt-mean-its-inevitable.html. *Offering a beacon of hope*: Chester E. Finn, Bruno V. Manno, and Gregg Vanourek, *Charter Schools in Action: Renewing Public Education*, reprint ed. (Princeton, NJ: Princeton University Press, 2001), 13.

23. Joanna Smith et al., *Mapping the Landscape of Charter Management Organizations: Issues to Consider in Supporting Replication*, Issue Brief (Los Angeles: National Resource Center on Charter School Finance & Governance, University of Southern California Center on Educational Governance, March 26, 2010); Julie Kowal et al., "Investing in Charter Schools: A Guide for Donors," Prepared by Public Impact for Philanthropy Rountable, Washington, DC, April 2009.

24. Barack Obama, "Presidential Proclamation—National Charter Schools Week, 2012," The White House, Office of the Press Secretary, May 7, 2012, https://www.whitehouse.gov/the-press-office/2012/05/07/presidential-proclamation-national-charter-schools-week-2012.

25. Public Agenda, "Charter Schools in Perspective."

26. CREDO, *National Charter School Study 2013*: The results were 0.01 standard deviations higher than traditional public schools on reading tests and 0.005 standard deviations lower on math tests in the 27 states that were a part of their study. For a breakdown of what this means, Tom Loveless of the Brookings Institution helped translate what changes in standard deviation mean to the rest of us who are not statisticians: "The national average on the 2011 NAEP eighth grade reading test was 265, with a SD of 34. That means a gain of 0.01 SD is about one-third of a single point (0.34) on the NAEP scale. A gain of 0.03 SD is approximately one point . . . The national NAEP score for 4th grade math, on the other hand, increased by 28 points from 1990 to 2011. That's the equivalent of 0.875 SD (using the 1990 SD of 32)—or more than 87 times larger than the charter-TPS difference." From: Tom Loveless, "Charter School Study: Much Ado About Tiny Differences," The Brookings Institution, July 3, 2013, http://www.brookings.edu/research/

papers/2013/07/03-charter-schools-loveless. Andrew Maul of the University of Colorado Boulder provides another example: "A student correctly answering a single additional question (out of 54) on the SAT Math test would boost her standardized score by anywhere from 0.05 standard deviations to more than 0.30 standard deviations." From: Andrew Maul and Abby McClelland, *Review of National Charter School Study 2013* (Boulder, CO: National Education Policy Center, 2014).

27. Julian R. Betts and Y. Emily Tang, *A Meta-Analysis of the Literature on the Effect of Charter Schools on Student Achievement* (Seattle, WA: Center for Reinventing Public Education, August 2014).

28. Philip Gleason et al., "The Evaluation of Charter School Impacts: Final Report. NCEE 2010-4029," National Center for Education Evaluation and Regional Assistance, 2010, http://eric.ed.gov/?id=ED510573.

29. *Most charter studies focus on test scores:* Public Agenda, "Charter Schools in Perspective"; CREDO, *Urban Charter School Study Report on 41 Regions* (Palo Alto, CA: Center for Research on Educational Outcomes, Stanford University, 2015), 41; Caroline M. Hoxby, Sonali Murarka, and Jenny Kang, *How New York City's Charter Schools Affect Achievement* (Cambridge, MA: New York City Charter Schools Evaluation Project, September 2009), 1–85. *Higher high school graduation and college enrollment percentages:* Ron W. Zimmer et al., *Charter Schools in Eight States: Effects on Achievement, Attainment, Integration, and Competition* (Santa Monica, CA: Rand, 2009); Joshua D. Angrist et al., *Charter Schools and the Road to College Readiness: The Effects on College Preparation, Attendance and Choice* (Boston, MA: NewSchools Venture Fund and the Boston Foundation, 2013), https://www.tbf.org/~/media/TBFOrg/Files/Reports/Charters%20and%20College%20Readiness%202013.pdf. *Lower rates of teen pregnancy and incarceration:* Will Dobbie and Roland G. Fryer Jr, "The Medium-Term Impacts of High-Achieving Charter Schools on Non-Test Score Outcomes" (working paper, National Bureau of Economic Research, October 2013), http://www.nber.org/papers/w19581.

30. Public Agenda, "Charter Schools in Perspective"; CREDO, *National Charter School Study 2013*; Furgeson et al., "Charter-School Management Organizations"; Scott, "Charter Schools."

31. Stephanie Simon, "Special Report: Class Struggle—How Charter Schools Get Students They Want," Reuters, February 15, 2013, http://www.reuters.com/article/2013/02/15/us-usa-charters-admissions-idUSBRE91E0HF20130215.

32. Martin Carnoy et al., *The Charter School Dust-up: Examining the Evidence on Enrollment and Achievement* (Washington, DC: Economic Policy Institute, and New York: Teachers College Press, 2005); Robert Bifulco and Helen F. Ladd, "Institutional Change and Coproduction of Public Services: The Effect of Charter Schools on Parental Involvement," *Journal of Public Administration Research and Theory* 16, no. 4 (October 1, 2006): 553–76, doi:10.1093/jopart/muj001; Courtney A. Bell, "All Choices Created Equal? The Role of Choice Sets in the Selection of Schools," *Peabody Journal of Education* 84, no. 2 (April 10, 2009): 191–208, doi:10.1080/01619560902810146; Erica Frankenberg, Genevieve Siegel-Hawley, and Jia Wang, "Choice without Equity: Charter School Segregation," *Education Policy Analysis Archives* 19 (2011): 1.

33. "NYC Charters Retain Students Better Than Traditional Schools," WNYC, March 15, 2016, http://www.wnyc.org/story/nyc-charter-school-attrition-rates/?utm_source=sharedUrl&utm_medium=metatag&utm_campaign=sharedUrl.

34. Sarah Darville, "The Quieter Charter School Divide: What You Need to Know about 'Backfill,'" Chalkbeat New York, March 11, 2014, http://ny.chalkbeat.org/2014/03/11/the-quieter-charter-school-divide-what-you-need-to-know-about-backfill/; Robert Pondisco, "Charter Schools and Backfill: The Debate We're Not Having," Thomas B. Fordham Institute, April 15, 2015, http://edexcellence.net/articles/charter-schools-and-

backfill-the-debate-were-not-having; Leo Casey, "Student Attrition and 'Backfilling' at Success Academy Charter Schools: What Student Enrollment Patterns Tell Us," Shanker Institute, February 18, 2016, http://www.shankerinstitute.org/blog/student-attrition-and-backfilling-success-academy-charter-schools-what-student-enrollment.

35. Will Dobbie and Roland G. Fryer Jr., "Getting Beneath the Veil of Effective Schools: Evidence from New York City" (working paper, National Bureau of Economic Research, Cambridge, MA, December 2011), http://www.nber.org/papers/w17632.

36. Will S. Dobbie and Roland G. Fryer Jr., "Charter Schools and Labor Market Outcomes" (working paper, National Bureau of Economic Research, Cambridge, MA, 2016), http://www.nber.org/papers/w22502.

37. Lake, "In the Eye of the Beholder"; Scott Ellison, "Hard-Wired for Innovation? Comparing Two Policy Paths toward Innovative Schooling," *International Education* 39, no. 1 (2009): 2; Courtney Preston et al., "School Innovation in District Context: Comparing Traditional Public Schools and Charter Schools," *Economics of Education Review*, Special Issue: Charter Schools, 31, no. 2 (April 2012): 318–30, doi:10.1016/j.econedurev.2011.07.016.

38. Doug Lemov, *Teach Like a Champion: 49 Techniques That Put Students on the Path to College*, 1st ed. (San Francisco: Jossey-Bass, 2010), 360–361.

39. Kate Taylor, "At Success Academy Charter Schools, High Scores and Polarizing Tactics," *New York Times*, April 6, 2015.

40. Geoff Decker, Stephanie Snyder, and Sarah Darville, "Suspensions at City Charter Schools Far Outpace Those at District Schools, Data Show," Chalkbeat New York, February 23, 2015, http://ny.chalkbeat.org/2015/02/23/suspensions-at-city-charter-schools-far-outpace-those-at-district-schools-data-show/; Advocates for Children of New York, *Civil Rights Suspended: An Analysis of New York City Charter School Discipline Policies* (New York: Advocates for Children of New York, February 2015). Provides a breakdown of behaviors that charters can suspend or expel students for that public schools cannot.

41. Emma Brown, "D.C. Charter Schools Expel Students at Far Higher Rates Than Traditional Public Schools," *Washington Post*, January 5, 2013, http://www.washingtonpost.com/local/education/dc-charter-schools-expel-students-at-far-higher-rates-than-traditional-public-schools/2013/01/05/e155e4bc-44a9-11e2-8061-253bccfc7532_story.html?hpid=z2.

42. Bruce D. Baker and Richard Ferris, *Adding Up the Spending: Fiscal Disparities and Philanthropy among New York City Charter Schools* (Boulder, CO: National Education Policy Center, 2011), http://eric.ed.gov/?id=ED515469.

43. Bruce D. Baker, Ken Libby, and Kathryn Wiley, *Spending by the Major Charter Management Organizations: Comparing Charter School and Local Public District Financial Resources in New York, Ohio, and Texas* (Boulder, CO: National Education Policy Center, 2012, http://eric.ed.gov/?id=ED531789.

44. Gary Miron and Charisse Gulosino, *Profiles of For-Profit and Nonprofit Education Management Organizations*, 14th ed. (Boulder, CO: National Education Policy Center, 2013), http://nepc.colorado.edu/files/emo-profiles-11-12.pdf

45. Marian Wang, "When Charter Schools Are Nonprofit in Name Only," *ProPublica*, December 9, 2014, http://www.propublica.org/article/when-charter-schools-are-nonprofit-in-name-only.; Marian Wang, "Charter School Power Broker Turns Public Education Into Private Profits," *ProPublica*, October 15, 2014, http://www.propublica.org/article/charter-school-power-broker-turns-public-education-into-private-profits. *Ohio:* Catherine Candisky and Jim Siegal, "Charter School's Lease Deals Scrutinized," *The Columbus Dispatch*, October 12, 2014, http://www.dispatch.com/content/stories/local/2014/10/12/charters-lease-deals-scrutinized.html. *Philadelphia:*Alex Wigglesworth and Ryan Briggs, "Charter Schools: Prefer Building Booms to Classrooms?," *Philadelphia Inquirer*, September 14, 2015, http://www.philly.com/philly/education/Philly_Charters_schools_build-

ing_boom.html.. *Washington, DC:* Emma Brown, "D.C. Officials Seek Stronger Oversight of Charter Schools after Recent Fraud Allegations," *Washington Post*, June 15, 2014, http://www.washingtonpost.com/local/education/dc-officials-seek-stronger-oversight-of-charter-schools-after-recent-fraud-allegations/2014/06/15/fb5e1042-f0b4-11e3-bf76-447a5df6411f_story.html.

46. Center for Popular Democracy and the Alliance to Reclaim Our Schools, *The Tip of the Iceberg: Charter School Vulnerabilities to Waste, Fraud, and Abuse; Escalating Fraud Warrants Immediate Federal and State Action to Protect Public Dollars and Prevent Financial Mismanagement* (Washington, DC: Center for Popular Democracy, and the Alliance to Reclaim Our Schools, April 2015), http://www.reclaimourschools.org/sites/default/files/Charter-Schools-National-Report_rev2.pdf.

47. Robert Bifulco and Randall Reback, *Effect of Charter Schools on School District Finance* (Albany, NY: New York State Education Department and The Education Finance Research Consortium at SUNY Albany, December 31, 2011).

48. Juan Perez Jr., "CPS Lays Off More Than 500 Teachers, Another 500 School-Based Workers," Chicagotribune.com, August 5, 2016, http://www.chicagotribune.com/news/local/breaking/ct-chicago-schools-teacher-layoffs-0806-20160805-story.html.

49. Greg Hinz, "See How Your School Fares in the New Round of CPS Budget Cuts," *Crain's Chicago Business*, July 13, 2015, http://www.chicagobusiness.com/article/20150713/BLOGS02/150719965/see-how-your-school-fares-in-the-new-round-of-cps-budget-cuts.

50. Lauren FitzPatrick, "School Budgets Show CPS Still Losing Students," *Chicago Sun-Times*, July 14, 2016, http://chicago.suntimes.com/politics/school-budgets-show-cps-still-losing-students/.

51. Julie Bosman, "Crumbling, Destitute Schools Threaten Detroit's Recovery," *New York Times*, January 20, 2016, http://www.nytimes.com/2016/01/21/us/crumbling-destitute-schools-threaten-detroits-recovery.html.

52. Richard D. Kahlenberg, "The Charter School Idea Turns 20," *Education Week*, March 26, 2008, http://www.edweek.org/ew/articles/2008/03/26/29kahlenberg_ep.h27.html; Finn, Manno, and Vanourek, *Charter Schools in Action*.

53. Stan Karp, "Charter Schools and the Future of Public Education," *Rethinking Schools*, Fall 2013, http://www.rethinkingschools.org/archive/28_01/28_01_karp.shtml.

54. Richard D. Kahlenberg and Halley Potter, *A Smarter Charter: Finding What Works for Charter Schools and Public Education* (New York: Teachers College Press, 2014).

55. Lake, "In the Eye of the Beholder"; Lubienski, "Innovation in Education Markets."

56. Dobbie and Fryer Jr., "Getting Beneath the Veil of Effective Schools."

57. WestEd, *Successful Charter Schools* (Washington, DC: U.S. Department of Education, Office of Innovation and Improvement, June 2004). A great narrative example of the power of extra staffing at charter versus district schools can be found in Dale Russakoff, *The Prize: Who's In Charge of America's Schools?* (Boston: Houghton Mifflin Harcourt, 2015).

58. *Principals:* Lesli A. Maxwell, "Principals Pressed for Time to Lead Instructional Change—Education Week," *Education Week*, March 26, 2014, http://www.edweek.org/ew/articles/2014/03/26/26principals_ep.h33.html; Steve Farkas, Jean Johnson, and Ann Duffett, "Rolling Up Their Sleeves: Superintendents and Principals Talk about What's Needed to Fix Public Schools," Public Agenda, 2003), http://eric.ed.gov/?id=ED482266. *Teachers:* Miriam Greenberg, "Teachers Want Better Feedback—Education Week," *Education Week*, August 19, 2015, http://www.edweek.org/ew/articles/2015/08/19/teachers-want-better-feedback.html.

59. Hoxby, Murarka, and Kang, *How New York City's Charter Schools Affect Achievement*; Matthew DiCarlo drilled down to isolate how time itself, rather than pedagogy, was a factor in the increased achievement scores, using the CREDO study. The additional time

that successful charter schools offered was about equivalent to the "days of added learning" that the CREDO study found within the test scores. For example, New York City's oversubscribed charters add the equivalent of 56 extra days of instruction, on average. If you take the CREDO findings as they are, these 56 added days of instruction resulted in just 28 days' gain of reading and 40 days' gain in math on the test. Meanwhile, the results for nontested subjects, including social studies and science, showed no statistically significant impact. See: Matthew DiCarlo, "Estimated Versus Actual Days of Learning in Charter School Studies," Shanker Institute, March 19, 2014, http://www.shankerinstitute.org/blog/estimated-versus-actual-days-learning-charter-school-studies. *District schools are adopting*: David Farbman et al., *Learning Time in America: Time to Reform the American School Calendar—A Snapshot of Federal, State and Local Action* (Washington, DC: The National Center on Time & Learning, Education Commission of the States, 2015).

60. WestEd, *Successful Charter Schools*.

Chapter 4

1. Daniel L. Duke, *The Children Left Behind: America's Struggle to Improve Its Lowest Performing Schools* (Rowman & Littlefield, 2016), 7–10.

2. *No Child Left Behind Act of 2001*, 2002, 1440, http://bulk.resource.org/gpo.gov/laws/107/publ110.107.pdf.

3. "Fast Facts: Closed Schools," *National Center for Education Statistics, Institute of Education Sciences*, 2016, https://nces.ed.gov/fastfacts/display.asp?id=619.

4. Journey for Justice Alliance: Kenwood Oakland Community Organization, Coalition for Community Schools, Conscious Citizens Controlling Community Changes, New Jersey Parents Unified for Local School Education, "Re: Civil Rights Complaint, Title IV and Title VI of the Civil Rights Act of 1964," May 13, 2014, http://b.3cdn.net/advancement/2 4a04d1624216c28b1_4pm6y9lvo.pdf.

5. Anthony S. Bryk et al., *Organizing Schools for Improvement: Lessons from Chicago* (Chicago: University of Chicago Press, 2010).

6. Elizabeth A. Harris, "Where Nearly Half of Pupils Are Homeless, School Aims to Be Teacher, Therapist, Even Santa," *New York Times*, June 6, 2016, http://www.nytimes.com/2016/06/07/nyregion/public-school-188-in-manhattan-about-half-the-students-are-homeless.html.

7. Communities for Excellent Public Schools, *Our Communities Left Behind: An Analysis of the Administration's School Turnaround Policies* (Washington, DC: Communities for Excellent Public Schools, July 2010).

8. Douglas N. Harris, *Ending the Blame Game on Educational Inequity: A Study of "High Flying" Schools and NCLB* (Tempe, AZ: Education Policy Research Unit, 2006), http://eric.ed.gov/?id=ED508527.

9. Sean F. Reardon, *School District Socioeconomic Status, Race, and Academic Achievement*, Preliminary Draft (Palo Alto, CA: Stanford Center for Education Policy Analysis, April 2016).

10. Paul Farhi, "Flunking the Test," *American Journalism Review*, May 2012, http://ajrarchive.org/Article.asp?id=5280.

11. James D. Anderson, *The Education of Blacks in the South, 1860–1935*, 1st new ed. (Chapel Hill: The University of North Carolina Press, 1988); Gilbert G. Gonzalez, *Chicano Education in the Era of Segregation*, reprint ed. (Denton: University of North Texas Press, 2013); Julie L. Davis, *Survival Schools: The American Indian Movement and Community Education in the Twin Cities* (Minneapolis: University of Minnesota Press, 2013); Jeannie Oakes and John Rogers, *Learning Power: Organizing for Education and Justice* (New York: Teachers College Press, 2006).

12. Pam Key, "Condi Rice: Today's True Racists Are Liberals Who Defend Teachers'

Unions," Breitbart, November 10, 2014, http://www.breitbart.com/video/2014/11/10/condoleezza-todays-true-racists-are-liberal-who-defend-teachers-unions/.

13. Shelby Dietz, *How Many Schools Have Not Made Adequate Yearly Progress Under the No Child Left Behind Act?* (Washington, DC: Center on Education Policy, 2010), http://eric.ed.gov/?id=ED508803.

14. David J. Hoff, "Schools Struggling to Meet Key Goal on Accountability: Number Failing to Make AYP Rises 28 Percent," *Education Week* 28, no. 16 (January 7, 2009).

15. Andrew Calkins et al., "The Turnaround Challenge: Why America's Best Opportunity to Dramatically Improve Student Achievement Lies in Our Worst-Performing Schools.," Boston: Mass Insight Education & Research Institute, 2007), http://eric.ed.gov/?id=ED538298.

16. George W. Bush, "Remarks on Signing the No Child Left Behind Act of 2001 in Hamilton, Ohio," The American Presidency Project, January 8, 2002, http://www.presidency.ucsb.edu/ws/?pid=73220.

17. Government Accountability Office, *No Child Left Behind Act: Education Should Clarify Guidance and Address Potential Compliance Issues for Schools in Corrective Action and Restructuring Status* (Washington, DC: Government Accountability Office, September 2007), https://swap.stanford.edu/20110202173808/http://www.gao.gov/new.items/d071035.pdf.

18. William J. Mathis, *NCLB's Ultimate Restructuring Alternatives: Do They Improve the Quality of Education?* (Lansing, MI: The Great Lakes Center for Education Research & Practice, April 2009), http://eric.ed.gov/?id=ED507355; Angela Minnici and Deanna D. Hill, *Educational Architects: Do State Education Agencies Have the Tools Necessary to Implement NCLB?* From the Capital to the Classroom: Year 5 of the No Child Left Behind Act (Washington, DC: Center on Education Policy, May 2007); Lucy M. Steiner, *State Takeovers of Individual Schools: School Restructuring Options Under No Child Left Behind: "What Works When?"* (Naperville, IL: Learning Point Associates, 2005), http://eric.ed.gov/?id=ED489527.

19. Barack Obama, "Remarks by the President in State of the Union Address," *Whitehouse.gov*, January 27, 2010, https://www.whitehouse.gov/the-press-office/remarks-president-state-union-address.

20. Barack Obama, "Remarks to the National Education Association Annual Meeting in Philadelphia," The American Presidency Project, July 5, 2007, http://www.presidency.ucsb.edu/ws/?pid=77006.

21. George A. Scott, *School Improvement Grants: Early Implementation Under Way, but Reforms Affected by Short Time Frames,* Report to Congressional Requesters, GAO-11-741 (Washington, DC: U.S. Government Accountability Office, 2011), http://eric.ed.gov/?id=ED522156.

22. SIG Grants: U.S. Department of Education, Office of Elementary and Secondary Education, "Guidance on School Improvement Grants Under Section 1003(g) of the Elementary and Secondary Education Act of 1965," December 18, 2009, revised June 29, 2010, http://www2.ed.gov/programs/sif/sigguidance05242010.pdf; Steven Hurlburt et al., "Baseline Analyses of SIG Applications and SIG-Eligible and SIG-Awarded Schools," National Center for Education Statistics, Institute of Education Sciences, U.S. Department of Education, May 2011; Susanne James-Burdumy and Thomas E. Wei, "Usage of Policies and Practices Promoted by Race to the Top and School Improvement Grants," National Center for Education Evaluation and Regional Assistance, Institute of Education Sciences, U.S. Department of Education, September 2015.

23. Charles T. Clotfelter et al., "Do School Accountability Systems Make It More Difficult for Low-Performing Schools to Attract and Retain High-Quality Teachers?" *Journal of Policy Analysis and Management* 23, no. 2 (March 1, 2004): 251–71, doi:10.1002/pam.20003; Jennifer K. Rice and Betty Malen, "The Human Costs of Education Reform: The Case of

School Reconstitution," *Educational Administration Quarterly* 39, no. 5 (December 1, 2003): 635–66, doi:10.1177/0013161X03257298.

24. Emma Brown, "High-Poverty Schools Often Staffed by Rotating Cast of Substitutes," *Washington Post*, December 4, 2015, https://www.washingtonpost.com/local/education/how-can-students-learn-without-teachers-high-poverty-schools-often-staffed-by-rotating-cast-of-substitutes/2015/12/04/be41579a-92c6-11e5-b5e4-279b4501e8a6_story.html?tid=pm_local_pop_b. One student at an understaffed school noted, "You're looking at test scores, but we didn't have a stable teacher."

25. Ginger Moored, "NCTQ Teacher Trendline: Substitute Teachers," National Council on Teacher Quality, *TQB: Teacher Quality Bulletin Newsletter* (May 2013), http://www.nctq.org/commentary/article.do?id=67.

26. Caitlin Scott, *A Call to Restructure Restructuring: Lessons from the No Child Left Behind Act in Five States* (Washington, DC: Center on Education Policy, 2008), http://eric.ed.gov/?id=ED503798; Mathis, "NCLB's Ultimate Restructuring Alternatives"; Heinrich Mintrop and Tina Trujillo, "Corrective Action in Low Performing Schools: Lessons for NCLB Implementation from First-Generation Accountability Systems," *Education Policy Analysis Archives* 13 (2005): 48; Tina Trujillo and Michelle Renée, *The Research on Turnarounds Doesn't Show What Arne Duncan Thinks It Shows* (Boulder, CO: National Education Policy Center, 2012); Tina Trujillo, *Review of Dramatic Action, Dramatic Improvement* (Boulder, CO: National Education Policy Center, 2015). About two-thirds of SIG schools made small gains or no gains at all, a result similar to struggling schools who received no SIG money, and the remaining one-third got worse: Caitlin Emma, "Here's Why $7 Billion Didn't Help America's Worst Schools," *POLITICO*, November 3, 2015, http://www.politico.com/story/2015/11/failing-schools-education-white-house-214332.

27. Ronald C. Brady, *Can Failing Schools Be Fixed?* (Washington, DC: Thomas B. Fordham Foundation, 2003), http://eric.ed.gov/?id=ED498798; Tina Trujillo and Michelle Renée, "Irrational Exuberance for Market-Based Reform: How Federal Turnaround Policies Thwart Democratic Schooling," *Teachers College Record* 117 (2015): 060304.

28. Andy Smarick, "The Turnaround Fallacy: Stop Trying to Fix Schools. Close Them and Start Fresh," *Education Next*, Winter 2010, http://educationnext.org/the-turnaround-fallacy/; Kenneth K. Wong and Francis X. Shen, "Does School District Takeover Work? Assessing the Effectiveness of City and State Takeover as a School Reform Strategy.," *State Education Standard*, 2002, http://www.researchgate.net/profile/Kenneth_Wong19/publication/234591079_Do_School_District_Takeovers_Work_Assessing_the_Effectiveness_of_City_and_State_Takeovers_as_a_School_Reform_Strategy/links/54caa5e80cf2517b755f3e57.pdf.; Mathis, "NCLB's Ultimate Restructuring Alternatives."

29. Arne Duncan, "Turning Around the Bottom Five Percent," (Speeches and Testimony, April 15, 2011), http://www2.ed.gov/news/speeches/2009/06/06222009.html.

30. See, for example, the Broad Foundation's guide to closing schools: *School Closure Guide: Closing Schools as a Means for Addressing Budgetary Challenges,* Education Reform Toolkits: Resources to Achieve Results (Los Angeles: The Broad Foundation, September 15, 2009).

31. The Schott Foundation, "The Color of School Closures," *The Schott Foundation for Public Education Blog*, April 23, 2013, http://schottfoundation.org/blog/2013/04/05/color-school-closures.

32. Andy Smarick, "Wave of the Future: Why Charter Schools Should Replace Failing Urban Schools," *Education Next*, Winter 2008, http://educationnext.org/wave-of-the-future/; Jelani Cobb, "The Life and Death of Jamaica High School," *The New Yorker*, August 31, 2015, http://www.newyorker.com/magazine/2015/08/31/class-notes-annals-of-education-jelani-cobb.

33. Marisa De la Torre et al., *Turning Around Low-Performing Schools in Chicago: Research Report* (Chicago: University of Chicago Consortium on School Research & American Institutes for Research, 2013), 19–28, http://eric.ed.gov/?id=ED542565. Additional stories on Chicago: Marisa De la Torre and Julia Gwynne, *When Schools Close: Effects on Displaced Students in Chicago Public Schools. Research Report.* (Chicago: University of Chicago Consortium on School Research, 2009), http://eric.ed.gov/?id=ED510792. Example of new schools opening, receiving outsized budgets and resources and the slots are going to white students: Tim Novak and Chris Fusco, "White Students Getting More Spots at Top CPS High Schools," *Chicago Sun-Times*, April 28, 2014, http://www.suntimes.com/27028503-761/watchdogs-whites-getting-more-spots-at-top-cps-high-schools.html.

34. Kate Taylor and Anna M. Phillips, "54 New Schools to Open in Fall, Bloomberg Says," *New York Times*, April 17, 2012, http://www.nytimes.com/2012/04/18/nyregion/54-new-schools-to-open-in-fall-bloomberg-says.html.

35. Edward Skyler, Robert Lawson, and Susan Byrnes, "$51 Million Grant from the Bill & Melinda Gates Foundation to Support Small Dynamic High Schools to Boost Student Achievement" (Bill & Melinda Gates Founation, September 17, 2003), http://www.gatesfoundation.org/Media-Center/Press-Releases/2003/09/New-York-City-Department-of-Education-Receives-Grant.

36. Urban Youth Collaborative, *No Closer to College: NYC High School Students Call for Real School Transformation, Not School Closings* (New York: Urban Youth Collaborative, April 2011); Clara Hemphill and Kim Nauer, *The New Marketplace: How Small-School Reforms and School Choice Have Reshaped New York City's High Schools* (New York: New School Center for New York City Affairs | The New School, 2009), 35–41.

37. The New York Immigration Coalition and Advocates for Children of New York, *So Many Schools, So Few Options: How Mayor Bloomberg's Small High School Reforms Deny Full Access to English Language Learners* (New York: The New York Immigration Coalition & Advocates for Children of New York, Chhaya Community Development Corporation, Chinese Progressive Association, Chinese-American Planning Council, Council of Peoples Organization, Haitian Americans United for Progress, Make the Road by Walking, Metropolitan Russian American Parents Association, November 2006); Elissa Gootman, "City's New Small Schools Are Focus of a Bias Inquiry," *New York Times*, June 16, 2006, sec. New York Region, http://www.nytimes.com/2006/06/16/nyregion/16schools.html.

38. Kim Sweet, *Testimony to Be Delivered to the Education Committee of the New York City Council Re: The Department of Education's Monitoring of Students at Closing Schools, Int. 354, and Int. 364* (New York: Advocates for Children of New York, 2011); Hemphill and Nauer, *The New Marketplace*, 35–41; Michael Powell, "In Schools Cut by New York City's Ax, Students Bleed," *New York Times*, April 16, 2012, http://www.nytimes.com/2012/04/17/nyregion/in-schools-cut-by-new-york-citys-ax-students-bleed.html; Communities for Excellent Public Schools, "Our Communities Left Behind: An Analysis of the Administration's School Turnaround Policies."

39. American Federation of Teachers, *Closing Schools to Improve Student Achievement: What the Research and Researchers Say*, Research Summary (Washington, DC: American Federation of Teachers, 2012), http://eric.ed.gov/?id=ED538666; B. Kirshner, M. Gaertner, and K. Pozzoboni, "Tracing Transitions: The Effect of High School Closure on Displaced Students," *Educational Evaluation and Policy Analysis* 32, no. 3 (September 1, 2010): 407–29, doi:10.3102/0162373710376823; John Engberg et al., "Closing Schools in a Shrinking District: Do Student Outcomes Depend on Which Schools Are Closed?" *Journal of Urban Economics* 71, no. 2 (March 2012): 189–203, doi:10.1016/j.jue.2011.10.001; Matthew F. Larsen, *Does Closing Schools Close Doors? The Effect of High School Closings on Achievement and Attainment* (New Orleans: Department of Economics, Educa-

tion Research Alliance for New Orleans, Tulane University, 2014), http://www.tulane. edu/~mflarsen/uploads/2/2/5/4/22549316/mflarsen_schoolclosings.pdf.

40. Russell W. Rumberger, *Student Mobility: Causes, Consequences and Solutions* (Boulder, CO: National Education Policy Center, June 2015), http://www.greatlakescenter.org/docs/ Policy_Briefs/Rumberger-Student-Mobility.pdf.

41. De la Torre and Gwynne, *When Schools Close*; Jessica Sherrod and Shelby Dawkins-Law, *After School Closure: Tracking the Academic Performance of Displaced Students* (Raleigh, NC: Public Schools of North Caroline, State Board of Education, Department of Public Instruction, August 2013), http://www.dpi.state.nc.us/docs/intern-research/reports/ schoolclosure.pdf.

42. "For Some New Orleans Students, School Choice Means Pre-Dawn Bus Pickups, The Lens Reports," *Times-Picayune | Nola.com*, August 26, 2013, http://www.nola.com/education/ index.ssf/2013/08/for_some_new_orleans_students.html.

43. "Derrion Albert's Death May Be Rooted in School Closures," NBC Chicago, October 7, 2009, http://www.nbcchicago.com/news/local/holder-arne-duncan-fenger-city-hall-daley-63642507.html; Darlene Hill, "Derrion Albert's Mother Speaks Out Against CPS Closures," Fox 32 News, May 2, 2013, http://www.ctunet.com/blog/derrion-alberts-mother-speaks-out-against-cps-closures.

44. Kristen Mack, Azam Ahmed, and Annie Sweeny, "Fenger Beating Death: Violence, Tension Had Been Building over Years," Tribunedigital-Chicagotribune, September 30, 2009, http://articles.chicagotribune.com/2009-09-30/news/0909290482_1_violence-school-officers-students.

45. Cami Anderson, "An Open Letter to Newark Families," February 25, 2015, http://assets. njspotlight.com/assets/14/0225/2342.; linked from: John Mooney, "Fine Print: Anderson Says She'll No Longer Attend School Board Meetings - NJ Spotlight," *NJ Spotlight*, February 26, 2014, http://www.njspotlight.com/stories/14/02/26/fine-print-cami-anderson-open-letter-to-newark-families-says-she-ll-no-longer-attend-school-board-meetings/.

46. Dale Russakoff, *The Prize: Who's in Charge of America's Schools?* (Boston: Houghton Mifflin Harcourt, 2015).

47. Alliance to Reclaim Our Schools, *Out of Control: The Systematic Disenfranchisement of African American and Latino Communities Through School Takeovers* (The Alliance to Reclaim Our Schools, August 2015).

48. Kristen Buras, "Race, Charter Schools, and Conscious Capitalism: On the Spatial Politics of Whiteness as Property (and the Unconscionable Assault on Black New Orleans)," *Harvard Educational Review* 81, no. 2 (2011): 296–331.

49. Kristen McQueary, "Chicago, New Orleans, and Rebirth," *Chicago Tribune*, August 13, 2015, http://www.chicagotribune.com/news/opinion/commentary/ct-chicago-katrina-financial-disaster-landrieu-new-orleans-mcqueary-emanuel-pers-20150813-column.html: "I find myself wishing for a storm in Chicago—an unpredictable, haughty, devastating swirl of fury. A dramatic levee break. Geysers bursting through manhole covers. A sleeping city, forced onto the rooftops . . . An underperforming public school system saw a complete makeover. A new schools chief, Paul Vallas, designed a school system with the flexibility of an entrepreneur. No restrictive mandates from the city or the state. No demands from teacher unions to abide. Instead, he created the nation's first free-market education system."; Jim Stergios, "Not Grateful for 'Charter School Cap Lift,'" *Rock the Schoolhouse Blog*, May 8, 2012, http://www.boston.com/community/blogs/rock_the_ schoolhouse/2012/05/not_grateful_for_charter_schoo.html: "Lawrence is Massachusetts' 'Katrina moment'" . . . The question for Massachusetts is, why can't we apply the same reform to Lawrence? Its performance is every bit as bad as was New Orleans' before the natural disaster that hit the city. "Do we have to wait for an act of god before we act?"

50. Dana Brinson et al., *New Orleans–Style Education Reform: A Guide for Cities, Lessons Learned 2004–2010* (New Orleans: New Schools for New Orleans, January 2012), 25.

51. Nathan Barrett and Douglas Harris, *Significant Changes in the New Orleans Teacher Workforce* (New Orleans: Education Research Alliance, August 24, 2015).; For more on these changes, see: Buras, "Race, Charter Schools, and Conscious Capitalism."

52. Caitlin Emma, "The New Orleans Model: Praised but Unproven," *POLITICO*, April 16, 2015, http://www.politico.com/story/2015/04/the-new-orleans-model-praised-but-unproven-116982.html; Alliance to Reclaim Our Schools, *Out of Control*.

53. Daarel Burnette, "Chris Barbic on Leading Tennessee's Achievement School District and Its Daunting Turnaround Task," Chalkbeat Tennessee, April 7, 2015, http://tn.chalkbeat.org/2015/04/07/chalk-talk-chris-barbic-on-leading-tennessees-achievement-school-district-and-its-daunting-turnaround-task/.

54. Lori Higgins, "DPS Board Files Federal Lawsuit Against State," *Detroit Free Press*, April 7, 2016, http://www.freep.com/story/news/education/2016/04/07/dps-school-board-lawsuit/82725586/.

55. Erin Richards, "Abele Gears Up for Role as Overseer of Troubled Schools," *Journal Sentinel*, August 14, 2015, http://www.jsonline.com/news/education/chris-abele-gears-up-for-role-as-overseer-of-troubled-milwaukee-schools-b99554280z1-321896481.html; Don Behm, "Abele Gets Earful on New School Role During Budget Session," *Milwaukee Journal Sentinel*, August 19, 2015, http://www.jsonline.com/news/milwaukee/abele-gets-earful-on-new-school-role-during-budget-session-b99560407z1-322331361.html; Don Behm, "Abele: Officials Close to Identifying Schools Needing Services," *Journal Sentinel*, March 15, 2016, http://www.jsonline.com/news/milwaukee/chris-abele-officials-close-to-identifying-schools-needing-services-b99687959z1-372166911.html. As of this writing, the county executive was holding off on using the authority given through the law to create such a district, despite the hopes of Republican legislators in Wisconsin.

56. Grace Tatter, "More States Look to Tennessee's Achievement School District as a School Turnaround Model," Chalkbeat Tennessee, July 7, 2015, http://tn.chalkbeat.org/2015/07/07/more-states-look-to-tennessees-achievement-school-district-as-a-school-turnaround-model/; *North Carolina:* Jess Clark, "Lawmaker Stands Behind Plan for Charter School Takeover, Despite Lackluster Results," WUNC.org, April 4, 2016, http://wunc.org/post/lawmaker-stands-behind-plan-charter-school-takeover-despite-lackluster-results; Kelly Hinchcliffe, "Lawmakers Considering New Management for NC's Lowest-Performing Schools," WRAL.com, January 27, 2016, http://www.wral.com/lawmakers-considering-new-management-for-nc-s-lowest-performing-schools/15284298/.

57. Max Brantley, "Following the Money on the Walton-Hutchinson Takeover of Little Rock Schools," *Arkansas Times*, March 15, 2015, http://www.arktimes.com/ArkansasBlog/archives/2015/03/15/following-the-money-on-the-walton-hutchinson-takeover-of-little-rock-schools; Kali Holloway, "How the Billionaire Kingpins of School Privatization Got Stopped in Their Own Back Yard," AlterNet, September 1, 2015, http://www.alternet.org/education/how-billionaire-kingpins-school-privatization-got-stopped-their-own-back-yard.

58. Ron Zimmer et al., *Evaluation of the Effect of Tennessee's Achievement School District on Student Test Scores* (Nashville, TN: Tennessee Consortium on Research, Evaluation and Development, Vanderbilt University, December 2015).

59. Sneha Shankar, "US DoJ, FBI Investigate Education Achievement Authority, Detroit Public Schools for Corruption," *International Business Times*, October 21, 2015, http://www.ibtimes.com/us-doj-fbi-investigate-education-achievement-authority-detroit-public-schools-2149821.

60. Higgins, "DPS Board Files Federal Lawsuit Against State."

61. Emma, "Here's Why $7 Billion Didn't Help America's Worst Schools."

62. Bryk et al., *Organizing Schools for Improvement.*

63. Communities for Excellent Public Schools, *A Proposal for Sustainable School Transformation* (Washington, DC: Communities for Excellent Public Schools, July 2010).

64. Kristin Anderson Moore, *Making the Grade: Assessing the Evidence for Integrated Student Supports* (Bethesda, MD: Child Trends, February 2014); Martin J. Blank et al., *Making the Difference: Research and Practice in Community Schools* (Washington, DC: Coalition for Community Schools, 2003); Sebastian Castrechini and Rebecca A. London, "Positive Student Outcomes in Community Schools," Center for American Progress, 2012, http://eric.ed.gov/?id=ED535614.

65. Patrick Wall, "Why Non-Academic Needs Matter, Too," *The Atlantic*, February 26, 2016, http://www.theatlantic.com/education/archive/2016/02/nyc-community-schools/471114/.

66. SETSS: Special Education Teacher Support Services.

67. I use this designation here to signal the multiple schools that shared the same organizational partner at the time, though we were not referred to as an empowerment network.

68. New York State standardized exams.

69. After years of argument, Forrest Park was finally renamed in 2013, but the statue remains.

70. David M. Herszenhorn, "Bloomberg Wins on School Tests After Firing Foes," *New York Times,* March 16, 2004.

71. Randi Kaye, "All Teachers Fired at Rhode Island School," CNN, February 24, 2010, http://articles.cnn.com/2010-02-24/us/rhode.island.teachers_1_teachers-union-troubled-school-reading-specialists.

72. Yoav Gonen, "Andy Throws Mike a Timely LIFO Line," *New York Post*, March 4, 2012, http://nypost.com/2011/03/04/andy-throws-mike-a-timely-lifo-line/; Danielson 2014-15 Rubric, http://www.cfn107.org/uploads/6/1/9/2/6192492/danielson_2014-2015_rubric.pdf

73. Philissa Cramer and Rachel Cromidas, "Arbitrator Rules for Unions: Turnaround Firing, Rehiring Reversed," Chalkbeat, June 29, 2012, http://gothamschools.org/2012/06/29/arbitrator-rules-for-unions-turnaround-firing-rehiring-reversed/.

74. Elissa Gootman and Jennifer Medina, "50 New York Schools Fail Under Rating System," *New York Times,* November 6, 2007, http://www.nytimes.com/2007/11/06/education/06reportcards.html?pagewanted=all.

75. "Why 'A' Isn't Enough" *New York Post*, January 25, 2012, http://nypost.com/2012/01/25/why-a-isnt-enough/.

76. See Virginia P. Collier, "How Long? A Synthesis of Research on Academic Achievement in a Second Language," *TESOL Quarterly* 23, no. 3 (September 1989): 509–531.

77. Cramer and Cromidas, "Arbitrator Rules for Unions."

78. Philissa Cramer and Rachel Cromidas, "Judge Ends Year's Turnaround Saga with a Fast, Firm 'No' to the City," Chalkbeat, July 24, 2012, http://gothamschools.org/2012/07/24/judge-ends-years-turnaround-saga-with-a-fast-firm-no-to-city/.

79. Dana Goldstein, "NYC to Release Teachers' 'Value-Added' Ratings: Why It's Not Fair," *The Nation,* February 24, 2102, http://www.thenation.com/blog/166453/nyc-release-teachers-value-added-ratings-why-its-not-fair#.

80. Kathleen Megan and Jon Lender, "Former Candidate For New London Superintendent Sues School Board, Seeks Damages," *The Hartford Courant*, November 19, 2014, http://www.courant.com/education/hc-new-london-carter-sues-1120-20141119-story.html.

81. In this story, the names of the people and schools have not been changed.

Chapter 5

1. Barack Obama, "Remarks of the President to the United States Hispanic Chamber of Commerce," Marriott Metro Center, Washington, DC, March 10, 2009, https://www.whitehouse.gov/the-press-office/remarks-president-united-states-hispanic-chamber-commerce.

2. George W. Bush, "Remarks to the Hispanic Scholarship Fund" (Speech, Indian Treaty Room in the Dwight D. Eisenhower Executive Office Building, Washington, D.C., May 22, 2001), http://www.presidency.ucsb.edu/ws/?pid=45897.

3. Gloria Ladson-Billings, "From the Achievement Gap to the Education Debt: Understanding Achievement in U.S. Schools," *Educational Researcher* 35, no. 7 (October 1, 2006): 3–12, doi:10.3102/0013189X035007003; Amity L. Noltemeyer, Julie Mujic, and Caven S. McLoughlin, "The History of Inequity in Education," in *Disproportionality in Education and Special Education,* eds. Amity L. Noltemeyer and Caven S. McLoughlin (Springfield, IL: Charles C. Thomas Publisher Ltd., 2012), 3.

4. Steve Suitts, *A New Majority: Low Income Students Now a Majority in the Nation's Public Schools* (Atlanta, GA: Southern Education Foundation, January 2015).

5. "Table 203.50. Enrollment and Percentage Distribution of Enrollment in Public Elementary and Secondary Schools, by Race/Ethnicity and Region: Selected Years, Fall 1995 through Fall 2025," Digest of Education Statistics, National Center for Education Statistics, Institute of Education Sciences, U.S. Department of Education, 2016, 50, http://nces.ed.gov/programs/digest/d15/tables/dt15_203.50.asp.

6. Child Trends Data Bank, *Immigrant Children: Indicators on Children and Youth* (Bethesda, MD: Child Trends, October 2014).

7. William J. Hussar and Tabitha M. Bailey, "Projections of Education Statistics to 2023," 43rd ed., National Center for Education Statistics, Institute of Education Sciences, U.S. Department of Education, April 2016, http://eric.ed.gov/?id=ED506451.

8. "The Condition of Education: Reading and Mathematics Score Trends," National Center for Education Statistics, Institute of Education Sciences, May 2015, http://nces.ed.gov/programs/coe/indicator_cnj.asp; Sean F. Reardon, "The Widening Academic Achievement Gap Between the Rich and the Poor: New Evidence and Possible Explanations," in *Whither Opportunity? Rising Inequality, Schools, and Children's Life Chances,* ed. Greg J. Duncan and Richard J. Murnane (New York: Russell Sage Foundation, 2011), 91–116; W. Steven Barnett and Cynthia E. Lamy, "Achievement Gaps Start Early: Preschool Can Help," in *Closing the Opportunity Gap: What America Must Do to Give Every Child an Even Chance,* 1st ed., ed. Prudence L. Carter and Kevin G. Welner (Oxford ; New York: Oxford University Press, 2013); Christina Samuels, "NAEP Scores for Students with Disabilities Show Wide Achievement Gap," *Education Week,* October 29, 2015, http://blogs.edweek.org/edweek/speced/2015/10/naep_scores_for_students_with.html.

9. Nailing Xia and Sheila Nataraj Kirby, *Retaining Students in Grade: A Literature Review of the Effects of Retention on Students' Academic Outcomes* (Santa Monica, CA: Rand Corporation, 2009), http://books.google.com/books?hl=en&lr=&id=LzAEjIJ3pD4C&oi=fnd&pg=PP2&dq=%22the+previous+year,+and,+thus,+students+should+be+less+at+risk+for+failure+when+they+go+on+to%22+%222003%E2%80%932004,+the+New+York+City+Department+of+Education+(NYCDOE)+implemented+a%22+&ots=6gi8jdLca4&sig=4N6on6t-RPsZQeip_AGfZG2Y7ec.

10. Jason A. Grissom and Christopher Redding, "Discretion and Disproportionality: Explaining the Underrepresentation of High-Achieving Students of Color in Gifted Programs," *AERA Open* 2, no. 1 (2016), doi:10.117/2332858415622175.

11. "The Condition of Education: High School Coursetaking," National Center for Education Statistics, Institute of Education Sciences, May 2016, http://nces.ed.gov/programs/coe/indicator_cod.asp.

12. Robert C. Pianta et al., "Opportunities to Learn in America's Elementary Classrooms," *Science* 315, no. 5820 (March 30, 2007): 1795–96, doi:10.1126/science.1139719.

13. "The Condition of Education: Public High School Graduation Rates," National Center for Education Statistics, Institute of Education Sciences, May 2016, http://nces.ed.gov/

programs/coe/indicator_coi.asp; "The Condition of Education: Status Dropout Rates," National Center for Education Statistics, Institute of Education Sciences, May 2016, http://nces.ed.gov/programs/coe/indicator_coj.asp; Schott Foundation, *Black Lives Matter: The Schott 50 State Report on Public Education and Black Males* (Cambridge, MA: Schott Foundation, 2015).

14. Complete College America, *Remediation: Higher Education's Bridge to Nowhere* (Indianapolis, IN: Complete College America, April 2012).

15. "The Condition of Education: College Participation Rates," National Center for Education Statistics, Institute of Education Sciences, May 2016, http://nces.ed.gov/programs/coe/indicator_cpb.asp; Erin Einhorn, "Rich School, Poor School: Looking Across the College-Access Divide," NPR.org, February 9, 2015, http://www.npr.org/sections/ed/2015/02/09/382122276/rich-school-poor-school.

16. Table 326.10: "Graduation Rate from First Institution Attended for First-Time, Full-Time Bachelor's Degree-Seeking Students at 4-Year Postsecondary Institutions, by Race/Ethnicity, Time to Completion, Sex, Control of Institution, and Acceptance Rate: Selected Cohort Entry Years, 1996 through 2008," Digest of Education Statistics, National Center for Education Statistics, Institute of Education Sciences, U.S. Department of Education, 2016, 10, https://nces.ed.gov/programs/digest/d15/tables/dt15_326.10.asp; Margaret Cahalan and Laura Perna, *Indicators of Higher Education Equity in the United States: 45 Year Trend Report* (Washington, DC: Pell Institute for the Study of Opportunity in Higher Education, 2015), http://eric.ed.gov/?id=ED555865; National Student Clearinghouse Research Center, "High School Benchmarks 2015: National College Progression Rates," National Student Clearinghouse, October 14, 2015. *Summary of English language learner gaps and needs:* Patricia Gándara, "Meeting the Needs of Language Minorities," in *Closing the Opportunity Gap: What America Must Do to Give Every Child an Even Chance*, 1st ed., ed. Prudence L. Carter and Kevin G. Welner (Oxford ; New York: Oxford University Press, 2013).

17. Prudence L. Carter and Kevin G. Welner, eds., *Closing the Opportunity Gap: What America Must Do to Give Every Child an Even Chance*, 1st ed. (Oxford ; New York: Oxford University Press, 2013), 3; Ladson-Billings, "From the Achievement Gap to the Education Debt."

18. Caroline Ratcliffe, *Child Poverty and Adult Success* (Washington, DC: Urban Institute, September 2015), http://www.urban.org/sites/default/files/alfresco/publication-pdfs/2000369-Child-Poverty-and-Adult-Success.pdf.

19. Yang Jiang, Mercedes Ekono, and Curtis Skinner, *Basic Facts About Low-Income Children* (New York: National Center for Children in Poverty, Mailman School of Public Health, Columbia University, February 2016).

20. No Kid Hungry, *Hunger in Our Schools 2015* (Washington, DC: No Kid Hungry, 2015).

21. Richard Rothstein, "Why Children from Lower Socio-Economic Classes, on Average, Have Lower Academic Achievement Than Middle Class Children," in *Closing the Opportunity Gap: What America Must Do to Give Every Child an Even Chance*, 1st ed., ed. Prudence L. Carter and Kevin G. Welner (Oxford ; New York: Oxford University Press, 2013)., 62-63

22. Pew Research Center, *Parenting in America: Outlook, Worries, Aspirations Are Strongly Linked to Financial Situation* (Washington, DC: Pew Research Center, December 17, 2015).

23. For a summary of recent research, see: Rothstein, "Why Children from Lower Socio-Economic Classes, On Average, Have Lower Academic Achievement Than Middle Class Children"; Reardon, "The Widening Academic Achievement Gap"; and Richard J. Coley and Bruce Baker, *Poverty and Education: Finding the Way Forward* (Princeton, NJ: Edu-

cational Testing Service, 2013). For further summary of recent research on the impacts of poverty on the brain and body, see Paul Tough, *Helping Children Succeed: What Works and Why* (Boston: Houghton Mifflin Harcourt, 2016).

24. Kimberly G. Noble et al., "Family Income, Parental Education and Brain Structure in Children and Adolescents," *Nature Neuroscience* 18, no. 5 (May 2015): 773–78, doi:10.1038/nn.3983.

25. Jack P. Shonkoff et al., "The Lifelong Effects of Early Childhood Adversity and Toxic Stress," *Pediatrics* 129, no. 1 (January 2012): e232–46, doi:10.1542/peds.2011-2663. See also: Center on the Developing Child, "Excessive Stress Disrupts the Architecture of the Developing Brain" (working paper no. 3, National Scientific Council on the Developing Child, Center on the Developing Child, Harvard University, 2014); and Center on the Developing Child, "Building the Brain's 'Air Traffic Control' System: How Early Experiences Shape the Development of Executive Function" (working paper no. 11, Center on the Developing Child at Harvard University, Cambridge, MA, February 2011).

26. Jiang, Ekono, and Skinner, *Basic Facts About Low-Income Children.*

27. Michael Leachman, Erica Williams, and Nicholas Johnson, "Governors Are Proposing Further Deep Cuts in Services, Likely Harming Their Economies," Center on Budget and Policy Priorities, March 21, 2011, http://www.cbpp.org/research/governors-are-proposing-further-deep-cuts-in-services-likely-harming-their-economies?fa=view&id=3389; Tracy Gordon, "State and Local Budgets and the Great Recession," The Brookings Institution, December 31, 2012, https://www.brookings.edu/articles/state-and-local-budgets-and-the-great-recession/; Nicholas Johnson, Phil Oliff, and Erica Williams, "An Update on State Budget Cuts," Center on Budget and Policy Priorities, February 9, 2011, http://www.cbpp.org/research/an-update-on-state-budget-cuts?fa=view&id=1214; Liz Scott and Misha Hill, "State General Assistance Programs Are Weakening Despite Increased Need," Center on Budget and Policy Priorities, July 9, 2015.

28. Amy Wilkins, "No Surrender," The Thomas B. Fordham Institute, September 21, 2005, https://edexcellence.net/commentary/education-gadfly-weekly/2005/september-22/no-surrender.html.

29. Jeanne Allen, "Race Is a Red Herring in the Battle for Better Schools," The Thomas B. Fordham Institute, June 2, 2016, https://edexcellence.net/articles/race-is-a-red-herring-in-the-battle-for-better-schools?utm_source=Fordham+Updates&utm_campaign=197367a658-20160605_LateLateBell_6_5_2016&utm_medium=email&utm_term=0_d9e8246adf-197367a658-71511041&mc_cid=197367a658&mc_eid=21b864b3fd.

30. Leila Morsy and Richard Rothstein, *Five Social Disadvantages That Depress Student Performance: Why Schools Alone Can't Close the Achievement Gaps* (Washington, DC: Economic Policy Institute, June 10, 2015); Robert D. Putnam, *Our Kids: The American Dream in Crisis* (New York: Simon & Schuster, 2015).

31. Gregory Camilli et al., "Meta-Analysis of the Effects of Early Education Interventions on Cognitive and Social Development," *Teachers College Record* 112, no. 3 (2010): 579–620; Pedro Carneiro and James Heckman, "Human Capital Policy" (working paper 9495, National Bureau of Economic Research Working Paper Series, Cambridge, MA, February 2003); Barnett and Lamy, "Achievement Gaps Start Early: Preschool Can Help"; James J. Heckman, "The Case for Investing in Disadvantaged Young Children," in *Big Ideas for Children: Investing in Our Nation's Future* (Washington, DC: First Focus, 2008), 49–58.

32. Joan Wasser Gish, Eric Dearing, and Mary Walsh, "Wraparound Services Still Worth It Even After Accounting for All Costs," The Brookings Institution, July 15, 2016, http://www.brookings.edu/blogs/brown-center-chalkboard/posts/2016/07/15-wraparound-services-accounting-costs-wassergish-dearing-walsh; Sebastian Castrechini and Rebecca A. London, "Positive Student Outcomes in Community Schools," Center for American Progress, February 2012, http://eric.ed.gov/?id=ED535614.

33. William Corrin et al., *Addressing Early Warning Indicators: Interim Impact Findings from the Investing in Innovation (i3) Evaluation of DIPLOMAS NOW* (New York: MDRC, 2016), http://www.mdrc.org/sites/default/files/Addressing_Early_warning_indicators_FR .pdf; *Absenteeism rates here:* Office for Civil Rights, *2013–2014 Civil Rights Data Collection: A First Look* (Washington, DC: U.S. Department of Education, Office for Civil Rights, June 7, 2016).

34. Equity and Excellence Commission, *For Each and Every Child: A Strategy for Education Equity and Excellence* (Washington, DC: U.S. Department of Education, 2013); Deborah A. Verstegen and Robert C. Knoeppel, "From Statehouse to Schoolhouse: Education Finance Apportionment Systems in the United States," *Journal of Education Finance* 38, no. 2 (2012): 145–66.

35. Beth Fertig, "Decision Reversed in NYC School Funding Case," WNYC, June 26, 2002, http://www.wnyc.org/story/85632-decision-reversed-in-nyc-school-funding-case/?utm_ source=sharedUrl&utm_medium=metatag&utm_campaign=sharedUrl.

36. Kristen A. Graham, "School-Funding System 'Broken,' Pa. Judges Hear," *Philadelphia Inquirer*, March 13, 2015, http://articles.philly.com/2015-03-13/news/60053382_ 1_plaintiffs-high-school-students-keystone-exams.

37. Bruce Baker et al., *Is School Funding Fair? A National Report Card*, 5th ed. (Newark, NJ: Education Law Center and Rutgers Graduate School of Education, March 2016).

38. Educational Finance Branch, *Public Education Finances: 2014* (Washington, DC: U.S. Census Bureau, June 2016), https://www2.census.gov/govs/school/14f33pub.pdf.

39. Lauren Camera and Lindsey Cook, "Title I: Rich School Districts Get Millions Meant for Poor Kids," *US News & World Report*, June 1, 2016, http://www.usnews.com/news/ articles/2016-06-01/title-i-rich-school-districts-get-millions-in-federal-money-meant-for-poor-kids.

40. Goodwin Liu, "Improving Title I Funding Equity Across States, Districts, and Schools," *Iowa Law Review* 93 (2008 2007): 973; Baker et al., *Is School Funding Fair?*

41. Natasha Ushomirsky and David Williams, *Funding Gaps 2015: Too Many States Still Spend Less on Educating Students Who Need the Most* (Washington, DC: The Education Trust, March 2016); Emma Brown, "In 23 States, Richer School Districts Get More Local Funding Than Poorer Districts," *Washington Post*, March 12, 2015, https://www. washingtonpost.com/news/local/wp/2015/03/12/in-23-states-richer-school-districts-get-more-local-funding-than-poorer-districts/.

42. Maura McInerney and Mike DeNardo, "Public Education Advocates Take Pennsylvania to Court over School Funding," CBS Philly, March 11, 2015, http://philadelphia.cbslo-cal.com/2015/03/11/public-education-advocates-take-pennsylvania-to-court-over-school-funding/.

43. Joe Guillen, "City Inspections of Detroit Schools Find Rodents, Mold," *Detroit Free Press*, January 25, 2016, http://www.freep.com/story/news/2016/01/25/city-inspections-detroit-schools-find-rodents-mold/79311004/; Eli Savit, "Why Detroit Schools Are Crumbling— Look at State's Funding Foundation," MLive.com, February 1, 2016, http://www.mlive. com/opinion/index.ssf/2016/02/why_detroit_schools_are_crumbl.html.

44. Amy Lange, "DPS Students Walk Out in Protest, Many Hit with Suspensions," WJBK, January 25, 2016, http://www.fox2detroit.com/news/local-news/82368501-story; Erin Einhorn, "Detroit Teachers Explain Why They're 'Sicking-Out,'" *Time*, January 29, 2016, http://time.com/4198582/detroit-public-schools-sick-outs-teachers-explain/.

45. "Fault Lines: America's Most Segregating School District Borders," EdBuild, August 2016, http://viz.edbuild.org/maps/2016/fault-lines/.

46. "Race and Hispanic of Latino Origin: 2010; Grosse Pointe Farms City and Detroit City, Michigan," American FactFinder, United States Census Bureau, 2012, https://factfinder. census.gov/faces/nav/jsf/pages/index.xhtml .

47. Bruce D. Baker, *Does Money Matter in Education?* 2nd ed. (Washington, DC: Albert Shanker Institute, 2016), http://eric.ed.gov/?id=ED528632; C. Kirabo Jackson, Rucker C. Johnson, and Claudia Persico, "The Effects of School Spending on Educational and Economic Outcomes: Evidence from School Finance Reforms" (working paper no. 20847, National Bureau of Economic Research, Cambridge, MA, January 2015), http://www.nber.org/papers/w20847; Julien Lafortune, Jesse Rothstein, and Diane Whitmore Schanzenbach, "School Finance Reform and the Distribution of Student Achievement," (working paper no. 22011, National Bureau of Economic Research, Cambridge, MA, February 2016), http://www.nber.org/papers/w22011; David Card and A. Abigail Payne, "School Finance Reform, the Distribution of School Spending, and the Distribution of Student Test Scores," *Journal of Public Economics* 83 (2002): 49–82.

48. OECD, "Viewing the United States School System Through the Prism of PISA 2012," in *Lessons from PISA 2012 for the United States* (Paris: OECD Publishing, 2013), http://dx.doi.org/10.1787/9789264207585-4-en.

49. Harvey Kantor and Robert Lowe, "Educationalizing the Welfare State and Privatizing Education: The Evolution of Social Policy Since the New Deal," in *Closing the Opportunity Gap: What America Must Do to Give Every Child an Even Chance*, ed. Prudence L. Carter and Kevin G. Welner, 1st ed. (Oxford ; New York: Oxford University Press, 2013), 31.

50. Gary Orfield, Susan E. Eaton, and Harvard Project on School Desegregation, *Dismantling Desegregation: The Quiet Reversal of* Brown v. Board of Education (New York: New Press, 1996); Nikole Hannah-Jones, "Lack of Order: The Erosion of a Once-Great Force for Integration," *ProPublica*, May 1, 2014, http://www.propublica.org/article/lack-of-order-the-erosion-of-a-once-great-force-for-integration; Charles T. Clotfelter, *After "Brown": The Rise and Retreat of School Desegregation* (Princeton, NJ: Princeton University Press, 2006); Matthew F. Delmont, *Why Busing Failed: Race, Media, and the National Resistance to School Desegregation* (Oakland, CA: University of California Press, 2016); Susan Eaton and Steven Rivkin, "Is Desegregation Dead?" *Education Next*, Fall 2010, http://educationnext.org/is-desegregation-dead/; Russell W. Rumberger and Gregory J. Palardy, "Does Segregation Still Matter? The Impact of Student Composition on Academic Achievement in High School," *Teachers College Record* 107, no. 9 (2005): 1999.

51. Gary Orfield et al., *Brown at 60: Great Progress, a Long Retreat and an Uncertain Future* (Los Angeles: The Civil Rights Project|Proyecto Derechos Civiles at the University of California, Los Angeles, May 15, 2014); Erica Frankenberg, Chungmei Lee, and Gary Orfield, *A Multiracial Society with Segregated Schools: Are We Losing the Dream?* (Cambridge, MA: Harvard Civil Rights Project, January 16, 2003), http://eric.ed.gov/?id=ED472347; Richard Rothstein, *For Public Schools, Segregation Then, Segregation Since: Education and the Unfinished March* (Washington, DC: Economic Policy Institute, August 27, 2013), http://www.epi.org/publication/unfinished-march-public-school-segregation/.

52. Nikole Hannah-Jones, "Segregation Now," *ProPublica*, April 16, 2014, http://www.propublica.org/article/segregation-now-full-text.

53. Orfield et al., *Brown at 60*; Derek Black, "Why Integration Matters in Schools," *Education Week*, May 14, 2014, http://www.edweek.org/ew/articles/2014/05/14/31black_ep.h33.html.

54. Ann Owens, Sean F. Reardon, and Christopher Jencks, *Income Segregation Between Schools and School Districts* (Palo Alto, CA: Stanford Center for Education Policy Analysis, May 2016); Ann Owens, "Inequality in Children's Contexts: Income Segregation of Households with and Without Children," *American Sociological Review*, April 27, 2016, doi:10.1177/0003122416642430; *Widening gulf:* OECD, *In It Together: Why Less Inequality Benefits All* (Paris: Organisation for Economic Co-operation and Development, 2015), http://www.oecd-ilibrary.org/content/book/9789264235120-en;

Dionne Searcey and Robert Gebeloff, "Middle Class Shrinks Further as More Fall Out Instead of Climbing Up," *New York Times*, January 25, 2015, http://www.nytimes.com/2015/01/26/business/economy/middle-class-shrinks-further-as-more-fall-out-instead-of-climbing-up.html; OECD, *OECD Economic Survey of the United States 2016* (Paris: OECD Publishing, 2016), http://www.oecd-ilibrary.org/economics/oecd-economic-surveys-united-states-2016_eco_surveys-usa-2016-en.

55. *Better Use of Information Could Help Agencies Identify Disparities and Address Racial Discrimination* (Washington, DC: Government Accountability Office, April 2016); Gary Orfield, John Kucsera, and Genevieve Siegel-Hawley, *E Pluribis . . . Separation: Deepening Double Segregation for More Students* (Los Angeles: The Civil Rights Project|Proyecto Derechos Civiles at the University of California, Los Angeles, October 18, 2012).

56. Amy Stuart Wells, Lauren Fox, and Diana Cordova-Cobo, *How Racially Diverse Schools and Classrooms Can Benefit All Students* (New York: The Century Foundation, February 9, 2016); Rumberger and Palardy, "Does Segregation Still Matter?"; Dana Goldstein, *The Teacher Wars: A History of America's Most Embattled Profession* (New York: Doubleday, 2014), 181.

57. Erica Frankenberg, Genevieve Siegel-Hawley, and Jia Wang, "Choice Without Equity: Charter School Segregation," *Education Policy Analysis Archives* 19 (2011): 1; Janelle Scott and Amy Stuart Wells, "A More Perfect Union: Reconciling School Choice Policy with Equality of Opportunity Goals," in *Closing the Opportunity Gap: What America Must Do to Give Every Child an Even Chance*, ed. Prudence L Carter and Kevin G. Welner, 1st ed. (Oxford; New York: Oxford University Press, 2013), 125, 129-135; Owens, "Inequality in Children's Contexts."

58. Orfield et al., *Brown at 60*; Stuart Wells, Fox, and Cordova-Cobo, *How Racially Diverse Schools and Classrooms Can Benefit All Students*; Rucker C. Johnson, "Long-Run Impacts of School Desegregation & School Quality on Adult Attainments" (working paper no. 16664, National Bureau of Economic Research, Cambridge, MA, 2011), http://www.nber.org/papers/w16664.

59. Stuart Wells, Fox, and Cordova-Cobo, *How Racially Diverse Schools and Classrooms Can Benefit All Students*; Genevieve Siegel-Hawley, *How Non-Minority Students Also Benefit from Racially Diverse Schools,* Issue Brief No. 8 (Washington, DC: National Coalition on School Diversity, 2012), http://www.fcps.net/media/1288141/jan15benefit.pdf.

60. Stuart Wells, Fox, and Cordova-Cobo, *How Racially Diverse Schools and Classrooms Can Benefit All Students*.

61. Ladson-Billings, "From the Achievement Gap to the Education Debt."

62. Andrew Ujifusa, "Report to Congress: Proposed Spending Rules Appear to Exceed ESSA Language," *Education Week*, May 16, 2016, http://blogs.edweek.org/edweek/campaign-k-12/2016/05/report_ed_depts_proposed_spend_essa.html; Cory Turner, "The 'Intolerable' Fight over School Money," NPR.org, May 18, 2016, http://www.npr.org/sections/ed/2016/05/18/478358412/the-intolerable-fight-over-school-money."

63. Michael Hilton, *Prioritizing School Integration in ESSA State Implementation Plans,* Issue Brief No. 6 (Washington, DC: National Coalition on School Diversity, May 2016).

64. Advancement Project, *Test, Punish, and Push Out: How Zero Tolerance and High Stakes Testing Funnel Youth into the School-to-Prison Pipeline* (Washington, DC: Advancement Project, March 2010); Jody Owens, "How Prison Stints Replaced Study Hall: America's Problem with Criminalizing Kids," *POLITICO Magazine*, March 15, 2015, http://www.politico.com/magazine/story/2015/03/criminal-kids-juvenile-justice-sentencing-reform-incarceration-116065.html.

65. Russell J. Skiba, Mariella I. Arredondo, and M. Karega Rausch, *New and Developing Research on Disparities in Discipline* (Bloomington, IN: The Equity Project at Indiana

University, 2014), http://www.indiana.edu/~atlantic/wp-content/uploads/2014/12/Disparity_NewResearch__Full_121114.pdf.

66. Russell J. Skiba et al., "The Color of Discipline: Sources of Racial and Gender Disproportionality in School Punishment," *The Urban Review* 34, no. 4 (November 2002), http://citeseerx.ist.psu.edu/viewdoc/download?doi=10.1.1.469.4065&rep=rep1&type=pdf ; Russell J. Skiba et al., "Race Is Not Neutral: A National Investigation of African American and Latino Disproportionality in School Discipline," *School Psychology Review* 40, no. 1 (2011): 85; Edward W. Morris, "'Tuck In That Shirt!' Race, Class, Gender, and Discipline in an Urban School," *Sociological Perspectives* 48, no. 1 (March 1, 2005): 25–48, doi:10.1525/sop.2005.48.1.25; Jason A. Okonofua and Jennifer L. Eberhardt, "Two Strikes: Race and the Disciplining of Young Students," *Psychological Science* 26, no. 5 (May 2015): 617–24, doi:10.1177/0956797615570365; Daniel Losen, *Discipline Policies, Successful Schools, and Racial Justice* (Boulder, CO: National Education Policy Center, 2011), http://escholarship.org/uc/item/4q41361g.pdf.

67. Julianne Hing, "The Shocking Details of a Mississippi School-to-Prison Pipeline," *Colorlines,* November 26, 2012, http://www.colorlines.com/articles/shocking-details-mississippi-school-prison-pipeline.

68. Daniel Losen et al., *Are We Closing the School Discipline Gap?* (Los Angeles: University of California, Center for Civil Rights Remedies, February 2015), https://escholarship.org/uc/item/2t36g571.pdf.

69. Edward W. Morris and Brea L. Perry, "The Punishment Gap: School Suspension and Racial Disparities in Achievement," *Social Problems* 63, no. 1 (February 2016): 68–86, doi:10.1093/socpro/spv026.

70. Advancement Project, *Test, Punish, and Push Out.*

71. American Psychological Association Zero Tolerance Task Force, "Are Zero Tolerance Policies Effective in the Schools? An Evidentiary Review and Recommendations," *The American Psychologist* 63, no. 9 (December 2008): 852–62, doi:10.1037/0003-066X.63.9.852; Council on School Health, American Academy of Pediatrics, ed., "Out-of-School Suspension and Expulsion," *Pediatrics*, February 25, 2013, doi:10.1542/peds.2012-3932.

72. Tough, *Helping Children Succeed*, 53–54; F. Chris Curran, "Estimating the Effect of State Zero Tolerance Laws on Exclusionary Discipline, Racial Discipline Gaps, and Student Behavior," *Educational Evaluation and Policy Analysis*, June 3, 2016, 0162373716652728, doi:10.3102/0162373716652728.

73. Matthew P. Steinberg, Elaine Allensworth, and David W. Johnson, *Student and Teacher Safety in Chicago Public Schools: The Roles of Community Context and School Social Organization* (Chicago: Consortium on Chicago School Research, 2011), http://eric.ed.gov/?id=ED519414; Brea L. Perry and Edward W. Morris, "Suspending Progress: Collateral Consequences of Exclusionary Punishment in Public Schools," *American Sociological Review* 79, no. 6 (December 1, 2014): 1067–87, doi:10.1177/0003122414556308.

74. Melinda D. Anderson, "Will School-Discipline Reform Actually Change Anything?" *The Atlantic*, September 14, 2015, http://www.theatlantic.com/education/archive/2015/09/will-school-discipline-reform-actually-change-anything/405157/; Lizette Alvarez, "Seeing the Toll, Schools Revise Zero Tolerance," *New York Times*, December 2, 2013, http://www.nytimes.com/2013/12/03/education/seeing-the-toll-schools-revisit-zero-tolerance.html; Stephanie Francis Ward, "Schools Start to Rethink Zero Tolerance Policies," *ABA Journal*, August 1, 2014, http://www.abajournal.com/magazine/article/schools_start_to_rethink_zero_tolerance_policies/.

75. Civil Rights Data Collection, *2013–2014 Civil Rights Data Collection: A First Look: Key Data Highlights on Equity and Opportunity Gaps in Our Nation's Public Schools* (Washington, DC: U.S. Department of Education, Office of Civil Rights, 2016).

76. W. David Stevens et al., *Discipline Practices in Chicago Schools: Trends in the Use of Suspensions and Arrests* (Chicago: University of Chicago Consortium on Chicago School Research, March 2015), https://ccsr.uchicago.edu/sites/default/files/publications/Discipline%20Report.pdf.

77. *Classroom management:* Elaine M. Allensworth et al., *Setting the Stage for Academic Challenge: Classroom Control and Student Support* (Chicago: The University of Chicago Consortium on Chicago School Research, September 2014). *Bias and empathy:* Jason A. Okonofua, David Paunesku, and Gregory M. Walton, "Brief Intervention to Encourage Empathic Discipline Cuts Suspension Rates in Half Among Adolescents," *Proceedings of the National Academy of Sciences* 113, no. 19 (May 10, 2016): 5221–26, doi:10.1073/pnas.1523698113.

78. Jeannie Oakes, *Keeping Track: How Schools Structure Inequality*, 2nd ed. (New Haven, CT: Yale University Press, 2005).

79. *Silent segregation:* Daniel J. Losen, "Silent Segregation in Our Nation's Schools," *Harv. CR-CLL Rev.* 34 (1999): 517. *Removes benefits of integration:* Karolyn Tyson, "Tracking, Segregation, and the Opportunity Gap: What We Know and Why It Matters," in *Closing the Opportunity Gap: What America Must Do to Give Every Child an Even Chance*, ed. Prudence L. Carter and Kevin G. Welner, 1st ed. (Oxford ; New York: Oxford University Press, 2013). *Negative impacts for students on lower tracks:* Oakes, *Keeping Track*. *Minimal overall effects:* John Hattie, *Visible Learning: A Synthesis of over 800 Meta-Analyses Relating to Achievement*, 1st ed. (London; New York: Routledge, 2008), 89–91.

80. Ning Rui, "Four Decades of Research on the Effects of Detracking Reform: Where Do We Stand? A Systematic Review of the Evidence," *Journal of Evidence-Based Medicine* 2, no. 3 (August 2009): 164–83, doi:10.1111/j.1756-5391.2009.01032.x.

81. A. Wade Boykin and Pedro Noguera, *Creating the Opportunity to Learn: Moving from Research to Practice to Close the Achievement Gap* (Alexandria, VA: ASCD, 2011); Helen P. Gouldner and Mary Symons Strong, *Teacher's Pets, Troublemakers, and Nobodies: Black Children in Elementary School* (Westport, CT: Greenwood Publishing Group, Incorporated, 1978); Charles M. Payne, *So Much Reform, So Little Change: The Persistence of Failure in Urban Schools* (Cambridge, MA: Harvard Education Press, 2008).

82. Boykin and Noguera, *Creating the Opportunity to Learn*, 78–79.

83. Seth Gershenson, Stephen B. Holt, and Nicholas W. Papageorge, "Who Believes in Me? The Effect of Student–Teacher Demographic Match on Teacher Expectations," *Economics of Education Review* 52 (June 2016): 209–24, doi:10.1016/j.econedurev.2016.03.002.

84. Lee Jussim, Jacquelynne Eccles, and Stephanie Madon, "Social Perception, Social Stereotypes, and Teacher Expectations: Accuracy and the Quest for the Powerful Self-Fulfilling Prophecy," in *Advances in Experimental Social Psychology*, vol. 28 (Cambridge, MA: Academic Press, 1996), 310, 315, http://linkinghub.elsevier.com/retrieve/pii/S0065260108602403.

85. Claude M. Steele, *Whistling Vivaldi: And Other Clues to How Stereotypes Affect Us* (New York: W. W. Norton & Company, 2011).

86. George W. Bush, "Remarks in a Discussion on Education at the National Institutes of Health in Bethesda, Maryland," Bethesda, MD, May 12, 2004, http://www.presidency.ucsb.edu/ws/?pid=62996; among many other speeches.

87. Gilberto Q. Conchas, *The Color of Success: Race and High-Achieving Urban Youth* (New York: Teachers College Press, 2006); Geneva Gay, *Culturally Responsive Teaching: Theory, Research, and Practice* (New York: Teachers College Press, 2000); Gloria Ladson-Billings, *The Dreamkeepers: Successful Teachers of African American Children* (New York: John Wiley & Sons, 2009); Lisa D. Delpit, *Other People's Children: Cultural Conflict in the Classroom*, 2nd ed. (New York: The New Press, 2006); Gary R. Howard, *We Can't*

Teach What We Don't Know: White Teachers, Multiracial Schools (New York: Teachers College Press, 1999). *Youth, hip-hop, and pop culture:* Ernest Morrell, *Linking Literacy and Popular Culture: Finding Connections for Lifelong Learning* (Norwood, MA: Christopher-Gordon Publishers, 2004); Christopher Emdin, *For White Folks Who Teach in the Hood . . . and the Rest of Y'all Too: Reality Pedagogy and Urban Education* (Boston: Beacon Press, 2016); Carol D. Lee, "Is October Brown Chinese? A Cultural Modeling Activity System for Underachieving Students," *American Educational Research Journal* 38, no. 1 (March 20, 2001): 97–141, doi:10.3102/00028312038001097; Carol D. Lee, "'Every Goodbye Ain't Gone': Analyzing the Cultural Underpinnings of Classroom Talk," *International Journal of Qualitative Studies in Education* 19, no. 3 (May 1, 2006): 305–27, doi:10.1080/09518390600696729; Carol D. Lee, *Culture, Literacy, and Learning: Taking Bloom in the Midst of the Whirlwind*, 62314th ed. (New York: Teachers College Press, 2007).

88. Boykin and Noguera, *Creating the Opportunity to Learn.*, 69-138
89. James Baldwin, *The Price of the Ticket: Collected Nonfiction, 1948–1985* (New York: Macmillan, 1985), 325.
90. Rhonda Rosenberg, "The Great Divide in High School College Readiness Rates" *EdWize,* June 27, 2013, http://www.edwize.org/the-great-divide-in-high-school-college-readiness-rates.
91. "College Completion: Who Graduates, Who Doesn't and Why It Matters," The Chronicle of Higher Education, 2010.
92. Jeff Davis, *The First-Generation Student Experience* (Sterling, VA: Stylus Publishing, LLC, 2010).
93. Miep Gies, "Raul Wallenberg Lecture," Wallenberg Legacy, University of Michigan, Ann Arbor, MI, October 11, 1994.
94. Howard Zehr, *The Little Book of Restorative Justice,* rev., updated ed. (Brattleboro, VT: Good Books, 2015).
95. Nancy Riestenberg, *Circle in the Square: Building Community and Repairing Harm in School* (St. Paul, MN: Living Justice Press, 2013).
96. Jay MacLeod, *Ain't No Makin' It: Aspirations and Attainment in a Low-Income Neighborhood,* 2nd ed. (Boulder, CO: Westview Press, 1995).

Acknowledgments

First and foremost, a huge thank you to the contributors of this book. I am incredibly grateful for their generosity, expertise, brilliance, and patience. They are a truly incredible group, and I feel very lucky that they have shared their stories in this collection. A special shout-out to Kari Kokka, who has often gone above and beyond contributor duties to help make this collection a reality.

I'd also like to thank the many people who helped me to find these teacher-contributors, including a long list of professors, researchers, scholars, nonprofit professionals, community organizers, school workers, members of teacher organizations, journalists, union leaders, and more. I so appreciate that you responded to my cold-call email and took the time to connect me to the amazing people whose stories make up this book.

I owe thanks to a few people in the education publishing world: Rebecca Novack, who asked me some great questions in the earliest stages of forming the idea for this book, and Brian Ellerbeck, who helped me consider how teachers could share alternative practices and add new ideas to the national conversation. A huge thanks is due my editor Nancy Walser, who not only has been an enthusiastic supporter of the book and of highlighting teachers' voices, but has also been wonderful to work with at every stage of this process. Diane Frederick, your careful copyediting is very much appreciated, and Chris Leonesio, thanks for getting us to the finish line.

There are many people who encouraged me throughout this years-long process. Thank you to Tricia, Ethan, Dusty, and Buster, who generously gave up their space a number of times so I could have somewhere to write. To my mentor from college, Lee Anne Bell, who first inspired me to think about the power of storytelling and who graciously read through parts of this book. Thanks to the friends who heard about this the most, Alex, Jenni, and Christien, who collectively contributed a story, talked through ideas with me, provided feedback on drafts, and helped me brainstorm a title, and to my family, Jake and Jennifer, whose support has always been unfailing and full of love. To my favorite person in the world, Mary Angélica Molina: thanks for reading everything I write and for the countless other ways that you make my life better.

Finally, to the students whom I've been lucky enough to teach, thank you for all that you've given and taught me. I would not be who I am today without you, particularly Lisanny, Juana, and Denise. And to all of the students in schools now or who will be in the years to come, we'll keep fighting, because you deserve better.

About the Editor

Brett Gardiner Murphy is a former New York City public school history teacher with a background in urban studies and education. She is currently the director of Strategic Projects at the Posse Foundation, where she designs, facilitates, and trains teams to implement curricula exploring identity, diversity, inclusion, youth development, and college access. Brett is also the coauthor of *The Storytelling Project,* a curriculum developed by a creative interdisciplinary team of artists, public school teachers, university faculty members, and students to address race and racism through storytelling and the arts.

Index